Pride and Pudding

The History of British Puddings
Savoury and Sweet

CONTAINING

ALL KINDS OF PUDDINGS AND HOW TO MAKE THEM

Foreword and Introduction
Notes on the recipes
Moulds
Boiled & steamed puddings
Baked puddings

Batter puddings
Bread puddings
Jellies, milk puddings
& ices
Sauces, pastry, etc.

The story of Pudding, savoury and sweet, giving the original recipes and historical background to each and every one of them. Celebrating the chefs to kings and queens, and the cookery book authors of times gone by.

With clear instructions to create the best steamed puddings and handmade ice creams, as in the olden days.

Written and photographed by Regula Ysewijn
with illustrations by Bruno Vergauwen

MURDOCH BOOKS
SYDNEY · LONDON

Pride
and
Pudding

This book is a tribute to the cookery writers of the past: the master chefs to kings and queens; the female cookbook writers – of whom there are surprisingly plenty; the confectioners; the physicians; the poets; the cookery teachers; and those writers – usually ladies, again – who were driven by a profound passion for British food.
Thank you for writing everything down.

The History of British Puddings Savoury and Sweet

Boiled & steamed puddings 64

Baked puddings 146

Batter puddings 192

Foreword

I love puddings. Sweet, savoury, boiled, steamed, baked and fried – I will eat all of them. But when I say pudding, I mean PUDDING. I don't mean sweets, or desserts. In modern Britain, pudding has come to mean anything sweet at the end of a meal. Pudding is shorthand for many things I don't like: overly sweet cakes, Americanised brownies, fruit in anything but its most raw form ...

When I want a pudding, I want something solid, something fuelling, something so quintessentially British that it reinforces who I am at a very basic level; and yet it's something that is so hard to define that in many ways those feelings are the definition.

Pudding's had a bad press. Someone described as a pudding is overweight, rotund. If a substance is puddinglike, it's solid, unyielding, stodgy. But there's something glorious about those very aspects of pudding. Pudding fills the stomach. Pudding salves the soul. Pudding's very solidity grounds us, and its traditional round or oval shape is unflinchingly simple.

Pudding cuts right to the heart of Britishness. In the eighteenth century, when British cuisine was growing up and developing an identity, pudding was central to British gastronomy. It represented British simplicity, adaptability and perhaps a little bit of thuggishness in the face of the prevailing fashion for French food, criticised as fanciful, wasteful and full of deception. It appeared in satires as a symbol of the Empire, and illustrations as a symbol of family.

The Victorians had puddings for every occasion, recognising that no matter what class you were, and what position you occupied, with a pudding on the table you were all as one. The decline of the pudding, in some ways, echoes a confusion over what nationality and national identity means in the modern world, and whether they are even useful ideas at all.

Of course, we can read too much into it. But I do think that pudding and Britishness are intrinsically linked, and that were we to talk about 'getting a British', in the same way we in Britain talk about 'getting an Indian' or 'getting a Chinese' [meal], then what we'd be getting would be a pudding. And I'd be okay with that.

Prejudiced I may be, but I'm pretty proud of my country's pudding heritage. You'll see as you peruse this book, there's a lot more to pudding than meets the eye. For me, seeing pudding through the eyes of someone who has come to love it, despite the breadth of the North Sea between herself and Pudding Central, is a glorious way to appreciate it even more. Delve in (preferably with a spoon), and enjoy. Here's to pudding!

Dr Annie Gray, food historian

Pudding & me

For nearly two years, my life has revolved around the British pudding. A political pamphlet of the 1700s said, 'The Head of Man is like a Pudding' (*A Learned Dissertation on Dumpling*, 1726); and on many occasions while writing this book my head did feel like a pudding. One with delightful air holes, speckled with currants and covered in rich eggy custard sauce.

The task of uncovering the history of the British pudding consisted of ploughing through about two hundred books: some historical and some written about history or people; some books were poems, diaries and political pamphlets. I started collecting the antique cookery books I couldn't consult online or at libraries; handwritten notebooks and postcards; looking for clues in every imaginable place. Then I set out to collect the original moulds in which these puddings had been made through the ages. Needless to say, when you are dealing with such rarities they take a long time to gather and a greedy bite out of your savings too.

But this wasn't all: the book needed pictures, and as I am a food and lifestyle photographer, I did the photography for my own book – and the design for that matter – and my husband, a talented illustrator, created the wicked illustrations that tell part of the story.

But the recipe shots all needed plates and things, and I wanted them all to be of English make, so I needed to collect those too. Burleigh, one of England's oldest surviving potteries (with whom I have a lovely relationship), kindly sent me some pottery, and the rest I gathered from markets and the usual online sources.

This was going to be a fairly straightforward project: a pudding book, except it became a project that would be with me for two years, and one that would dictate my life and my dreams at times. It has been an education. And although my quest has occasionally been nerve-racking – partly because I do not live in Britain, but mostly because I do not come from a scholarly background – I would dip my spoon in this bowl again.

Luckily I had a base to start from: I already knew a lot about British food and culture, having blogged about it for five years. I have been an Anglophile since I was a little girl; I loved England before I knew what the word love meant. We travelled around England, Scotland and Wales and I saw many beautiful villages, castles and poetic landscapes. I enjoyed the regional food and pub classics, and as I was a picky eater, getting me to eat was no easy task. I remember my mum telling me one time that all my childhood memories seem to be connected to the food I ate. So food was always on my mind, even then.

Writing at first for an international audience, I needed to paint a picture of Britain's – in particular, England's – social history. This is important, to show how the pudding evolved from the times of the Roman occupation until the present day. But it is also important to give some kind of explanation about why British food went from being the lauded subject of diarists and letter writers to a subject of ridicule.

This book is a tribute to the English cookery writers of the past. The master chefs to kings and queens, the female cookbook writers – of which there are surprisingly plenty – the confectioners, the physicians, the poets, the cookery teachers and those writers – usually ladies again – who were driven by a profound passion for English food.

One of these women, Florence White, established the English Folk Cookery Association in 1928 and published a compendium of traditional English recipes in *Good Things in England* (1932) as well as several other works on cookery. Florence perfectly expressed my feelings for this project of mine:

> I am not blowing my own trumpet; gladly and gratefully I acknowledge that the cookery wisdom in this book is the heritage of all of us from Yesteryear. My job has simply been to select and record it.
> *Good English Food*, 1952

There are enough books with exciting new recipes, but I think it is important to revive these historical recipes, which are equally special, if not more special because they were lovingly prepared so long ago. It fits into my philosophy of 'be happy with what you have' and that is what this is all about. I am blowing new life into something that was already there for us to enjoy, but is so often overlooked or forgotten.

Why British food?

So why would a Flemish girl dive into British food and not the more fashionable and socially acceptable French or Italian cookery?

British food has evolved much more than French or Italian food. First by the different invaders of the island who each brought their own culture with them; then by the religious consequences of the Protestant Reformation, which forbade the richly spiced cuisine of medieval times. Before the Reformation, most recipes in English, French and Italian recipe books were similar and in some cases the same. Blancmange is a great example, as the name of this dish is identical in all these nations' cookbooks, and it can even be found in Spanish, Portuguese, Italian, Dutch and Scandinavian books.

Most of these early cookery books also had dishes that were especially designed for Lent, as the Catholic faith forbade the consumption of warm-blooded animals and eggs on the fast days that took up nearly a third of the year. After the Reformation, when England became Protestant – and especially during the reign of the Puritan Cromwell – this changed. Not only was the use of dried fruits and spices deemed too excessive and opulent, 'Lenten dishes' – which often involved counterfeit meat dishes – were found too fussy, too Catholic and too French. As France was a Catholic nation that had always tried to gain power over England – and vice versa – it was considered the enemy.

So what's the original story of this Catholic–French vendetta? Charles I was beheaded for treason, one of the reasons being the reintroducing of several Catholic rituals following his marriage to a Catholic French princess. His son, the future king, fled to France; a Puritan republic took over under rule of Lord Protector Oliver Cromwell to rid England of the frivolous Catholic ways ... and Catholic people. Cromwell died and the exiled Charles II was restored to the throne. With the return of the king came an appetite for French food and fashion and the approval of the food ways of pre-Cromwell and pre-Reformation England, which were now just assumed to be French.

But England's cuisine had evolved and the simpler and more honest way of cooking that was favoured after the Reformation continued as common fare and was joined by some of the foods the English had loved from the centuries before.

The love–hate relationship continued when James succeeded Charles II. The political elite found James too pro-French, and when he produced a Catholic heir, tempers rose. Eventually he was deposed and fled to France. After a Protestant invasion, his Protestant daughter Mary became a true Protestant queen and no other Catholic would ever sit on the British throne.

How all of this affected the pudding and British food you can read in the pages of this book, where I go into further detail, explaining how enclosures of common land drove people to capitalism and others to starvation.

Today, Britain is full of small independent cafés and restaurants serving up beautiful regional food such as Lancashire hot-pots, Melton Mowbray pies, Aylesbury duck and Bakewell pudding. The capital has an exciting scene of restaurants cooking up modern British food and also the newest of the cuisines from all over the world. You can taste the world in Britain, but you can also taste Britain in Britain.

And this is the strength of the cuisine. Young people in Britain will eat a steamed bun or a bowl of ramen one day, fish and chips on the next, and on a Saturday evening they will go in to town to enjoy some exciting new British cuisine, prepared with regional ingredients to be proud of. On Sunday they will close the week with a proper home-cooked Sunday roast with Yorkshire puds and more pud for pudding.

There was a time when Europe laughed at British food, and there was a moment when even a lot of Brits were starting to laugh at it. But that time has changed, and will continue to change.

I am a Flemish girl writing this, brought up on Belgian food, which is in its essence French. But I love British food: I love jellied eels, traditional pie and mash, a proper fish and chips, venison pudding, steak and ale pie, and a proper roasted loin of pork with crackling and Yorkshire puddings to soak up all the juices. I love the honesty of the food, the tradition and the history, and I hope you will too.

Regula Ysewijn

All the proofe of a pudding, is in the eating

William Camden, *Remaines of a Greater Worke*, 1605

English Proverb

Meaning: you can only judge something after you have experienced it.

Origin: the earliest version was a medieval proverb, quoted in the poem *Kyng Alisaunder* (transcribed by Henry Weber, 1810):
"Hit is y-writein, Every thyng, Himseolf sheweth in tastyng."

Blessed be he
that invented pudding

When we speak of pudding we will all, British or not, think of a sweet course concluding a meal. But the term 'pudding' has only been connected to this last part of the meal since the twentieth century. In its early days, pudding started out as a savoury dish which was mostly meat-based, such as a haggis or a sausage.

The etymology of the English word pudding leads in several directions. A very possible explanation for its ancestry is the Latin word *botellus*, meaning sausage, from which very likely came the French word *boudin*. Another option is the West Germanic stem *pud* which meant 'to swell', or the Westphalian dialect *puddek* meaning 'lump'. One that is very close is the Low German *pudde-wurst* which was the word for their black pudding.

Basically, pudding is the name of a mixture that is prepared either in animal skins like a sausage or haggis, wrapped in a pudding cloth or in a vessel such as a tray, pastry casing or mould. In *A Book of Cookrye* from 1584 (by A.W.) we find recipes for puddings made in vegetables, much like the Mediterranean stuffed vegetables we know today. There have also been medieval recipes for fish, game or large birds prepared 'with a pudding in their belly', which can be compared to the stuffing for a Christmas turkey. The word pudding has an ambiguous nature as it also refers to the intestines of a man or animal in some old texts. This could very well be the reason why pudding is named as it is, as the earliest ones were prepared in intestines – indeed, some still are – and became filled puddings.

To explain how the pudding evolved from being a savoury sausage-like preparation to being a synonym for all kinds of sweet stuff, we have to take a journey through Britain's rich culinary and cultural past. Pudding is one of the most characteristic dishes of British cuisine. It has been favoured for so many centuries that we see it pop up in literature throughout the ages.

Quite extraordinarily, it would be a Frenchman visiting England in the 1690s who would write about the British pudding in a lyrical manner:

> **Blessed be he that invented pudding,** for it is a Manna that hits the palates of all sorts of people; a manna better than that of the wilderness, because the people are never weary of it. Ah what an excellent thing is an English pudding! To come in pudding-time, is as much as to say, to come in the most lucky moment in the world. Give an English man a pudding, and he shall think it a noble treat in any part of the world.
>
> Francois Maximilian Misson, *Mémoires et observations faites par un voyageur en Angleterre*, 1698

So what is a pudding?

Let us first take a look at what we categorise as puddings today. Although the term 'pudding' has become synonymous with dessert in Britain, not all puddings are desserts, while all desserts are puddings in the modern sense of the word.

Boiled and steamed puddings

Early puddings are, as I explained, sausage-type dishes, which were usually boiled, then often smoked, or roasted. They were either made with meat, blood or entirely from rice, spelt or other grains stuffed into some kind of intestine or cloth bag. These puddings were always flavoured in one way or another, either using herbs or spices. Later, candied fruits, fortified wines and liqueurs were added and the puddings nearly all lost their meat content. Steaming them in a basin or mould became the favoured method over boiling, when the technique was developed. Today's steamed puddings are usually made of a sponge cake batter, or a rich fruitcake batter and are made either in large pudding moulds, or small individual ones. Savoury versions still exist under the name haggis, blood pudding and white pudding. Dumplings are also puddings.

Baked puddings

Baked puddings are those in which the pudding mixture is placed in either a bowl or tray, which is sometimes prepared with a layer of pastry, making it more of a tart or a pie. Today, most tarts and pies are considered 'pudding' as they fit into the dessert category. They are of course all baked.

Bread puddings

Bread puddings are made by including bread – stale or fresh – as a primary ingredient. Some previously named types of pudding can also contain breadcrumbs, but that doesn't make them bread puddings. In a bread pudding, the bread is usually, but not always, left whole and often acts like a crust encasing some kind of cream or egg mixture or fruit. Bread puddings are often baked.

Batter puddings

These are made by making a light pancake-type batter which is then baked or fried in butter or fat. These can be Yorkshire puddings, but also fritters.

Milk puddings

The sweet and delicately flavoured puddings made with animal milk, almond or oat milk include creams, custards and ice creams.

Jellies

These are sweet puddings set with either vegetable or grain starches, or animal-derived gelatine. They are often boldly coloured and shaped in a mould for dramatic effect. They can encase fruit and in medieval times they often encased meat or fish, much like aspic, although they are no longer known as jellies.

The early years

To talk about the prehistoric settlers of England we must refer to archaeological finds and their different interpretations – therefore much is based on speculation. It is hard to get a complete picture as small animal and fish bones may have decayed completely, leaving us to think that some animals weren't eaten. Also, vessels made out of certain materials might not have survived because they were less sturdy, which makes us wonder what was used and how they made them and if they existed or how common they were. Grimston Lyles Hill made the earliest ceramics in Britain, dated to around 4000 BCE. Pots of this ware were found throughout Britain, so it is likely a trade was established. Again, the way these pots were used in cookery is uncertain. Archaeologists have suggested a method with 'pot boilers': stones that were placed in the fire and then added to the liquid in the pot to warm it. Others have said the pottery vessels were fired in such a way that they could have been placed on the embers of a fire directly to cook meals, without them breaking. Whatever happened, we know for certain that there was a culture in cooking. Quite extraordinarily, while I was in the final stages of writing these pages, scientists found evidence of wheat in Britain 8000 years ago. This suggests the grain was traded with people from the East, long before it was grown by the first British farmers. In ancient times man had to rely largely upon hunting and gathering, but things changed once he was able to farm, raise cattle and establish trades in food.

We don't know if these prehistoric people made puddings. I can only assume they did, as no part of an animal would be wasted and stuffing intestines or skins with blood other foods such as offal, berries and grains seems like a very logical thing to do.

British cuisine evolved from the same place as French, Italian and other European cuisines: Ancient Greece, Rome and Persia. But, as you may expect, due to climate, type of soil and taste, it evolved differently.

The very first time that a pudding appeared in European literature was in Homer's saga *The Odyssey* in about 800 BCE. This story from classical antiquity tells of the Greek hero Odysseus (known as Ulysses in Roman myths) and his journey returning home to Ithaca after the fall of Troy. Assumed dead during his 10-year absence, his house was filled with suitors hoping to marry his wife, Penelope. The men competed for Penelope's hand while also taking advantage of her hospitality by feasting on meat and drink. One of the passages speaks of preparing black pudding: 'there are some goats' paunches down at the fire, which we have filled with blood and fat, and set aside for supper.' (Translation by Samuel Butler, 1900.)

Roman puddings

When the Romans arrived in Britain around 43 CE many things changed: Beef and pork were the preferred meats of Roman Britain, and also a part of the rations of a Roman soldier. Consequently, cattle-rearing and other forms of meat farming became more regulated. New animal species, vegetables, herbs and fruit trees were introduced and a new system of farming brought in, creating enclosures around farmsteads. Some of those enclosures were leporaria or 'hare gardens', and deer parks were established too.

The Romans also brought with them one of the first sets of recipes: *De Re Coquinaria*, a cookbook credited as a kind of homage to the gourmet Apicius, is a set of 10 books on Roman cookery believed to date from the late fourth or early fifth century CE. The topics vary from 'The Careful Housekeeper' to 'The Fisherman'. The number of different spices and herbs used in the recipes of this book is significant. It is commonly assumed that Europe was introduced to spices during the Crusades. It is true that the Crusades had an impact on the people's taste for exotic flavours, but spices and aromatics were introduced by the Romans centuries before.

In Book II, titled 'The Meat Mincer or Minces', we find a number of recipes for minced meat and seafood dishes, stuffed animal intestines and the first instructions to make sausages. We also find the first recipes for a black pudding and a white pudding; the black pudding using blood, cereals and spices and the white pudding sometimes entirely cereal in composition or using white meats such as chicken, pork or pheasant. It shows that this part of the gastronomy was favoured and not feared, whereas we now often find guts and offal unappetising.

> Botellum sic facies
> sex ovi vitellis coctis, nucleis pineis concisis cepam, porrum concisum, ius crudum misces, piper minutum, et sic intestinum farcies. Adicies liquamen et vinum, et sic coques.
> The first black pudding recipe, as given in Apicius: *De Re Coquinaria*

It is believed that the Celtic Britons ate differently from the Romans, even after years of Roman occupation. Not only did the Roman villas have much better-equipped kitchens (the Romans introduced the first ovens to England), there was also a difference in taste. The Romans preferred beef and pork, while the remains of Celtic victims of the Roman invasion – buried with joints of mutton in Maiden Castle in Dorset – tell us that mutton might have been prized enough to be deemed an important burial gift. The Celts also continued to speak their own language and live with their own traditions.

Cattle-rearing must have provided the Celtic Britons with most of their meat, but hunting, fishing and foraging would still have provided them with a lot of their food, especially for those who did not have access to farmyard animals or money to purchase meat. Castorware pottery from the Nene Valley in Northamptonshire of that time is illuminated with hunting scenes of dogs pursuing deer or hares, which is either because hunting was common, or they tried to copy the natural or mythical world scenes on much of the pottery imported from Gaul.

Cauldrons, though produced since the late Bronze Age, began to be manufactured on a much larger scale so that they became more widely used. But one single pot was usually all people had to cook all of their food in and, for centuries to come, this would hardly change for regular folk.

Some of the recipes for Roman sausages and puddings hardly change at all over the next few centuries and it's hard to believe that the Celtic Britons didn't cook puddings or sausages before the Romans came; however, we do not have written proof, only speculation and logical thinking.

Making puddings gave people the opportunity to cook something else along with the main dish they were cooking in their one pot. Animal intestines would provide the vessel in which they could stuff the minced offal, offcuts of meat and blood left over from slaughtering. This they would have flavoured with herbs, usually sweet ones, and the odd bit of pepper or any other spice they were lucky enough to get their hands on.

Adventus Saxonum 410 CE

When the Romans retreated from Britain after nearly 400 years of occupation, the Saxons, Angles and Jutes began to arrive with their boats from the areas around South Denmark. The Venerable Bede, a monk from the then Kingdom of Northumbria, wrote that their nation came to Britain, leaving their own lands empty. The invaders were referred to as Anglo–Saxon, and called themselves Englisc, from which the word English and England derives.

A lot of them were already in Britain under the 'Foederati' or 'Treaty of Alliance', where tribes who were neither from Roman colonies nor beneficiaries of Roman citizenship would provide warriors to fight in the Roman armies in exchange for certain benefits. In short, they were mercenaries. During these treaties the tribes often rebelled, and there was a constant threat from northern tribes such as the Picts and the Scots. As a result, Hadrian's Wall was built by the Emperor Hadrian as a military defence from these barbarian northerners and other invaders from the sea.

When the threat became too large, the Romans retreated and left the Britons to the mercy of the invaders. Roman cities decayed, their villas and farms were abandoned, imported animal breeds merged with the native ones and the vulnerable ones were killed. Cultivated plants and herbs previously grown on Roman estates started to grow wild and so the land became richer as fruit trees and crops were able to grow outside their enclosed orchards. The population of England shrunk drastically after the Romans left, leaving much of the arable land deserted and prone to being consumed by woodland again, where wolves and bears were lord and master.

Because we have no recipes other than a few medical texts that give instructions for food for invalids, it is not certain whether the puddings and sausages of the Romans were still being made, or if they were ever popular with the Britons and later the Saxons. What remained of Roman cookery were most likely those dishes that were easiest to prepare, that had been around before but were adapted and those that were most favoured. But surprisingly little else remained.

Other works that give us some glimpses of daily life in Anglo–Saxon England are *Aelfric's Colloquy* (translated by Ann Watkins), which took the form of a dialogue game for young monks and novices to practise Latin. The pupil has to explain the duties of the working day acting as a farmer, hunter, fisherman or cook, but sadly no puddings are mentioned.

The Monasteriales Indicia (Debby Banham, ed., 1991) is a book with a monastic sign language used by Catholic monks during times when the Benedictine Rule forbade them to speak. These signs not only give us an insight on what was eaten in the monasteries, but they also provide clues as to how some foods looked. For example, the illustration in the *Monasteriales Indicia* of the sign for bread shows us that bread in that period was only the size of a circle one could make by putting one's index fingers together and doing the same with the thumbs. Of course this doesn't tell us what regular people ate, as monastic food was very different and often much richer. Sadly again, there was no illustrated sign for a pudding, but that doesn't mean there were none.

The Viking Age

T he Vikings were raiders or pirates from Scandinavian countries. In 793 CE a few boats arrived and Vikings raided the abbey on the holy island of Lindisfarne in Northumberland. This was recorded in the *Anglo–Saxon Chronicle*, an account of events in Anglo–Saxon and Norman England. The Vikings weren't planning on staying, they initially just wanted to plunder and take riches back to their homelands across the sea; however, many did stay eventually as some were looking for land to farm.

The Vikings coming to England were mostly Danes. They chased away or massacred the Saxons, as the Saxons had done to the Britons earlier, though genetic research shows that in some areas these different peoples remained to live with their own kin. No entire tribe of people was completely wiped out, as was previously assumed of the Saxons and the Britons.

The colonisation of England had begun and the new invader charged the Anglo–Saxons 'Danegeld', or tribute, a kind of tax paid in order to keep their villages safe from being ravaged. The wealth of the Saxon nobles declined because of the Danegeld. Trade and commerce, including that of spices, is believed to have nearly disappeared during this time and the land was struck by decades of floods, snow and frost.

Cooking would still have been done in the one cauldron over an open fire. The Danes would also have brought with them the culinary traditions of their homeland. They introduced more fish to the diet of the English and developed the fishing trade further. Exact accounts of what was eaten are as good as nonexistent so we have no way of knowing that they would have made puddings, but again I'm inclined to believe they did.

The Norman Conquest

William the Conqueror's invasion of England in 1066 destroyed England's links with Scandinavia, and brought the country in closer contact with the continent, in particular France. William wanted to know the exact value of the riches of England so he ordered the compilation of a survey giving him information on who owned what throughout the country, and who owed him tax and how much. This record, now named *The Domesday Book*, was compiled around 1086. It also noted how many farm animals, ploughs, mills and so on that each manor or village had. *The Domesday Book* therefore gives historians a detailed picture of what life was like in England in the eleventh century.

The Norman nobility developed a rich and lavish cuisine. They brought with them the recipes and ways they had adopted and adapted from the Mediterranean areas they conquered, such as the Arab cuisine they savoured in conquered Sicily. The spiced foods of Persia were so loved by the Anglo–Normans that naturally they brought more influences and spices back with them to England during the Crusades. The spice trade was very important and pepper was often used as currency, and later as spice rents. During the reign of King John, the royal accounts listed pepper, almonds, cumin, rice, cloves, ginger, saffron and nutmeg.

It is important to note, though, that the elite had been using many spices in their kitchens since Roman times, although they temporarily disappeared during the rule of the Danes.

Pudding or pudingis

The earliest recipes we have all come from the kitchens of the elite, and the ones we can date most accurately are those of Alexander Neckham. Around 1190, Neckham wrote several works but in his *Nominibus Utensilium* he gives an insight into the upkeep and the design of an Anglo–Norman manor house or castle. He gives us some of the first actual recipe instructions: slicing vegetables, how to prepare fish and a list of domestic utensils such as pots and pans.

When talking about the kinds of preserved foods used to fill the castle storehouses, Neckham states some of the following foods: 'vino, pernis, baconibus, carne in succiduo posita, hyllis, salsuciis, tucetis, carne suilla, carne arietina, carne bovina, carne ovina et leguminibus diversis'.

The three words that were of interest to me were 'hyllis, salsuciis, tucetis': translated into Anglo–Norman French in Thomas Wright's *Dictionary of Obsolete and Provincial English* (1857) to 'aundulyes, saucistres, pudingis'. But Wright's book is known to be one of the least reliable sources with often flawed and misleading translations. The Neckham text was used as a Latin learning text for centuries, so there are many translations or 'glosses' of his words. Often, however, different scribes give different or several glosses.

Although I was excited to finally find an early reference to the word pudding, I discovered that the gloss 'pudingis' for the Latin 'tucetis' is not correct. Help came from a man named Dave Rainer who is able to read medieval Latin. He kindly provided me with his own translation of Neckham's words. Still of particular interest to me were those three words, which he translated to 'small sausages, large sausages, preserved beef'. So I had found an early twelfth century record of puddings after all. These puddings, or sausages as they most likely were, were probably of the smoked and cured kind as the text does refer to foods suitable for a castle storehouse.

City food differed from that in the country as towns, short of arable land, could not feed themselves and relied on imports. In great cities like London, public eating-houses were established. William Fitzstephen, cleric and administrator to Thomas Becket (who became Archbishop of Canterbury in 1162), wrote about these in his description of London:

> There is also in London, on the bank of the river, amongst the wine shops, which are kept in ships and cellars, a public eating-house; there every day, according to the season, may be found viands of all kinds, roast, fried and boiled, fish large and small, coarser meat for the poor, and more delicate for the rich, such as venison, fowls and small birds. If friends, wearied with their journey, should unexpectedly come to a citizen's house, and, being hungry, should not like to wait till fresh meat be bought and cooked.
>
> William Fitzstephen, *A Survey of London*, 1598

We find some more clues to the gastronomy of Anglo–Norman England in the thirteenth century *Treatise* of Walter of Bibbesworth. This was a book written in verse in the 1230s to help a widowed English mother teach her two children the then-fashionable French of the nobility. The work is of significance as it shows that the mother's language in the early thirteenth century was English and not French and that it is possible that the usage of French was already declining in popularity and only being taught to use in matters of managing an estate.

Bibbesworth's poem suggests that the term haggis – a stuffed stomach of a sheep, filled with kidneys, heart, suet and herbs – was commonly known in English and French of that time as there are no glosses provided for the word. Haggis is the pudding that would, centuries later, become the national treasure of Scotland and be dubbed a 'Scottish dish'.

By the 1280s the eating-houses had moved away from the Thames and towards the centre of London, where they remained, and we find references to commercial cooks, cook-shops and street sellers. The *Norwich Leet Roll of 1287–88* (William Hudson, ed., 1891) mentions a mustard-seller, and sellers of pork sausages and puddings: these would most likely have been meat puddings like haggis.

The Forme of Cury

The fourteenth century started with one failed harvest after another, causing the Great Famine. The year 1348 marked the arrival of an even greater evil, the Black Death. Two years later the disease had wiped out nearly half the population of England. The social change in the aftermath of the Black Death, and the further crippling high taxes resulting from the Hundred Years' War with France, led to the Peasants' Revolt. The peasants were angry that they had to suffer so that the elite could wage war and feast in their great halls.

Ten years after the Revolt a book was compiled by the master cook of King Richard II. We know it today as *The Forme of Cury*: 'the method of cooking'. The book, of which there are a number of different incomplete vellum manuscripts, is the earliest surviving book on cookery in the English language. It is considered one of the most important manuscripts of the Middle Ages, along with the earliest French recipe collection *Le Viandier* and the Latin *Liber de Coquina*. All three recipe collections have quite a few near-identical recipes.

The Forme of Cury is, however, not a cookery book as we know them today. Most common dishes would not feature in this book as they were considered to be general knowledge in the kitchens. Before the early eighteenth century, cookbooks weren't seen as collections of instructions but as aide-memoires for seasoned cooks, to help them recall the more elaborate, uncommon and complicated dishes that didn't appear on the dining table on a regular basis.

This book also doesn't tell us anything about what the ordinary people ate, as this was court cookery at its best. The recipes in *The Forme of Cury* appear luxurious and feature Blank Mange (see page 254), a dish of significance that would become a favourite pudding during the course of the centuries, up to the present day. Baked custards, either with meat or without, were also featured and also the first rice pudding (see page 310). Another great pudding was a Sambocade (see page 150) an early cheesecake flavoured with elderflower. For fritters, which are batter puddings very popular with the rich crowd of the Middle Ages, *The Forme of Cury* gives several recipes.

Many people picture medieval food as unsophisticated and plain, but the recipes and ingredients of *The Forme of Cury* have an exotic and elegant feel. Remember that the Romans brought aromatic spices and herbs to England. And when the Normans invaded they brought Arabic influences to English shores from occupied Sicily and southern Italy, which was ruled by the Arabs prior to Norman rule.

We can see that Arabic influence in some of *The Forme of Cury*'s recipes. Professor Melitta Adamson notes that the recipe called 'Maumenee', can also be found in *Liber de Coquina* where it is called Malmoma and presumed a variant of blancmange by its editor. The Arab name for this dish is Ma'muniya; it is a sweet porridge thickened with white meat, rice flour, almonds, spices and coloured with saffron. Looking at the ingredients it does seem like a blancmange; however, these dishes weren't European versions of Arab dishes, they were merely inspired by them. The close relation between the dishes in name, could have been a coincidence. As you can see, English cuisine is clearly fusion by nature so couldn't have been anything but imaginative and rich. Tasty too.

introduction |

Medieval feasting: a dinner theatre

By the fifteenth century, more manuscript recipe books were written, or more survived, and therefore we have more data to interpret. These writings, however, are mainly focused on the food of the elite, while peasants would mostly have survived on their daily pottage which was made with grains or pulses and flavoured with herbs.

Meals of the upper class were not defined by a system of courses as we know them today. Nor was division made between sweet and savoury. Meat dishes often contained sugar and dried fruits, and sweet puddings could contain some form of meat or fish, often used as a thickener. Savoury meat puddings were made in intestines, but so, too, were custards and rice puddings.

The bills of fare in the early texts described that the dishes were placed on the table in banquet style, with each course containing vegetables, grains, fish, meat and sweet dishes for the guests to choose from. The food would be eaten off a 'trencher' or 'manchet', a thick piece of bread serving as a plate, or from a communal vessel. For the latter, a strict etiquette was followed.

In 1407, for the installation feast of the Bishop Clifford, a spectacular jelly was made in the shape of a castle with a devil and a priest in the midst of a custard-filled moat. Theatrical ornate creations like this accompanied every course and were called 'subtleties'.

To give you an idea of these elaborate meals, the following dishes are those served to King Richard II on a feast at the Bishop's place of Durham in London in 1387, according to Thomas Austin in *Two Fifteenth-century Cookery-books* (1888): The first course was venison with furmenty (a pottage made of cracked wheat), a meat pottage, boars' heads, roasted haunches of meat, and roasted swans and pigs. Finally, there was also a custard tart called a crustade lumbard in paste and a subtlety, which is sadly not described. The second course was a pottage called gele (probably a slightly set stew with meat or fish), a pottage de blandesore (a white soup), roasted cranes, pigs, pheasants, herons, chickens and bream. There were tarts, carved meats and roasted two-year-old rabbits and another subtlety. The third course consisted of almond pottage, Lombardian stew, roasted venison, chickens, rabbits, partridge, quails, larks, payne puff (a fritter), a jelly, long fritters, and, lastly again, a subtlety. After great feasts, all leftovers would have been put into alms vessels and distributed to the poor.

A variety of dishes were presented at meals so that each diner could eat according to their own 'humoral temperament'. The four humours of Hippocratic medicine were based on the assumption that the world was made up of four elements: water, fire, air and earth, which were connected to our body's wellbeing. These elements stood for four temperaments: sanguine, choleric, phlegmatic and melancholic; each corresponding to one of the body's humours: blood, yellow bile, phlegm and black bile. They were believed to be created by the body when food was digested. This could either provide good humoral balance, which meant that you were healthy, or could make the body out of balance, which meant you were unwell. This holistic approach, with links to Ayurvedic medicine, was adopted by Greek, Roman and Persian physicians.

Beasts & wonders

The medieval food of the rich was highly extravagant and decorative in order to impress and entertain guests. Not only were tables adorned with imposing subtleties shaped like castles, eagles and other grand creations, centrepieces such as peacocks, swans and other large animals were often sewn back into their own feathers after roasting so that they appeared alive. Sometimes an entirely fictive creature would be created by sewing parts of different animals together. One of these curious dishes, 'the cockatrice', is one of the most intriguing dishes dating from this period.

One recipe for a cocatrice (translated by Constance B. Hieatt in *Cocatrice and Lamprey Hay*, 2012) instructed the cook to recreate this fantastical creature by sewing five different parts of animals to each other: a pig's head, the forequarters of a pig, the hindquarters of the cock, the forequarters of a cock (strangely used in reverse order) and the hindquarters of a pig. The pig's head has to come first and the last part should be the pig's tail.

Imagine your dining table with this creature staring you in the face! It might sound like a strange thing to do to a main course but I find it highly inventive and it shows how much effort was put into a feast. Heston Blumenthal constructed a fire-breathing cockatrice for one of his television programs. The guests were entertained and intrigued: a meal like this certainly wouldn't be boring!

Another theatrical aspect of the dinner table was the illusion dish, designed to fool either the eye or the palate. These elevated the cook to the status of an artist. To serve one thing under the guise of another was something that would continue to feature in English cuisine in the centuries to come.

But often these illusion dishes were also there to solve the problem of fasting days. Imitations such as a blancmange made of fish instead of capon are simple examples but certainly not the most inventive. Fish meat was also moulded to look like meatloaf, roast beef or game birds.

Eggs in Lent is a dish of counterfeit eggs, made of almond cream in real eggshells. This mid-fifteenth century recipe is from Thomas Austin's *Two Fifteenth-century Cookery-Books* compiled from several manuscripts in 1888.

> Eyroun in Lentyn
> Take eggs, and blow out that is within at the other end; then wash the shell clean in warm water; then take good milk of almonds, and set it on the fire; then take a fair canvas, & pour the milk thereon, & let run out the water; then take it out on the cloth, & gather it together with a platter; then put sugar enough thereto; then take half of it, & color it with saffron, a little, & do thereto powder cinnamon; then take & do the white in the nether end of the shell, & in the middle the yolk, & fill it up with the white; but not too full, for going over; then set it in the fire & roast it, & serve forth.

These illusory eggs would reappear in the eighteenth century as an impressive-looking pudding made to look like a hen's nest with straw made of lemon peel and eggs made of flummery (see page 269).

introduction

We find some more interesting pudding-related things in a cookery book written entirely in verse called *Liber Cure Cocorum* dating from around 1430, where we find the first recipe for a haggis (see page 76). The recipe is simple and easily reproduced today; I am particularly fond of the usage of the fresh herbs. Haggis has strong ties with the puddings from Roman times and it appears it can be said that haggis was a type of pudding under which a number of variations existed. Just like there are a variety of different types of sausages.

In the Austin manuscripts (*Two Fifteenth-century Cookery-books*, 1888), we find a blancmange made with either fish or lobster for fish days. The church dictated fasting, which meant the abstinence from meat, for nearly half the days of the year, including every Friday, Saturday and often Wednesday as well as during Lent and Advent. Recipes would therefore often appear in texts alongside versions suitable for fast days. Often it would even just be a sentence added to the end of the recipe giving an option to replace some ingredients with others suitable for Lent.

Another significant moment for this century is the first time a written record can be found of the use of a pudding cloth instead of animal intestines to cook a pudding in. Up until very recently, it was assumed the pudding cloth first appeared in books at the start of the seventeenth century. People would, however, continue to prepare puddings in skins when they were available and one cannot forget that the skins were also used for their nutritional value. The use of the pudding cloth would allow the pudding dishes to evolve as they could be made more often and by those with no access to animals.

The food of the upper class remained highly spiced, as it had been since the Roman occupation, – and focused on sweet-and-sour flavour combinations. Sugar remained in use like spice and was used sparingly because it was so expensive. Common seasonings included verjuice, wine and vinegar in combination with honey, herbs and spices. Those spices were also used in the puddings, jellies and fritters.

The Northumberland Household Book, written towards the end of the fifteenth century (edited in 1905 by T. Percy), tells us exactly which spices, and how many of them, they bought in a year. The account lists pepper, mace, cloves, ginger, cinnamon, nutmeg, grains of paradise (a kind of pepper), long pepper, turnsole, saunders, ground aniseed, galingale, saffron and sugar. Dried fruits and nuts such as currants, prunes, dates and almonds were also named amongst them. Almonds were used as a thickener in puddings and also in soups, stews and sauces. Almonds were also made into almond milk, which was used in many dishes. Saffron was one of the most favoured spices and people experimented with growing it in various places in England; we can still see evidence of that in the town of Saffron Walden in Essex. In recent years saffron is being grown again in England on a very small scale.

The theory that food was spiced to disguise the flavour of rotting meat has been discarded in recent years. Those households that could afford precious spices would certainly have been able to afford fresh meat. In fact, when recipes constantly call for a clean bowl, or a clean pot, or give instructions to wash things very clean, it would be hard to believe they would have, at the same time, use a spoiled piece of meat.

The Reformation's influence on food

The Tudor King Henry VIII was crowned in 1509 and the sixteenth century was a period of change in many respects. After four years on the throne he successfully invaded France, only to sign the Treaty of London in 1518, uniting the kingdoms of western Europe in the face of a greater threat, the Ottomans. Peace with France was, however, short-lived: it was France after all, and there was history.

Foods from the New World were introduced and graced the tables of the impressive feasts Henry VIII was famous for. Francesco Chieregati, a papal emissary visiting England, was particularly impressed with the English ways of throwing a party:

> The banquet which followed in the Palace of Whitehall was on a magnificent scale; the gold and silver plate; piled on the sideboard was worth a king's ransom, and every variety of meat, poultry, game, and fish was served at table. All the dishes were borne before the King by figures of elephants, panthers, tigers, and other animals, admirably designed.
> Letter to Isabella d'Este, 1517

But the finest things in Chieregati's eyes were the jellies made in the shape of castles, towers, churches, and animals of every variety, 'as beautiful and closely copied as possible'. He must have been really impressed during his time at the court as he then goes on to state: 'most illustrious Madama, here in England we find all the wealth and delights in the world. Those who call the English barbarians are themselves barbarians!'

The Church of England was established in 1534 when England broke away from the Catholic Church so Henry could marry the second of his six wives, Anne Boleyn. Henry became the head of the church instead of the pope in Rome. This initiated the English Reformation and resulted in the Dissolution of the Monasteries. The treasury gained great wealth from plundering the monasteries, and those who showed their loyalty to the king were rewarded with former monastic estates and riches. This created a new breed of elite: the wealthy middle class. As Protestantism took over from Catholicism, strict fast days were no longer fixed. This brought a change in the kitchen. Before the Reformation, dishes were more complicated, and one had to be able to cook grand dishes using fish on the many fast days. These 'made dishes' were now deemed deceitful and Catholic and French. Meat became favoured over fish and great efforts were put into properly roasting a joint. This proper honest English cooking, along with having the sovereign as head of the church instead of the pope, became a form of nationalism.

All the cooking was still conducted over a fire, or in front of it using the radiant heat. Roast beef. or any other roasted meat. would become a dish for which England would be famous for in the seventeenth century. The fast-day recipes were forgotten by many after the Reformation, as only those who remained Catholic would continue to cook according to the pre-Reformation style. Remarkably, cooking became a political statement. To cook in the old manner or even the French manner would have shown that you were Catholic and not loyal to the king.

It wouldn't have mattered much to the peasants whether or not it was a fast day, they were lucky to have meat at all in their pottage, which had been their staple food for centuries.

Elizabethan Times

E lizabeth I was said to have such a sweet tooth that by the end of her life her teeth were black. This would have been the case with many of her contemporaries and, curiously, it became a sign of wealth. Highly refined white sugar arrived from the continent in the shape of cones called sugar loaves – these are still produced in Arab countries to the present day. The increase in the use of sugar brought a very big change in the eating habits. Sugar went from being used sparingly, like an expensive spice, to being liberally used in dishes such as sugared flower petals, comfits, and fruit roasted in syrup. Decorations and elaborate 'subtleties' made completely out of sugar, were made for the most lavish feasts. Although edible, they would not have been created to be eaten as they were in the thirteenth and fourteenth centuries, they were meant just for show. A whole new profession, that of confectioner, emerged to feed the need for these imposing sugar creations. The term banquet came to stand for both the course itself and the sweetmeats served at it.

Elizabeth reintroduced Lent and fast days on which fish should be eaten, in order to save the declining coastal towns and fishing industry. She needed fishermen to maintain her naval fleet and the people were probably all too happy to be able to practise their fast days again.

Just over a dozen cookery books were printed in the sixteenth century and manuscript recipe books from this period are also very rare. Recipes in books remain spiced, but slightly less than pre-Reformation medieval recipes. From now on, recipes for haggis, black pudding and white pudding, cooked in animal guts, appear regularly. In *A Book of Cookrye* (by A.W., 1584) we find recipes for a pudding in a turnip, a carrot and a cucumber. These recipes can be compared to Mediterranean stuffed vegetables. Also in this book is the first recipe for Hogs Pudding, a dish popular in the West Country today. Thomas Dawson in *The Good Huswifes Handmaide for the Kitchin* (1594) gives us a recipe 'To boil a conie with a pudding in his bellie' which confirms the ambiguous nature of the word pudding. Another interesting pudding in his book is 'To boyle a legge of Mutton with a pudding'. In this case the vessel is the leg of mutton: he instructs to remove the skin, parboil it, then mix it with suet, herbs and spices, currants and minced dates, before stuffing it into the leg of mutton and boiling it in broth. What an exotic sounding dish!

Dawson also gives us the first recipe for a trifle (see page 290) although at this time the method is more like that of another pudding, a fool (see page 296). As there still wasn't a method for preserving milk, the cream would go straight to the manorial estates for their puddings and tarts, and butter and cheesemaking remained the most important way to process milk. Sweet milk puddings such as flummeries and possets, which were flavoured, coloured and decorated with flowers and almonds, must have looked beautifully dainty on the table of the lord of the manor.

Recipes for tansies (see page 206) appear more often after their first appearance in 1430. They are intriguing because we have a similar dish in Flanders, the 'kruidkoek', which is still popular around the town of Averbode today. Tansies are omelette or pancake-style dishes which originally, as in the Flemish recipe, contained the bitter herb tansy. Interestingly, as with so many other puddings, the tansy wasn't a pudding when it first started to appear in recipe books, but soon it started to be associated with being a sweet dish and recipes for tansy puddings were published.

Seventeenth Century

E ngland would see three monarchs and a republic in the seventeenth century. The Protestant King James I was nearly killed by rebelling Catholics in the famous Gunpowder Plot to blow up the House of Lords in 1605. The thwarted plot is still remembered every year on Bonfire Night, the 5th of November.

In 1625 Charles I succeeded his father, James I. Charles, probably in an attempt to bring his people together, married the Catholic Henrietta of France. But he was showing too much affinity with the Catholic ways, reintroducing several Catholic rituals. France was still considered synonymous with Catholicism, and therefore the enemy. Charles I was eventually beheaded for treason and Britain became a republic for a decade under the Puritan, Oliver Cromwell. Cromwell famously 'cancelled' Christmas and banished Friday and Lenten fasts, and their associated traditional dishes. The Puritans wanted a purer worship without rituals and icons and the festivities of Christmas and Easter were too lavish and Catholic for them. The Reformation and the Puritan rule changed English ways and food by making it more simplified and less extravagant.

Le Cuisinier François, written by Francois la Varenne, was the first French cookery book to be translated into English at the beginning of Cromwell's Puritan rule in 1653. The book, however, essentially showed the dishes that had been known in pre-Reformation England as well. This gave English–Catholics the opportunity to eat like Catholics under the guise of French cuisine, with fast-day dishes and spices. French medieval food and English medieval food had been very much the same.

France had remained a Catholic nation, and therefore the cuisine of that period changed little. The English Catholic gentry employed French chefs so that they could eat according to the Catholic ways without anyone suspecting they weren't loyal to Protestantism.

introduction

A sugar loaf in traditional blue paper is pictured with
a sugar snapper to cut pieces of sugar from the cone,
a 'toleware' spice dungeon and a matching nutmeg grater

Even back then, the French were chauvinistic about their cuisine. La Varenne stated in the dedication of his book: 'Of all cookes in the world, the French are esteem'd the best.' Ironically, many of the dishes in that book for which the author was credited had already appeared in English cookery books long before that time.

When Charles II was restored to the throne, English gastronomy of the upper class became even more influenced by the French. Charles had been living in exile in France and had developed a taste for French fashion and cookery.

Quite a number of British cookery writers still produced books with pre-Reformation recipes. Robert May's book, *The Accomplisht Cook*, was published in 1660, the year of the Restoration, still holding onto the pre-Reformation medieval custom of using spices, dried fruits and candied peels and fish-day recipes. His book also has a huge number of pudding recipes in it. Hannah Wolley's book, *The Queen-Like Closet* of 1670, was the first printed cookery book by a woman. It was also full of those types of recipes, as if the Reformation had never happened.

A great number of the cookbooks published in the seventeenth century were actually written by women. This was a phenomenon totally unknown in France at that time, when high-standard cookery was very much a male thing. In fact it remained fairly uncommon in France until the nineteenth century.

For our pudding, this century would mean even more evolution with more books published and written than ever before. The traditional white and black puddings would continue to pop up in books, as would the haggis, and new and exciting puddings would emerge.

An overview

1615

The first fool recipe is published in *The English Huswife* (Gervase Markham). It was then called a Norfolk Fool. Markham also gives us some of the first recipes for trifle and flummery in the same book, as well as a white-pot, which was a bread and butter pudding prepared in a pot, pan or dish. John Murrell publishes his 'pudding in a frying-panne' and a peculiar 'pudding stued between two dishes' in his book *A Newe Booke of Cookerie*. He is also the first to give a recipe for Cambridge pudding. He is the first to confine the puddings in his book into a pudding chapter.

1645

Colonel Norwood is the first to mention a Christmas pudding in his diary, 'A Voyage to Virginia'.

1660

The earliest English ice-cream recipe is written down by Lady Ann Fanshawe in her manuscript recipe book. She calls it an Icy Cream. Robert May, in *The Accomplisht Cook*, tells us to mould jellies in scallops and other kinds of seashells and also provides us with templates for making tarts in fancy-shaped pastry casings.

1661

William Rabisha's book *The Whole Body of Cookery Dissected* gives instructions to create a tart of jelly and leach (see page 248). By the mid-seventeenth century isinglass, hartshorn and ivory were added to jellies to give them a firmer set, allowing for even more elaborate creations to be made.

1672

The first recipe for a Sussex Pond pudding can be found in *The Queen-Like Closet*, a book written by Hannah Wolley.

1681

A milk pudding called a syllabub and the gooseberry fool appear in a book called *The Compleat Cook*, by Rebecca Price. In this book we also find the first printed recipe for a Quaking Pudding and several other puddings.

1690

French visitor Francois Maximilian Misson raves about pudding in his *Mémoires et Observations*: 'The pudding is a dish very difficult to be described, because of the several sorts there are of it; Flower, Milk, Eggs, Butter, Sugar, Suet, Marrow, Raisins, etc. etc. are the most common Ingredients of a pudding. They bake them in the oven, they boil them with meat, they make them fifty different ways.'

Pictured overleaf: the kitchen of Cotehele Castle, Cornwall, England

Eighteenth Century

Plots and politics may hurt us, but Pudding cannot.

The Head of Man is like a Pudding: And whence have all Rhimes, Poems, Plots and Inventions sprang, but from that same Pudding. What is Poetry, but a Pudding of Words.

The Law is but a Cookery of Quibbles and Contentions. Some swallow every thing whole and unmix'd; so that it may rather be call'd a Heap, than a Pudding. Others are so Squeamish, the greatest Mastership in Cookery is requir'd to make the Pudding Palatable: The Suet which others gape and swallow by Gobs, must for these puny Stomachs be minced to Atoms; the Plums must be pick'd with the utmost Care, and every Ingredient proportion'd to the greatest Nicety, or it will never go down.

Henry Carey, *A Learned Dissertation on Dumpling; its Dignity, Antiquity and Excellence with a Word upon Pudding*, London, 1726

In this satirical political pamphlet the author displays a considerable knowledge of cookery in London and in general; he insinuates that to love pudding is to love corruption. It also shows how much pudding is intertwined with being English. This was a time of vast changes in the political and social landscape. Scotland and Wales joined England as Great Britain. Of course all these changes had an influence on diet.

Peasant cooking

Industrialisation and the increasing enclosure acts, which privatised common land that had previously been available to all, deprived most of the people of access to agricultural land and therefore delivered a giant blow to the peasantry and rural cuisine.

Those peasants who did have land, known as 'yeomen' since the sixteenth century, now became large landowners. The aristocracy became wealthier too. The regular people, often robbed of their land and villages, moved to the industrial towns. But there they were even more restricted in the ways they could feed themselves. They would be worse off because in towns they had no way at all of growing a few vegetables or keeping a chicken to sustain themselves. They now had little or no access to the food they were cooking with in the country, and as recipes in the working-class homes were transmitted orally from mother to child, a lot of these recipes were simply forgotten and knowledge tragically lost.

According to Colin Spencer (*British Food*, 2011), it was a devastation not yet seen in continental countries such as France or Italy, both praised for their peasant cooking. These countries didn't see their open fields and common land divided and privatised so people could no longer farm, hunt and gather wild plants. If there is little or nothing to cook with, how can you pass on recipes?

Marxist historians have suggested that the rise of capitalism started earlier in Britain than in any other country because of the social changes induced by the enclosure acts. People increasingly had to depend on buying food at markets and the desire of obtaining commodities rose with it.

introduction |

Ah, the French

Another influence on British cuisine of this period was the war with France ... again. What demonstrated Britain to be a culinary nation was the fact that patriotism was still shown in the manner of cooking. Possession of French cookery books would show your allegiance to France and the Catholic faith. English–Catholics had always looked up to France, as it was a country where their faith was allowed to be practised to the full. Those of the elite who possessed French cookery books now hid them from sight and quintessentially English dishes such as roast beef and plum pudding became an absolute testimony of loyalty to king and country and appeared often in political cartoons of the period.

Many French dishes that had infiltrated the British cookery books remained in custom. So much so, that some of them disappeared from French cookery books entirely and became traditional British recipes. An example of this is the Tort de Moy (see page 166).

Hannah Glasse made her dislike of French food clear in her book *The Art of Cookery, Made Plain and Easy* (1747) while Eliza Smith, a few years earlier in 1727, had written *The Compleat Housewife,* a book which was very much pre-Reformation in its usage of spices and dried fruits in recipes. Mrs Raffald, 20 years after Glasse, didn't mention French food or its influence in her book *The Experienced English Housekeeper*, but did mention a couple of dishes by their correct French name.

Georgian splendour

The great dinners in Georgian England remained focused on spectacle. For the kitchen and the table, new items were developed as ironworking improved. Patty pans, cake hoops, pastry wheels and jiggers were being produced to aid the cook with his or her daily tasks. When a copper mine was discovered in Anglesey, frying pans began to be made in larger numbers.

Fragile glassware was made into elegant custard, syllabub and jelly glasses. The blancmanges, jellies and flummeries took on dramatic forms of temples and castles for which special moulds were produced by the Staffordshire potteries. Some moulds were large to impress and others tiny, to fool the dinner guests with their appearance, just like the subtleties from the Middle Ages. Some looked like playing cards, some like little fish in a pond of water. And some flummery puddings were even made to look like bacon and eggs (see page 272), just like the 'mock eggs' for Lent in medieval times. Illusion and theatre was what mattered on the Georgian dinner table.

James Woodforde, who documented 45 years of his life starting from 1758 in *The Diary of a Country Parson*, mentions eating several types of puddings. Hash mutton with plain suet pudding, plum puddings with roast beef, pease pudding, batter pudding, boiled beef and suet pudding, rabbit pudding and black pudding. He also mentions a pike with a pudding in his belly, which tells us that the word pudding still means a stuffing too. He also enjoyed several sweet puddings: rice pudding, bread pudding, cherry pudding, a baked plum pudding, damson pudding, orange pudding, a number of fruit tarts, blancmange, puffs, fritters, creams and plenty of jellies. The puddings appear in each course, showing us that in the eighteenth century the pudding was still not considered only to be a dessert. In fact, they appeared mostly in the second course. This manner of courses, which each included sweet and savoury dishes as well as fruit at times, was called 'service à la Française'.

For example, on Christmas Day 1774 the first course served to Woodforde consisted of roast beef, pea soup and orange pudding. The second course was roasted wild ducks, lamb and salad. The meal ends with 'a fine plumb cake'. This was a modest meal as many other meals in his diary consisted of many extra dishes in each course. On another occasion, custard puddings were served along with the first course, and a trifle with cheesecakes, blancmange and raspberry tartlets as part of a second, and concluding the meal was simply fresh fruit.

Puddings stuffed in animal casings always had been cooked along with whatever else was in the solitary pot, but the wider use of the pudding cloth had allowed pudding to appear on the table more often. People would have either two courses or an accompaniment to their meat or pottage. Ordinary people saw those grand dinners their lords enjoyed and wanted to mimic that by creating a way to have more than one dish on the table too. Therefore pudding gave them a sense of luxury and became a much-loved and anticipated part of the meal. When the pudding didn't contain any meat but only breadcrumbs or oatmeal, suet, spices (for those who could afford them) and raisins, it would be boiled, then cooled and often roasted by the fire. This plum pudding would be served before the meat or as a side dish. A man once told me that he and his family still ate a plum pudding this way in the 1970s!

Another popular pudding to make as an accompaniment to the meat was the Yorkshire pudding. These puddings were around for many years before they first made their appearance in print in Hannah Glasse's book in 1747. Before Glasse mentioned the recipe in her book, they were known simply as 'dripping puddings'. We find the first recipe for one of those in *The Whole Duty of a Woman* in 1737, where the anonymous author instructs to place the pudding under a shoulder of mutton instead of a dripping-pan. Dripping puddings were also popular in Scotland where they were called 'fired puddings'; there they were often made of mashed potato, which had by this time become common, and milk.

Pudding chapters in books would now appear more often, and become larger and larger; however, sweet and savoury puddings continue to feature together in those chapters. Recipes for one type of pudding now also started to appear with two ways of preparation: boiled or baked.

Around this period the Swedish explorer and agriculturalist, Pehr Kalm, wrote in his account of his visit to England in 1748 (translated by Joseph Lucas, 1892) about the English love for pudding and roast meat. His words give us an understanding of the way puddings were eaten:

> Puddings, being plain batter puddings or plum puddings, were prepared by either boiling them in skins or cloth in the pot along with the boiling meat, or roasted under the dripping of the joint of meat before the fire. It was the custom to have pudding and gravy as a kind of starter. It meant that, by the time the meat came to the table, one had already feasted on pudding; this made one joint of meat stretch for longer. Any leftover pudding could be saved, roasted the next day or enjoyed as a treat drizzled with honey, pudding sauce or the very precious sugar, if one was lucky enough to get it.

Victorian splendour: slums and starvation

Nineteenth century England saw a rapid growth of population and urbanisation, stimulated by the Industrial Revolution. The elite became wealthier and the poor became poorer. In many ways, the lower classes hadn't been in this dire a situation since the Middle Ages. Peasant cooking had been largely forgotten and the daily pottage, which had sustained people as a staple food for centuries, had disappeared from the table. Eliza Acton noted in her book, *Modern Cookery for Private Families* (1845), that soups or pottage were hardly eaten. The poor didn't have the means to heat up the dish, and often they didn't have access to the ingredients to make a soup. This was an era marked by slum housing, hard labour, starvation and disease.

Street sellers of hot food, who had been around since medieval times, were there to feed those who had the money to purchase it but not the stove to cook it on themselves. In the book *London Labour and the London Poor*, Henry Mayhew interviews and lists the street sellers and the destitute of Victorian London. This gives us a unique insight into what the lower class were eating and what they paid for their food. Hot eels and pea soup, plum duff (see page 120), meat pudding, tarts, savoury and sweet pies were sold on the streets from steaming baskets and kettles, ready to eat. Their customers were mostly fellow street sellers who had had a good day selling; and they were often young children who had been up since the crack of dawn in every kind of weather. When times were hardest, the meat in the pies and puddings of the street sellers and pie houses, was of questionable quality. It could have been spoiled, could have contained stray cats or, in the case of the tale of Sweeney Todd, even worse ...

Changes in farming

Peasants in Georgian times would have been better off than people of a similar class living in towns, but this changed too. Tenant farmers no longer paid their farm labourers with room and board, they now paid wages under contract. Being paid a wage meant they no longer lived as a part of the household, they were now merely staff and were often worse off.

We can see this shift in culture in Thomas Hardy's *Tess of the d'Urbervilles*. Tess first works as a milkmaid and lives along with the other milkmaids in the farmhouse of their employer. Life is merry because the familial bond makes life more pleasant and there is a mutual respect between employer and employee. Meals are frequent and eaten together, and cooking would probably have been done together. Later, Tess finds herself working under contract for a tenant farmer: she receives a small wage, living conditions are bad and the work rough. Although she probably earns more money, she would have considered herself far richer before. Without any means to cook she now eats poorly in a pub, which probably would have cost her a fair penny too.

One of the reasons for this change in farming was the greater food demands from the bigger cities like London. This changed the nature of farming and was the origin of a modern problem, factory farming. Dairy farms changed the way they worked by making the cows have extra calves in autumn so they would have milk all year round. Steam power led to mechanisation that dramatically reduced the workforce. Gone were the days when farmwork was dictated by the forces of nature. The railways were developed to bring the produce to the cities, so that produce no longer stayed within the localities where it was harvested or caught.

Changes on the dinner table

Not only did farming change, food production in general experienced a major revolution. The technique of preserving food in glass and cans came into use and soon vegetables, meat and fish were canned. Originally canning was a solution to provide ships on long sea journeys with enough food, but it soon crept into the normal household too. Towards the end of the nineteenth century, as freezing techniques evolved, meat started to be imported from further afield. Additives such as chalk, powdered bones and ground stone were used to whiten flour because of a preference for using cheaper high-gluten 'hard wheat' from the US in combination with 'modern' milling techniques, which made the flour brown.

For the upper classes, the Victorian era was a slightly more pleasant time to live. These people were deeply religious and had a fear of experiencing pleasure or of expressing emotion because it was considered vulgar. The fashion was to show enormous restraint and this also expressed itself in the food. The Victorians were afraid of food that was too raw, too spicy, too delectable. The food had to look good, but the flavour was often secondary!

At the start of this century the theatrical banqueting style that had been popular for centuries (service à la Française) evolved into service à la Russe. Unlike the banqueting style, with service à la Russe the chef would have more control over what dishes would be combined. So as not to completely take the choice away from the diner, there were sometimes two or three options from which one could choose. Written menus became an absolute necessity for dining à la Russe because guests could no longer see the dishes on the table and needed to make a choice before the serving trays of food arrived. Later, this kind of service would evolve to the plated service we know today, where the chef has absolute control over how the food looks on the plate and how the items on the plate are combined. It is most certainly the case that this evolution is connected to the phenomenon of celebrity chefs. Before this, the cook was just a servant, but now chefs were brought in due to the reputation of their food. Those cooking for the monarchy and other influential people and societies would also publish their own books, and variations on their books for the lower middle class with less elaborate dishes.

There was also a change for our humble pudding. More books were being published and at lower prices, so they were no longer the privilege of stately homes and the elite. Not only would there be a pudding course at dinner, pudding chapters now appeared as standard in cookery books and were often very large. From the mid-nineteenth century there would be books entirely devoted to puddings. The manufacturing of pewter, copper and earthenware ice-cream moulds grew to create blancmanges, jellies and steamed and iced puddings in ornate shapes. The plum pudding took its iconic place at the Christmas feast, with its popularity shown in greeting cards depicting puddings as centrepieces on the festive table. This was before the Christmas tree appeared and became the symbol of the holiday season.

The pudding would continue to feature on satirical cards in which political feuds were addressed, just as in *A Learned Dissertation on Dumpling* nearly a century before.

introduction |

Fancy Ices and inspiring women

A new kind of pudding was emerging, though it had its origins a few centuries earlier. Ice cream became popular in the eighteenth century when people experimented with technique and with flavours. From the nineteenth century these ices took on more impressive shapes thanks to the production of special pewter moulds, and ice-cream puddings were born. Queen Victoria's chef, Charles Elmé Francatelli, created many majestic ice-cream puddings for the court. He published them in several of his books. Another significant Victorian cookbook author, Mrs Agnes B. Marshall, published two books on the subject of ice cream alone, *The Book of Ices* (1888) and *Fancy Ices* (1894). She sold the moulds she mentioned in the books in her shop and taught people how to use them in her own cookery school.

Another lady worth mentioning again is Eliza Acton. Her big volume *Modern Cookery for Private Families* was published in 1845 and was dedicated to the housekeepers of England. It became an enormously popular book until its success was smothered by Mrs Beeton's clever publishers (see page 44). The book was intended for the home cook and gives clear instructions and guidance, written in the most elegant manner. The book reads like a Jane Austen novel minus the mentions of handsome-yet-stern young men and rainy walks. A dish to use up leftover plum pudding she calls 'The Elegant Economist's Pudding' and another is named 'The Printer's Pudding'. Just as wittily named are 'The Young Wife's Pudding' or 'The Good Daughter's Mincemeat Pudding'. The 1855 edition of the book had added sections on 'foreign food', including many recipes for curry dishes and Jewish cooking.

Eliza Acton was progressive and made no secret about the fact that she disliked the food adulterations of that era. She was forward-thinking when she claimed that store-bought bread contributed to malnutrition. This inspired her to write *The English Bread Book* in 1857, which has become, just as her previously named book, a very rare find in the book store.

In this era a whole range of pudding books would be published, probably prompted by the number of different moulds that were being made, and also as testimony to the British love for pudding. Georgiana Hill published *Everybody's Pudding Book* in 1862. Massey and Son published their *Comprehensive Pudding Book* around 1865. Mary Jewry had a pudding chapter in *Warne's Model Cookery Book*, with one of them bearing my favourite name for a pudding: 'General Satisfaction' (see page 176).

New puddings came out of these books and steaming became the preferred method of cooking. The jam roll would evolve into the roly-poly pudding (see page 116). The first recipes for spotted dick (page 128) and treacle sponge pudding (page 130) popped up and filled suet puddings such as steak and kidney pudding became increasingly popular. Blancmange would now be made with cornflour (cornstarch) and flavourings, rather than meat, fish and almond milk. This after some genius marketing from the largest cornflour brands, providing recipe books and moulds.

Mrs Beeton and clever marketing

Considered one of the most famous and influential English cookery writers, Isabella Beeton published the most iconic book on British food in history. But her book has also been partly blamed for giving English food a bad name. Her husband was a publisher and at his request Isabella, in her early twenties, started to write articles on cooking and household management for one of his publications. It was something she knew barely anything about but Isabella and her husband wanted to cash in on the fact that ladies weren't mere ornaments anymore, they were now suddenly expected to manage the household and cook or at least brief the cook and staff. Those articles and supplements were then published as a single volume in *The Book of Household Management* in 1861.

Mrs Beeton died in her late twenties, before her book received any kind of recognition. She never gave cookery demonstrations to entire halls of people, as Mrs Marshall did, and in her lifetime she never had the status in British food that she is wrongly credited for today. She also wasn't the first cookery author to list the ingredients at the beginning of each recipe. And according to Kathryn Hughes, – who wrote *The Short Life and Long Times of Mrs Beeton* in 2006 – many of her recipes were taken from other books.

So how is it that hers is still the best-known book on British food? The answer is a smart publisher. The notable Ward Lock bought the rights of the book from Isabella's husband, Sam Beeton, after she had died at 29, and immediately started to edit and add to the book, to the extent that very little remained of the original. Mrs Beeton became a brand, and a brand that sold, although she didn't have anything to do with it anymore.

But even before it was severely altered by Ward Lock, the book was flawed. Of course not all of the recipes in her original book were bad; in fact, some are simply delicious. But her recipes often failed or resulted in overcooked vegetables. She made a big thing about cooking with leftovers and gave it respectability, so much so that some restaurants of the time thought it was acceptable to start using old meat rather than fresh, selling it as a Mrs Beeton recipe.

How different British food would have been in the early twentieth century if Ward Lock had chosen another cookery writer to endorse! The entrepreneurial Mrs Marshall would have been a much more deserving recipient for this status, running her own cookery school and shop with kitchen appliances she designed; or Eliza Acton with her two delightful books about cookery.

Mrs Beeton's book was published two years after Acton's death and Jill Norman, in her introduction to the most recent edition of *Modern Cookery for Private Families* (2011), explains that when Eliza complains in her preface about other cookery writers stealing her recipes without any acknowledgement, Isabella Beeton would prove to be 'one of the worst offenders'.

Twentieth Century

Although the nineteenth century had done a lot of damage to British cuisine, the disappearance of domestic servants in the twentieth century only accelerated its decline. The lady of the house now had to try to cook those often time-consuming and labour-intensive dishes herself. Boiling puddings was hardly ever done, and preference was given to steaming in basins or baking. Plum pudding would be for festive occasions only and black, white and haggis-type puddings could be bought from the butchers' shops.

Powdered custard and blancmange, junket tablets and ready-made jelly packets took over from the real thing to aid convenience. They were boldly coloured and artificially flavoured; nothing of their ancestors' delicacy and splendour remained.

A new development in the preparation of puddings came with the invention of a pudding basin by Grimwades pottery around 1911. This basin, named Grimwade's Quick-Cooker, no longer required a pudding cloth and illustrated the need for a more simple form of cooking that people were searching for at this time. Grimwades and Brown & Polson created moulds with instructions to aid people who wanted to prepare dishes from scratch rather than using the prepacked processed powders on offer.

Wartime austerity

Two world wars didn't help the quality of British food either. Imports were disrupted and rationing imposed into the 1950s for some products, which made it hard to cook as normal. Entire generations of people didn't learn how to cook properly as so many ingredients just weren't available.

Alarmed by malnutrition, the government founded the Ministry of Food and, for the first time in history, food was distributed fairly to all people from all walks of life. Booklets were published with recipes on how to cook with war rations, and people were advised to grow their own vegetables. Contradicting Mrs Beeton, who instructed people to cook vegetables to a mush, people were told to cook vegetables briefly to retain as many vitamins as possible.

Ironically, research shows that the British people had never been healthier than during those years of war rationing. Because of new developments in science, nutrition could be monitored by the Ministry of Food and people were no longer starving in the streets while others feasted in their great glittering dining rooms. Deficiencies were countered by allowing only wholegrain bread and fortifying margarine with vitamins.

Although Spam, corned beef and other inferior canned meat products and packet shortcuts were dominating the food landscape of this time, quite a few great works were published on British food. First came Mrs C.F. Leyel's extraordinary books – including *Puddings: baked boiled, fried, steamed, iced* (1927) – which would influence a young Elizabeth David. Then Florence White founded the English Folk Cookery Association, asking people to send in their traditional

English recipes, the result being compiled into the book *Good Things in England*. Both of these ladies ignored Mrs Beeton's book entirely. May Byron published her *Pudding Book* in 1917, as part of a series of books on cake, potatoes and so on.

In 1945 the Second World War ended and the women who had been working in the factories didn't enjoy being placed back at the stove again; they wanted to keep their right to be independent and work. Often, those who had worked in domestic service before the war didn't return to their jobs. Food rationing only formally ended in 1954, and some food production, such as artisan cheeses, would continue to feel the influence of the war for decades afterwards.

London Cordon Bleu

In the 1950s, Constance Spry and Rosemary Hume's cookery book *The Constance Spry Cookery Book* was published. It was notable for including the recipe for Coronation Chicken that had been served at Queen Elizabeth II's coronation lunch in 1953.

Rosemary Hume was a graduate of Paris cookery school Le Cordon Bleu, and she founded Le Cordon Bleu school in London. This was more a kind of finishing school for young upper-class girls than a serious education in cookery. Teachers often didn't even comprehend the dishes they were teaching. Anne Willan, whom I had the pleasure of meeting at the Oxford Food Symposium, writes in her book *One Soufflé at a Time: A Memoir of Food and France* (2013) that after she had finished her three-month course at London Cordon Bleu, she was hired as a teacher for the professional course and had to teach dishes she had never even made herself. Later she had to teach a pastry class when she had no clue at all about pastry and most of the dishes she had to prepare she had never even seen before. This makes me wonder about the quality of the education that was given at this otherwise respectable and posh school.

Rosemary Hume and Constance Spry made it clear that they preferred French cookery. In their recipes they use French names for dishes that could easily be British, and discard the many beautiful British recipes of the past. This produced a different reason for embracing French culinary cuisine, one we still know today: snobbery.

Meat for the masses

The common belief arose throughout most of Europe and America that we should eat more protein to remain healthy. As the demand grew, more meat needed to be produced, with catastrophic consequences for animal welfare and the rise of factory farming. More animals in tight living spaces meant that there was a greater need for antibiotics to control disease. Needless to say, the quality of meat declined, as did the respect for animals. Food production became increasingly mechanised and additives and preservatives became standard.

The popularity of supermarkets meant food had to be presliced and prepacked, creating more waste, and more need for plastic wrapping material. Fast-food chains popped over from the US and were embraced as new and exciting. Convenience food took over and more knowledge of cooking was lost.

The organic food and health food movement, which emerged in the 1960s, was a reply to the decline in food quality. People became concerned by one food scandal and health scare after another. Organic eggs and vegetables began to be produced on a small scale and free-range farms were once again founded and preferred by a select few. But the food quality continued to be influenced by an increasingly growing world population and the connected need for food.

Elizabeth David

For those who have never read any work of Elizabeth David, I can only tell you to go and buy one of her books immediately. Her writing in postwar Britain shows the longing for a full and flavoursome cuisine at a time when food culture in Britain had become bleak due to rationing. People increasingly stopped cooking from scratch because they lacked the knowledge and ingredients and the offering of convenience food was there. I guess the fussy overcomplicated dishes and French terminology in *The Constance Spry Cookery Book* didn't help to get people cooking at home either.

The making of one of the greatest food writers started when a young David received a copy of *The Gentle Art of Cookery* by Hilda Leyel (1925) as a gift from her mother. She later spoke about this gift (as quoted in Artemis Cooper's biography, 2011) saying, 'I wonder if I would have ever learned to cook at all if I had been given a routine Mrs Beeton to learn from, instead of the romantic Mrs Leyel with her rather wild, imagination-catching recipes.'

David had started travelling around the continent just before the war and savoured the foods of the sunny Mediterranean. When she finally returned home after six years, she didn't like the postwar Britain she found. Many vegetables and spices were simply not available in the 1950s and she had a dislike for things such as custard powder and other processed food.

Her first book was *Mediterranean Food* (1950), followed by *French Country Cooking* and *Italian Food* (both 1951), and *Summer Cooking* (1955). This showed that she missed the fresh fruit and vegetables she had access to when living abroad. *Spices, Salt and Aromatics in the English Kitchen* was her first book about English food, published in 1970. It showed that David had done years of research into the history of English food. Her next book – one I love dearly – *English Bread and Yeast Cookery* was of the same high standard, telling the history of wheat and milling, baking ovens and different styles of bread in Britain. The recipe section is a magnificent tribute to historical cookery writers such as Robert May, Hannah Glasse, Eliza Acton and many more. David shows that when before she might have preferred a more continental cuisine, knowledge of her own country's food had won her heart.

Jane Grigson

Jane Grigson was a contemporary of Elizabeth David and she wrote fantastic books such as *English Food* (1974) and *Charcuterie and French Pork Cookery* (1967), which would be the first book by an English food writer to be translated into French. Grigson and David were the first to write about food in a way that felt like someone telling you a story rather than instructing you while relaying some facts.

For example, Elizabeth David's introduction to a recipe for plum pudding in *Spices, Salt and Aromatics in the English Kitchen* (1970), tells the story of when she lived in Greece; the friends she had in the village requested first pickles and then a Christmas pudding, as it was one of the glories of Old English fare. She explains the pains she took to cook up this pudding, the time and the annoying little tasks like stoning raisins 'as sticky as warm toffee'. Jane Grigson says of her trifle recipe (in *English Food*) that it is 'a pudding worth eating, not the mean travesty made with yellow, packaged sponge cakes, poor sherry and powdered custards'.

These ladies' paragraphs were full of personal opinions and emotions: they were storytellers rather than mere recipe writers. They were the first true food writers.

David and Grigson would be an integral part of a new movement in food, together with Alan Davidson and his wife. Davidson wrote the *Oxford Companion to Food* (1999), a massive volume of information beautifully crafted into clean short paragraphs of delightful prose. He was one of the founders of The Oxford Symposium on Food and Cookery, Prospect Books and the *Petites Propos Culinaires* (*PPC*), a journal of food studies. The Oxford Symposium still continues; *PPC* still appears three times a year and Prospect Books continues to publish facsimiles of historical works on cookery and new books on the subject of food history and the ethnology of food, thanks to Tom Jaine who took over the reins in 2000 after Davidson's death.

We can only be thankful that these people had such deeply rooted passion for English food and food in general, that they have created a landscape of knowledge on which young people like myself – and many after me for decades to come – can build, .

What's for pudding?

Although puddings have stayed a firm favourite for centuries, by the 1980s you would have to try hard to find a restaurant serving British puddings. A trolley with all kinds of French-sounding gateaus and sweets were the rule by then. But somewhere in the picturesque Cotswolds a couple called Keith and Jean Turner, started a peculiar club to revive the great British pudding: The Pudding Club.

Thirty years on, The Pudding Club continues to meet once a week and on that evening seven puddings are tasted. The couple have published several books, and even launched a pudding of their own brand in a supermarket. People attend The Pudding Club meetings from all over the country and all over the world. They can stay in pudding-themed rooms at the hotel that is the home of the club and promise to stick to The Pudding Club rules in true Fight Club style.

The 1980s was the time that celebrated the arrival of many kitchen gadgets. The microwave had aided the mother of the house in her task of making sure the family was fed, although she had been going out to work during the day since the 1970s. Ready meals were phenomena that followed. Whereas before people sat down together to eat, now more often they would warm their plastic container of ready-made curry, lasagne or shepherd's pie, and eat it while the others were still waiting for theirs. Here lie the roots of eating in front of the telly and the declining importance that was given to the family dinner, during which people had conversations and thoroughly experienced the food on their table.

Special meals were prepared for dinner parties, and the new popular style 'Nouvelle Cuisine' was being mimicked in domestic kitchens by women desperately trying to impress family and friends. Fiddly French food was back, with overcomplicated dishes and tiny portions at premium prices. It is no wonder by the nineties people were sick of it and longed again for the proper honest grub of yesteryear: roast beef with Yorkshire puddings and gravy, honey-glazed vegetables, bangers and mash, proper pies and meat puddings with all kinds of fillings ... Food that fills you up and nourishes the soul.

Modern British food

On modern British food, a whole new book can be written. Celebrity chefs like the rockstar-looking Marco Pierre White and British food advocate Gary Rhodes brought a breath of fresh air to modern British food in the nineties. Pubs started to offer great food and the gastropub phenomenon took off. In one of these gastropubs a young Jamie Oliver was helping out his parents in the kitchen for pocket money. At the turn of the millennium, Oliver became a new force in British food and showed his pride and belief in the nation's gastronomy. He took people by storm worldwide with his new and fresh way of doing things and became the change British food was waiting for. British food was on its way to becoming cool again.

Today, restaurants proudly present you with their British food, which is, as you will know by now, fusion by nature. Chefs such as Heston Blumenthal have created a whole new restaurant concept around it, bringing dishes to the table that are inspired by historic British recipes. A small chain of country restaurants proudly presents a 20-mile menu, only using the food and drink from the surrounding landscape. Rare traditional breeds of farm animals have been revived and some saved from extinction. There are now more than 700 British cheeses, and the number is still growing. Craft beer breweries pop up everywhere and English sparkling wines can compete with any prosecco. Regional food, produced by the ever-growing group of passionate artisans, is what defines modern British food today.

British puddings are experiencing a revival too and are being noticed and respected again outside the family home. A dessert menu isn't complete without a couple of proper old-school puddings. It is the dish this country has been praised for, for many centuries. It is quintessentially British in its every form.

It is the pride of British gastronomy.

It is pudding.

Pride and pudding.

Notes on the recipes

When reading through historical recipes you will soon notice that the early ones, especially the ones from the Middle Ages, lack the essential weights and measures of each ingredient. Cookery books of that time were not written to give instructions to an inexperienced reader; they were written by the master cooks of large elite households to remind them of dishes that were complicated to create, or didn't appear on the dining table frequently, so as not to forget how to cook them. The weights, measures and cooking times were omitted as the cook would have known those by expertise. This also means that simple recipes and instructions didn't appear in those early manuscripts, as they were often cooked every day and didn't need remembering.

The most intriguing of those manuscripts is no doubt *The Forme of Cury* (edited by Samuel Pegge) which is the earliest surviving manuscript on cookery in the English language and attributed to the master cooks of King Richard II. The original manuscript, now lost, is believed to date back to around 1390.

Interpretation

Modern or period translations, interpretations and glosses of the most ancient manuscripts aren't always reliable. For example in Samuel Pegge's version of *The Forme of Cury* it is clear that the printer has forgotten to add parts of instructions while setting the text. Sometimes words would be replaced by another entirely and because they were often written down phonetically they could be interpreted wrongly. Therefore it is often hard to know, if you aren't an expert in the matter and haven't got original manuscripts at your disposal, what would be meant by the original author. Mistakes can be severe, such as naming oatmeal instead of dates. But also there are many words used in contemporary works that are not in use anymore; for example, the word 'coffin' or 'trap' for a pastry case.

Cooking technique

Another thing to take into account is the fact that cooking techniques are very different now. Whereas meat nowadays is usually roasted in an oven, which is actually more like baking it, historically, meat was roasted on a spit with the radiant heat of an open fire behind it. These two techniques give totally different results. In addition, the old technique gives you the chance to cook something else under the dripping of the joint: the wonderfulness that is the dripping pudding (see page 198).

Some historical dishes just can't be replicated with our modern techniques. The open fire, and the kind of heat and cooking preparation that comes with it, give you quite a few things you don't have in an enclosed oven with electrical heating.

Considering the issues of weights and measures, different cooking methods and vessels, environment as well as different produce and spices, it is safe to say that when recreating historical recipes we can probably never exactly follow the recipe to obtain the same result in flavour and texture as the original.

Therefore I have chosen to provide modernised versions of these historical recipes, after numerous attempts at testing and often guessing by placing myself in the mind of cooks long gone, and working out how intense the spices should be.

For the social, cultural and food history enthusiast, such as myself, and for the sake of painting the whole picture for you, my reader, I have chosen to also share with you the original text of historically important recipes in this book without changing the original words. This is because I have tried to go back to the primary source of recipes during my research, to recipes that were often wrongly interpreted during the last centuries. I have provided the original text so you can make up your own mind and try your hand at interpreting the recipe yourself, if you should wish to do so.

I will always stay as true to the original recipe as possible. For example, the slower method of stewing prunes for a couple of hours in an oven makes for a better prune compote than if you quickly stew them on a fast hob. Of course we need to consider the cost of energy in this modern day and age as well; therefore I would suggest you do as I do and place an earthen pot with prunes or other fruit you need in the oven while one of your stews slowly bubbles away.

Some ancient puddings have evolved over time because of the changes that have happened in our kitchens. They can be witnessed in their primitive form in the earliest cookery books and in their modern form in many books today.

A Yorkshire pudding is a good example of this evolution. Originally a dripping pudding, baked slowly under the fat dripping from the joint of meat, it is now often prepared in muffin tins for individual portions, in a quick oven using a vegetable oil. The original Yorkshire, or dripping, pudding as it was called before Hannah Glasse's *The Art of Cookery* was published in 1747, had a savoury note so ravishing it remained a much-loved part of the roast meal for so long that it evolved into a mandatory accompaniment to a Sunday roast today. Who wants roast without Yorkshire puds to suck up all the juices? Not me.

Modern tastes

Some of the recipes in this book might not appeal to modern tastes, and this is okay. Some dishes take a little getting used to because we have often forgotten how some things taste. An example is hogs pudding: while loved in the West Country in England, someone from Belgium might find the taste of the liver too strong, while West Country folk don't even notice. Some puddings are a bit stodgy and are included in this book for their part in the story. A plum duff might not be to anyone's taste today, but in Victorian times the children were very happy to have it. A few raisins in a bit of dough would have painted a smile on the little ones' faces back then, while today we would add sugar, sugar and more sugar. Toning down one's palate is a good thing and many sweet puddings in this book do not taste very sweet at all, but as I am used to having little sugar, they are plenty sweet enough for me.

Ingredients

Spices

In later recipes where weights and measures are specified, the quantities required – especially of spices – seem overgenerous and should be tested and altered today. This we can explain because in the old days spices took many months to arrive and were often poorly stored, which made the intensity of flavours weaker.

The variety of pepper used is worthy of note. There weren't just black or white peppercorns as we use today; there were 'long pepper' and 'cubeb'. Often when pepper is called for, long pepper is actually what would have been meant. Long pepper looks a little like a hazel-tree catkin, made of little grains of pepper. The flavour is pungent and fruity. It was frequently used by the Romans, which might have been how the long pepper arrived in Britain.

Cubeb or tailed pepper is another pepper that was popular during the Middle Ages. It was also used for medicinal purposes, to guard against demons and in love spells. During Victorian times cubeb was even used in the form of cigarettes to cure asthma and other ailments. Both cubeb and long pepper are very perfumed and are not exclusively used in savoury dishes.

Another spice you will encounter in this book is Grains of Paradise; technically a member of the ginger family, it is also often called Guinea pepper. Its flavour is peppery with a hint of coriander seed, coconut and citrus. Grains of Paradise were also used to add fictitious alcoholic strength to gins and cordials, which was an illegal practice by 1888 ('Grains of Paradise' in the *Encyclopædia Britannica*, 9th ed., Vol. XI. 1880). Today it is still found in some brands of gin, as are cubeb berries.

Flour

Where flours are used, including the traditional wheat but also spelt, rye, rice and cornflour, I choose to use organic flour, stone ground when possible and absolutely unbleached. Stone ground flour is more nutritious as the stones do not heat up the flour as industrial mills do. High temperatures during milling cause the oils in grain to turn rancid and make the flour spoil faster. Also make sure the flour isn't old, as fresh flour makes a difference in flavour and texture. In historical recipes it is often called for to heat the flour or sometimes bake it for a short while before using it. This is because flour was kept in a cold store to prevent it going dry, but to use it, it was often then needed to bring it to room temperature. Baking the flour, however, gives a nutty flavour and different texture to your baking. When a recipe states plain (all-purpose) flour, a white spelt flour can be used instead, as I often do.

Breadcrumbs

Where recipes ask for breadcrumbs, day-old or fresh bread, I prefer to use a home-baked loaf or one that came from an artisan baker. When using fast-proved bread from industrial bakeries – read factories – you will not get the same result. There will most certainly be less flavour and often the texture of the soaked bread will become gooey and unpleasant. If you want your pudding to be delicious, use the best products you can afford. It should be a treat, not something for every day.

Sweeteners

When using sugar, I will generally reduce the quantities in the old recipes. When triple-refined sugar, pounded sugar or loaf sugar is asked for in old texts, I will use raw cane sugar blitzed in a food processor or blender to create the fine result the servants got in the old days by grinding pieces of solid sugar from the loaf sugar in a mortar and pestle. If you want to try your hand at using loaf sugar, Arabic stores still sell large conical sugar loaves which are often given to a couple on their wedding day. When icing (confectioners') sugar is called for, I make it myself, also by blitzing caster (superfine) sugar in a blender. Store-bought icing sugar often contains cornstarch as an additive, and this isn't always clearly stated on the pack; therefore I avoid using it.

Verjuice

Some early recipes call for verjuice. This was a sour crabapple juice, used like vinegar. As this isn't readily available to all, I use apple cider vinegar.

Lemon

When lemon juice and lemon rind are used, I use unwaxed lemons.

Milk & cream

When I use cream, milk or yoghurt in recipes or for serving, it will always be of the full-fat variety. Skimming on fat is skimming on flavour. Where early recipes call for milk, I substitute thin (pouring) cream as store-bought milk today is far thinner than milk straight from a cow's udder. When cream is required, I use thick (double) cream with a fat content of at least 40 per cent; anything less will not do. I like to buy raw cream and milk from my local farm, but if you go to the store try to look for pasteurised, and not 'ultrapasteurised'.

Butter & lard

Butter used should always be the real thing, the best quality, no gruesome replacements such as margarine or baking spread!

Clarified butter is called for in some recipes: this is butter from which all milk solids have been removed by heating it. The result is a clear butter that can be heated to a higher temperature, which makes it ideal for frying. To clarify butter, heat unsalted butter in a saucepan over very low heat until it is melted. Let it gently simmer until a froth rises to the top and use a spoon to skim off the froth. You will notice a milky layer in the bottom of your pan. Carefully pour the clear liquid above it into a heatproof storage container, discarding the froth and the milky residue. Clarified butter keeps quite a long time in the fridge, and you can also freeze it.

Dripping or fat used should be lard. Lard is rendered pig fat and can be bought in a store or you can make it yourself by melting the fat of the belly or back of pork, and then letting it cool. This is called rendering and it takes a couple of hours, but it's totally worth it. Just pour into containers and freeze. Beef tallow can also be used.

NUTMEG

BAY LEAVES

LONG PEPPER

SAFFRON

CUBEB

ALLSPICE

SEA SALT

CLOVES

Suet

So what is suet? Suet is the hard fat found around the kidneys of cows or sheep. It's not commonly used outside Britain, where it has been used for making puddings since at least the sixteenth century. If I can't get it fresh from the butcher's, I will use 'shredded suet' from a store.

Suet is used for savoury and sweet puddings since it has a melting point of between 45 and 50°C (113–122°F). This makes it ideal to use for pastry and for deep-frying. When suet melts it leaves air holes to break up the dense structure of your baked goods, giving it a lighter texture. Other fats would melt sooner than suet, burn too fast and not leave the air holes in puddings.

Processing fresh suet

Fresh suet should be creamy white, not yellow, because that means it is old. To use fresh suet in your cooking, break up the lump of fat and select the whitest parts. When torn apart you will see the connective tissue, you need to remove this as much as possible. To use, just break off little pieces: the smaller the better when using fresh. The size of a pea is good.

If you want to process your suet for another day in the near future, you need to render it. To do this you need a cast iron pot, then put in the broken up suet; these pieces can be larger than peas as you are melting them. Melt the suet but make sure it doesn't boil. When melted, pour through a sieve to remove the last bits of connective tissue. The parts of connective tissue that are left behind in the strainer are called 'graves' and were used for fish bait in the eighteenth century.

Pour the strained fat into a mould – I use small cake tins – and allow it to harden into a block, then wrap it in paper. When cooled it becomes as hard as a bar of soap. This will enable you to grate it when you need to use it.

Shredded suet

Atora is the biggest and most iconic brand selling ready-shredded suet, and they have both a vegetarian and traditional beef version. To create shredded suet, the suet is heated and all the remaining blood vessels and connective tissue are removed, then a little flour is added to stabilise it. Although using ready-made shredded suet is what most people do, if you want to eat consciously you might prefer to go to your meat source, farm or butcher and ask him for kidney fat, but make sure they don't give you muscular fat as that won't work at all and doesn't firm up the way kidney fat does. I know there are a few farms selling higher welfare suet from their animals, so it is definitely worth an internet search to find them.

Bone marrow

Bone marrow from beef or veal should always be used. Ask your butcher for it and ask him to cut the bone into shorter chunks so you can extract the marrow with ease. It might sound strange to our ears today to use bone marrow in sweet dishes, but it does give an effect that is not easily achieved with, for example, butter. Once you are able to get over the fact that it is bone marrow, I promise you will love it.

Meat

The meat I use will always come either from a local farm where I buy it at the farm gate, or from other farms I pass when I am travelling around. To have the best result, you need the best quality and this doesn't mean more expensive meat but higher welfare meat. Look out for grass-fed meat. Animals reared on intensive farms are more prone to disease and therefore are more likely to have had antibiotics during their lifetime. The farmer at the farm where I buy my meat always says, 'The meat from animals you pass on the highway, stuffed in large trailers without space and dignity, is completely ruined and sour.' This comes from an old man who has got nothing to do with the whole new fashion of free-range meat, he just speaks out of common sense and, more importantly, experience.

Gelatine

To set jellies and flummeries, a number of different gelling agents were used in the past. Calves foot, hartshorn (deer antler), ivory and the bladder of a sturgeon are just a few things that have been used in history. But even as far back as the seventeenth century there were vegetarian options, such as agar-agar. Today I use either agar-agar, which is made from a seaweed, or regular gelatine leaves when the jelly needs to be strong enough not to collapse.

Rennet

When using rennet to set junket or curd cheese, I will always use vegetable rennet. Regular rennet is made from the lining membrane of the fourth stomach of a slaughtered, unweaned calf. This you can buy from specialist stores and some pharmacies. Vegetable rennet is not chemical and can be traced back to a mention in the ancient Greek *Iliad* by Homer. It can be made from a variety of thistles, nettles and even dried caper leaves. Nowadays it is easier to get than animal rennet, just check online.

Eggs

When eggs are used in the recipes they are from free-range hens and they are assumed to be 60–65 g (large/Grade 3) eggs.

Moulds

Sometimes multiple uses are possible for one kitchen object and this is true of the different pudding or jelly moulds out there.

We often assume moulds were only used for jelly-making, but those same moulds, whether they were copper, tin or ceramic, would have been used for moulded cakes, steamed puddings, milk puddings and ice creams as well as fruit cheeses or potted meats and terrines. Teacups were used as moulds, as instructed by Mary Eales, confectioner to Queen Anne, in her *Receipts*, published in 1718. Saucers were also used to make 'a pudding stued between two dishes' as noted by John Murrell, in *A Newe Booke of Cookerie* in 1615.

Moulds in carved wood, delicate salt-glazed stoneware and a more robust creamware pottery were produced from the early eighteenth century. Some were made into elaborate shapes, such as castles and temples. One of these producers was Wedgwood, who produced a Solomon's Temple mould for flummery dishes and many other shapes and forms. Small fish were made and Mrs Raffald, in *The Experienced English Housekeeper* (1769), used them to create a 'fish pond', fish made of flummery that were then gilded and placed on a pool of clear jelly as if they were swimming. This shows the great fantasy style in which dishes were presented to guests.

By the nineteenth century, moulds were being produced on a larger scale and this is directly linked to the invention of ready-made gelatine which made jelly-making a lot less tedious and no longer required people to process raw animal parts. Tin, copper and more robust stoneware pudding moulds were manufactured, with copper being mainly for the well-to-do household.

This page, top to bottom: Solomon's Temple mould and conical flummery mould; a wooden flummery mould; salt-glazed pottery fish moulds.

Opposite page, top to bottom: pewter swan ice-cream mould; Grimwade's Quick-Cooker; the Paragon Jelly mould, also from Grimwade; Brown & Polson's Corn Flour Blanc-Mange mould.

Catalogues with illustrations of all the different types of moulds were being produced by large manufacturers such as Benham & Froud and, in smaller scale, Agnes Marshall. They were expensive and the copper ones needed regular retinning on the inside.

Some moulds were very elaborately designed and sometimes even had multiple parts to create striking multicoloured jellies with. These were called 'Macedoine Moulds' and were unique to Britain. They were admired in other countries by important chefs. The jelly made in them could have different layers of colours and several kinds of fresh fruit added.

In the twentieth century, moulds were still expensive but the earthenware ones became more affordable for middle-class households. In 1911 Grimwades pottery won a gold medal for its 'Quick-Cooker', a lidded porcelain pudding steamer with the instructions for use printed all over it. They also had a jelly mould like this. Brown & Polson produced a pudding mould printed with the recipe of their 'Corn Flour Blanc-Mange'. This shows the need for guidance and a more simplified way of cooking without many domestic servants.

Twenty-first century moulds are made for nostalgic reasons and usually in aluminium to use for moulded cakes. It is very rare now that a blancmange or elaborate homemade jelly would feature on a dinner table. Powdered jelly is used for trifle and for small jellies and the moulds are usually from pliable silicone. But there is a revival coming: two British guys have started a company creating bespoke jelly moulds and jellies for special occasions and movies. It is still very niche but it shows the longing for a kind of splendour and theatre on the feast table that we have lost over the years. It is only a matter of time before it becomes a trend again, as so many retro things have in the past decades.

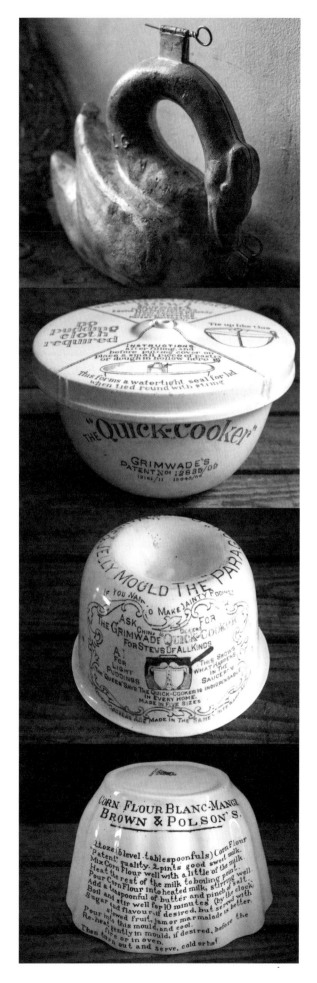

CHAPTER 1

BOILED & STEAMED

Boiled & steamed

Boiled puddings are the first and true puddings in the world. They come from the necessity and logic of using up every bit of an animal, meaning the blood, the offal and the guts. The ancestors of all puddings are the sausage-type stuffed guts of Ancient Greece and Rome. It is nearly impossible to know whether stuffed guts were eaten in England before the Roman pudding-eaters extraordinaire arrived. I just think it is probable and logical that they would have been, in order to eat from nose to tail.

Boiling a pudding made it possible to cook something along with whatever else was stewing in the pot. Households only had one cauldron in which they had to prepare everything over an open fire. Because these puddings would only be prepared when guts were available, they probably gained status as a special treat. The amount of care and preparation put into the puddings would most definitely have made a pudding the best meal a peasant could afford.

Pudding in your puddings

As mentioned in the introduction, in old texts the word 'pudding' also refers to the intestines of a man or animal. This could very well be the reason why puddings are named as such, as the earliest ones were prepared in intestines. Game animals, larger birds and fish were often prepared with a pudding – meaning a stuffing – 'cooked in their belly'. Stuffing for eggs, vegetables and roots were all also referred to as puddings in *A Book of Cookrye* in 1584.

The pudding cloth

When people wanted to have their favourite puddings and sausages more often, they searched for an alternative vessel to cook them in. Until recently, historians believed that the first mention of a pudding cloth appeared in Gervase Markham's oatmeal section of his fabulous book *The English Huswife* in 1615. However, it has come to light, in one of the last works of historian Constance Hieatt, that there was an earlier mention in *A Miscellany of Household Information*, which was compiled more than a hundred years earlier, in 1485. The recipe is for a boiled fish pudding for Lent, and uses cod, salmon, currants, salt and saffron.

The pudding cloth is one of the first evolutions of the boiled pudding; it was made from tightly woven linen and was reused each time a pudding was made. The cloth would have made it easier to prepare puddings and would allow for more recipes to be developed. The shortage of nutrition in the winter months when people had no meat left would also have meant that people with cattle often bled the already weak animals to bake the blood, mixed with cereal, into cakes for a much-needed hearty meal (see Black pudding in a tray and griddle cakes, pages 84–85).

The need for an easier method would develop puddings even more in later centuries. In the early years of the seventeenth century, a 'Pudding Pye' appears in Gervase Markham's book, published alongside the tarts and pies. He also gives a recipe for a 'White-pot', which was prepared in a pot, pan or dish. From then on, other baked puddings appear and the term 'puddings' is stretched to include pies and tarts, as well as custards. Of course, this evolution could only be noticed in the most lavish of households. The plain folk would have been happy if they had a small fire and a pot while the rich had ovens built into the heart of their kitchens.

By 1690 the words of a French visitor tell us that puddings are baked in the oven, boiled with meat and made in fifty different ways. Some puddings continued to be boiled throughout history; the plum pudding, suet puddings and haggis are great examples. In fact, haggis has changed little – it is still boiled in either a sheep's stomach lining or another large intestine such as ox bung – while the plum pudding lost its animal-derived casing and was prepared in a cloth, and later in a pudding basin (mould) when that method became the fashion.

One-pot meals

Plum puddings, plain suet puddings or dumplings were prepared alongside and sometimes even cooked in the pot with the meat or pottage, to act as a filler before or during the meal. People I have spoken to in England can still recall being presented roast or stewed beef with plum pudding or plain suet pudding in the mid-twentieth century. In Hungary and the Czech Republic the dumpling is a necessary part of a goulash, where the pudding is cut into slices and placed in a deep dish with the meat to soak up the bright red brothy paprika sauce.

When moulds started to be produced in the eighteenth century, people used them not only for moulded jellies but also for making cakes and boiling – and later steaming – puddings. By the nineteenth century, moulds were being produced on a larger scale and most books suggest using a mould, lined with a floured cloth or with the cloth wrapped around the basin.

Wartime shortages and shortcuts

The First and Second World Wars meant that the key ingredients for puddings were all rationed, with sugar and butter rationing continuing until 1953. This was a blow to pudding-making, but as they were so much a part of British culture the Ministry of Food issued several recipes using potato and other replacements in their leaflets to aid housewives to cook on war rations. After the war, many domestic servants didn't return to their positions in the households where they previously worked. More and more, the ladies of the house had to do their own cooking, so a more simplified way of pudding-making was desired. Shortcuts were invented, such as Bird's iconic custard powder.

When baking paper appeared, the need for a pudding cloth was no more; it remained in use only in the kitchens of nostalgic cooks. New and more reliable electric and gas ovens made the life of the cook even easier, and pudding-making with it.

Puddings were a little forgotten about in the early twentieth century, but they then became the staple of the school-dinner menu. Those who grew up on these puds re-created them at home and in their restaurants out of nostalgia. Steamed puddings saw a revival by the end of the twentieth century. They are simply good and, when prepared with care, they can be excellent.

I dare you to give boiled puddings a go. You won't look back after you've tasted a boozy, rich plum pudding and experienced the delights of a nicely soaked suet dumpling.

Steaming a pudding using a pudding basin

Preparing the basin

Generously grease the pudding basin (mould) with butter and cut a circle of baking paper the same size as the base of the pudding basin. Place the paper circle in the basin; it will stick perfectly to the butter. This will make it easier to get the pudding out of the basin.

Spoon the batter into the pudding basin, then cut another two circles of baking paper with a diameter about 8–10 cm (3¼–4 inches) larger than the top of the basin. Make a narrow fold across the middle to leave room for the paper cover to expand slightly. I like to use two layers of paper. Tie securely around the top of the basin with kitchen string, then cover with foil and tie kitchen string to create a handle so it will be easier to lift the basin out of the pan after steaming.

Now get yourself a pan large enough to hold your pudding basin(s) or, if you are steaming little ones all in one go, a large baking dish. I prefer to use the oven for this as I do not like to have a pot of boiling hot water on the stovetop for 2 hours or more, depending on the recipe.

Preheat the oven to 160°C (315°F) or the temperature suggested in the recipe.

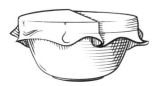

Stand the pudding basin on an inverted heatproof saucer, a jam-jar lid or trivet in the base of a deep ovenproof saucepan or pot.

Pour in boiling water to come halfway up the side of the basin. Cover the pan, either with its own lid or with foil, in order to trap the steam. Place in the preheated oven and leave for as long as your recipe states. This can be between 30 minutes and 7 hours depending on the size of your pudding.

When you are steaming little puddings, it is sufficient to place the puddings in a deep baking dish and fill the dish with boiling water once you have put them in the oven. Cover the dish with foil and steam for as long as your recipe states.

Unmoulding a pudding

Carefully remove the pudding from the pot while it is still in the oven. Have a tea towel (dish towel) at the ready to hold it safely and catch all the hot water that will drip from it. Leave the pudding to rest for a couple of minutes, so that it will cool off a bit and be easier to handle.

Have a plate ready. Remove the foil and string, then open the paper lid and turn the pudding out by carefully loosening it around the edges with a blunt knife.

Plum Pudding

Probably the most loved and internationally famed pudding of all is the plum pudding, or Christmas pudding. It has its roots in the ancient Roman and haggis-type puddings, but along the way it lost the meat and became a sweet dish. Originally boiled in skins, then in a cloth and later, when it became the fashion, in moulds, it has changed surprisingly little over the past 300 years.

There are a lot of legends and claims made about the origins of the plum pudding. Some say it evolved from plum porridge, a thick soup with similar ingredients, but I believe these are two separate dishes that coexisted with each other.

According to tradition, plum pudding should be made on 'Stir-up Sunday'. It is a custom that is believed to date back to the 1549 Book of Common Prayer; where a reading states 'stir up, we beseech thee'. The words would be read in church on the last Sunday before Advent and so the good people knew it was time to start on their favourite Christmas treat.

It was a family affair: everyone would gather to stir the pudding mixture from east to west, in honour of the Three Kings who came from the east. Sometimes coins or trinkets would be hidden in the dough; finding them on Christmas Day would bring luck and good fortune.

Some say it was King George I who requested plum pudding as a part of the first Christmas feast of his reign, in 1714. George I was christened 'the Pudding King' because of this myth but there are no written records prior to the twentieth century to tell us that this king deserved his title.

The first written record of a recipe for plum pudding as we know it today can be found in John Nott's *The Cooks and Confectioners Dictionary* from 1723:

> A Plum-pudding: Shred a Pound and a half of Suet very fine, and sift it; add a Pound and a half of Raisins of the Sun ston'd, six spoonful of Flour, and as many of Sugar, the Yolks of eight Eggs, and the Whites of five, beat the Eggs with a little Salt, tye it up close in a Cloth and boil it for four or five Hours.

There is, however, no suggestion that the pudding is associated with George I, the practice of Stir-up Sunday, or the Christmas feast.

An earlier reference in the diary of Henry Teonge, a British naval chaplain during the reign of Charles II, speaks of a Christmas Day dinner on board a ship in the year 1675. It comprised 'a rib of beef, plum puddings, mince pies and plenty of good wines'. This is the first time we find a plum pudding associated with Christmas, but at the same time it is not referred to as the Christmas pudding.

Around that same time, another man, on another ship, also writes about the celebration of Christmas, though his circumstances are rather grim compared to Henry Teonge's. Colonel Norwood's ship set sail for Virginia in 1649 but became lost and ran out of food and water.

On Christmas the near-empty barrels of flour – and whatever else they had – were scraped clean to make a plum pudding from the last of their store. It is an extraordinary account of a group of people living in fear that they might die on that ship, but still in the midst of all that despair they go to the trouble to create a plum pudding, which the diarist for the first time in history names 'Christmas Pudding'.

> Many sorrowful days and nights we spun out in this manner, tille the blessed feast of Christmas came upon us, which we began with a very melancholy solemnity; and yet, to make some distinction of times, the scrapings of the meal-tubs were all amassed together to compose a pudding. Malaga sack, sea water, with fruit and spice, all well fryed in oyl, were the ingredients of this regale, which raised some envy in the spectators; but allowing some privilege to the captain's mess, we met no obstruction, but did peaceably enjoy our Christmas pudding.
> 'A Voyage to Virginia', by Colonel Norwood, from *A Collection of Voyages and Travels by Awnsham Churchill and John Churchill*, Vol 6, 1745

This Christmas pudding must have been savoured by the passengers meant for America, on the quest for a new life after the civil war in England. It might have created a nostalgic moment, when they lingered on the memory of a sweet Christmas feast, safe and warm at home, before they had left on this terrible fatal journey that would kill most of them after Christmas.

In this era, plum puddings were a common companion to beef on festive days; they were eaten before or along with the meat, not after the meal topped with plenty of cream as we know it today. A plum pudding would often be sliced up and arranged under the dripping of a roasting joint of meat in front of the fire.

The 'Hack' or 'Hackin' pudding, a relative of the haggis and plum pudding from the north of England, was eaten in the same fashion. In 1732 Richard Bradley (*The Country Housewife and Lady's Director*) wrote down a letter from a gentleman in Cumberland – now Cumbria: 'It is a Custom with us every Christmas-Day in the Morning, to have, what we call an Hackin ...'. He then gives the recipe (see page 94) and goes on to explain: 'This is our Custom to have ready, at the opening of the Doors, on Christmas-Day in the Morning. It is esteem'd here; but all that I can say to you of it, is, that it eats somewhat like a Chriftmas-Pye, or is some-what like boil'd.'

It is possible that the tradition of eating a plum pudding with roast beef on festive occasions evolved to it becoming the highlight of the Christmas feast, inspired by customs in the north of England.

The Victorians' love of Christmas

By the Victorian era the Christmas pudding was well and truly the symbol of Christmas, although the Christmas tree would soon take its place. Printing methods improved and it became possible to print in various colours so Christmas cards became popular. Many of these depicted puddings as centrepieces on the festive table and cards featured puddings dressed up like little men. The pudding would also continue to grace satirical cards in which political feuds were addressed, as in *A Learned Dissertation on Dumpling* nearly a century before.

But what about the Pudding King?

It was not George I but his namesake George V who really made a difference in the pudding's tale. In 1927 he encouraged people to cook a Christmas pudding made from ingredients sourced in the British Empire. This was inspired by an earlier statement made by the British Women's Patriotic League, on how to show your patriotism. They commanded their followers to always buy British or Empire-made goods, as cheap imports from America were of no support to the Empire.

In the eighteenth and nineteenth centuries the British Empire had grown vast and during the First World War many of the member countries had suffered great losses. On Empire Day 1917, King George V made a proclamation to emphasise food economy in the British Empire. All over the Empire people were motivated to show patriotism in the way they bought food. In 1925 Australian fruit growers paraded a huge Christmas pudding through the streets of London. The top of the huge cannonball pudding was decorated with the Australian flag and the Union Jack and on the back of the pudding were the words 'make your pudding of Empire products'.

The Christmas pudding now became the Empire pudding, promoted by the Empire Marketing Board. Posters depicted Britannia holding a flaming plum pudding, sporting a Union Jack flag and the recipe to make the pudding.

In 1926 a propaganda film was made by Reginald Brabazon, 12th Earl of Meath. The film featured the making of the Empire pudding: people from all over the Empire brought a basket with an ingredient showing the name of the country to be stirred into the pudding. Brabazon used the family tradition of Stir-up Sunday as a tool to promote the idea that the Empire was one large family, creating this most iconic pudding together as one.

Plum pudding indeed became the symbol of patriotism as much as eating roast beef and plum pudding had done in the mid-eighteenth century when the French threatened British shores and plum puddings appeared in political cartoons.

During the First World War, women who worked in refugee camps in France and Belgium created the now sought-after 'WWI Silks' to show support for the troops fighting for their freedom. These postcards were made by framing the embroideries the women created and the themes were, of course, usually patriotic scenes with Belgian, French and British flags surrounded by garlands of flowers or ... a plum pudding bristling with flags.

The recipe for Empire pudding promoted later by George V was created by his head chef, Mr Cédard, and based upon the recipe earlier provided by the Empire Marketing Board. It adds a few more countries to the list. In 1930 a propaganda film called *One Family* was made to promote the pudding of George V and the Empire trade. Much of it was filmed in Buckingham Palace and tells the story of a boy dreaming he goes to Buckingham Palace and meets the king after finding the recipe for an Empire pudding in his father's newspaper. He is then sent on a quest to gather each ingredient for the Empire pudding in the producing countries.

boiled & steamed |

Clockwise from top left: WWI Silk postcard; Puddings, *by Mrs Leyel; late Georgian Christmas card; Atora shredded suet recipe booklet, 1929; Atmore's Mince Meat trade cards (early business cards); a Victorian Christmas card; another trade card from Atmore's; plum pudding illustration from* Warne's Model Cookery, *1868; James Gillray's 1805 illustration, 'The Plumb-pudding in danger' depicts William Pitt, wearing a regimental uniform and hat, sitting at a table with Napoleon; two more Victorian Christmas cards.*

Although nothing suggests that the day on which the Empire pudding had to be made was indeed Stir-up Sunday, I think when this tradition became common, this was the moment when preparing the pudding became a family affair and a celebration. To this day, most British families will enjoy their Christmas pudding and prepare it well in advance to soak it in rich booze until Christmas Day.

For this plum pudding, I started with one of the earliest recipes and it has evolved in my kitchen over the past few years. It is a favourite with my friends and family and I will often make several, either to give as gifts or keep for a few months, or even until the next Christmas, as the pudding only gets better and better.

Makes 2 puddings using 16 cm (6¼ inch/No. 36) basins (moulds), or 6–7 mini (150 ml/5 fl oz) puddings

200 g (7 oz) shredded suet

75 g (2¾ oz) plain (all-purpose) or spelt flour

150 g (5½ oz/2½ cups) fresh breadcrumbs

150 g (5½ oz) muscovado (dark brown) sugar

150 g (5½ oz) currants

150 g (5½ oz) raisins

40 g (1½ oz) candied orange peel

1 small dessert apple, grated

2 teaspoons mixed spice

½ teaspoon grated nutmeg

½ teaspoon sea salt

3 large eggs

150 ml (5 fl oz) brandy or dark rum

75 ml (2¼ fl oz) stout (beer)

butter, to grease the pudding basins

Plum pudding

Prepare the pudding basins for steaming, as explained on pages 68–69.

Mix together all the dry ingredients in a large bowl, then add the eggs, brandy and stout and mix well by gently stirring with a wooden spoon. You can stir from east to west if you fancy it. If you have the time, leave the mixture to rest overnight.

Preheat the oven to 160°C (315°F). Spoon the batter into the prepared pudding basins and proceed as instructed on pages 68–69. Steam for 3–4 hours for small puddings and 5–7 hours for large ones.

After the puddings are steamed you can either serve them straight away or, if Christmas is still a while off, cool the puddings in their basins, change the baking paper covers for clean ones and tie up. Store the pudding in a cool cupboard and, if you like a boozy pudding, feed it with a couple of teaspoons of brandy or rum once a week. This will also help preserve the puddings.

To serve on the day, steam for 1 hour and serve with custard sauce (see page 338), clotted cream (see page 336) or brandy butter and enjoy.

Use appelstroop (apple butter) instead of the dark sugar to give the pudding more depth of flavour. I also like to add a handful of walnuts or pecans. Combinations are endless; adding dried cranberries to the mix is lovely too, but stay away from glacé cherries as they make the dish far too sweet.

Haggis

Haggis might be one of the best-known puddings of Great Britain. Although the Scots have adopted it as their national dish, it is not very Scottish in origin at all. In fact, the first recipe published in Scotland was at the end of the eighteenth century, 300 years after it first appeared in an English text.

Haggis is a savoury pudding made of a sheep's stomach stuffed with the minced heart, liver and lungs from a lamb or sheep, onions, oatmeal, suet, spices and herbs. It's rather like a large sausage, which is boiled and then often toasted in front of the fire. The first mention of the word haggis can be found in Walter of Bibbesworth's thirteenth century book *The Treatise* (written in verse to help a woman teach her Anglo–Norman children French). The earliest recipe for a haggis can be found in a manuscript from circa 1430 and is written in verse. Similar puddings had been around for decades, even centuries, before that. The Romans had recipes for stuffed sow's womb and the ancient Greeks enjoyed a roasted stuffed sheep's stomach.

> For Hagese
> The heart of sheep, the kidneys you take, The bowel naught you shall forsake,
> In the vortex made, and boiled well, Hack all together with good parsley,
> Hyssop, savory, you shall take then, And suet of sheep take in, I teach,
> With powder of pepper and eggs good quantity, And seethe it well and serve it then,
> Look it is salted for good men. In winter time when herbs are good,
> Take powder of them I know indeed, As savory, mint and thyme, quite good,
> Hyssop and sage I know by the Rood.
>
> *Liber Cure Cocorum*, c. 1430, translated into modern English by Cindy Renfrow, 2002

But even in the rest of Europe and further afield there were and still are dishes that it is possible to categorise under the 'haggis' type of pudding. Norwegian lungemos, Swedish pölsa, Lebanese ghameh and Icelandic slátur – to name a few – are all very similar to the haggis. This shows again that our cuisine comes from similar if not quite identical backgrounds, but just evolved differently due to climate and culture.

The etymology of the word haggis is another thing to consider. Bibbesworth's mid-thirteenth century poem suggests that the term haggis was commonly known in English and French at that time as there are no glosses provided for the word. It could have been derived from a Frankish verb meaning 'to hack'. The etymologist Walter Skeat suggested Scandinavian origins and claimed that 'hag' is derived from the Old Norse 'höggva' which means to strike or hew, but this theory has been discarded by others. Therefore it is most probable that the word haggis came from the fact that one had to chop or hack up all the ingredients. In the north around Cumbria, a pudding with the name hack or hackin pudding (see page 94) existed and shares many similarities with the haggis.

As with many puddings, the haggis started off being savoured nationally before surviving only in localities like the north of England and Scotland. We have the Scottish poet Robert Burns to thank for this shift. In the eighteenth century he wrote a poem called 'To a Haggis' that started

Fair fa' your honest, sonsie face,
Great chieftain o' the puddin'-race!
Aboon them a' ye tak your place,
Painch, tripe, or thairm:
Weel are ye wordy o' a grace
As lang's my arm.

The Poetical Works of Robert Burns,
c.1856, George Routledge and Sons

the tradition of Burns Night suppers, when a large haggis would be served to the guests. The poem would be recited and afterwards the haggis would be roasted and eaten. Burns Night is an important part of Scottish culture and gives an occasion to celebrate that isn't related to politics or religion.

Haggis continues to appear in most historical cookery books, and most recipes remain very traditional, like the first in *Liber Cure Cocorum*. Robert May, in *The Accomplisht Cook* (1660), gives three recipe for 'Sheeps Haggas Puddings'. In his recipes he explains that for Lent you can use a cloth instead of the sheep stomach and leave out the suet. He also gives a recipe which makes a haggis entirely of oats, egg yolks and several fresh herbs.

Today haggis has many different regional variations and it can now also be found deep-fried, as a topping on pizza, in croquettes, burgers, and many other odd and creative fusion ways. The Scots continue to embrace the dish that has become such a big part of their culture and have brought it into the twenty-first century. Scottish friends tell me they usually buy their haggis rather than making it at home from scratch.

Do you have the guts?

If you're feeling a wee bit reluctant to use a lamb's stomach, you can either buy large ox bung (intestine) casings online or you can make an artificial gut out of plastic wrap! Place a pudding cloth or clean tea towel (dish towel) over a bowl, lay two sheets of plastic wrap over it, put the pudding mixture in the middle and close the plastic wrap around it. Now tie the cloth around the ball and proceed to boil the haggis.

Makes 2 large haggises, or 3 smaller ones. The large one would serve 6, or more if used as a starter or spread on oatcakes as an appetiser.

a sheep's stomach, ox bung (intestine) or plastic wrap and pudding cloth

2 lamb's kidneys, cleaned (about 80 g/2¾ oz when cooked)

2 lamb's hearts (about 90 g/3¼ oz when cooked)

1 pair of lamb's lungs (about 70 g/2½ oz when cooked)

2 onions, roughly chopped

1 tablespoon each of finely chopped parsley, savory, hyssop, sage and mint (if using dried herbs, use double)

1 teaspoon salt

1½ teaspoons black pepper

200 g (7 oz) shredded suet

200 g (7 oz) pinhead oatmeal (steel-cut oats), soaked in water overnight

4 eggs, beaten

Haggis

Note: For the offal, I'm giving you an estimated weight – measured when cooked – as the size of a lamb varies in different countries.

Soak the sheep's stomach or ox bung overnight in salted water, or prepare the plastic wrap on the day.

Rinse the offal, put it in a saucepan with cold water and bring to the boil. Leave to simmer for 1 hour. When cooked, allow to cool, then weigh the pieces. In the bowl of a food processor, combine the cooked offal, chopped onion and herbs and salt and pepper. Process until it forms fine grains. Taste and add more pepper or salt if you like. Then add the suet and oats, and fold in the beaten eggs. The mixture will still look quite dry, but that's okay.

Now stuff the stomach, bung or plastic wrap. Sew or tie up the casing using kitchen string, leaving some room for the pudding to expand.

Bring a large saucepan of water to the boil, turn down the heat and put in the haggis, tying it to the handle so it doesn't touch the bottom of the saucepan.

Simmer for 2 hours, if making three, or 3 hours if making two large ones. Very importantly, don't take your eyes off it: you need to prick the casing with a sharp needle or it will blow up. It needs pricking all over roughly every 10 minutes. In Scotland they call the haggis 'the Beast'; you need to keep an eye on 'the Beast'!

Serve with 'neeps and tatties' for a traditional Burns Night supper, or spread on oatcakes or toast as an appetiser. Haggis freezes well.

Black Pudding

Just like the haggis, the black pudding originated centuries before the first written word about it. A blood pudding appeared in Homer's *Odyssey* around 800 BCE, and the Romans had several recipes for it.

In times when food was scarce, animals would be bled to create black pudding in trays or as cakes. A little milk and oatmeal would be added, and the pudding would be the only source of protein. From letters of the period, we know this custom was still very much alive in the eighteenth century, particularly in the Scottish Highlands where the rough landscape made it difficult to grow crops and rear cattle.

It is in the north that the popularity of black pudding remains the greatest, with several counties preparing their own regional variety. Two particular rivals – Yorkshire and Lancashire – fight out the battle of the best black pudding by hosting the Black Pudding Throwing Championship each year. The rivalry dates back to the medieval Wars of the Roses, when the houses of York and Lancaster each made claim to the English throne, but it seems today the war is being fought on culinary grounds rather than the battlefield.

Black pudding was not just food for the peasantry, it was also fit for the most noble. The extravagant banquets held by King Henry VIII at Hampton Court included black pudding, and recipes for the dish appeared in cookery books aimed at court cooks rather than the amateur cook or domestic housewife. The spices used in those early recipes – cinnamon, cloves, mace, pepper and ginger – were all very expensive and a way for the king to show off his wealth and status. Regular folk would not have had access to those spices and would have used wild herbs such as pennyroyal, savory and fennel seeds, or no flavourings at all.

> To make blacke puddings.
> Take great otmeale and lay it in milke to steepe, then take sheepes bloud and put to it, and take Oxe white and mince into it, then take a fewe sweet hearbes and two or three leeke blades, and choppe them very small, and then put into it the yolkes of some egges, and season it with Cynamon, ginger, cloues, Mace, pepper and salt, and so fill them.
> Thomas Dawson, *The Good Huswifes Jewell*, 1596

Black pudding is certainly not a dish unique to Britain and Ireland; Belgium has its beuling, France its boudin, Finland has mustamakkara and Hungary has véres hurka. These are just a few examples. In fact, Sweden still makes cakes from blood: blodplättar are blood pancakes that can also be found in parts of eastern Europe, Finland and Estonia.

It is safe to say that using animal blood has been part of food culture for many centuries. As well as turning the blood into some kind of sausage or cake, Hungary, Sweden, Poland and a few Asian countries have a tradition of blood soups, or using blood to thicken sauces. In some parts of Italy, not only are several blood sausages made but the fresh warm blood is even mixed with milk and chocolate at pig-slaughtering feasts as a treat for the children.

Many of these dishes might sound strange to us; we have become so far removed from the fact that there are animals needed to provide us with meat that we no longer feel the need to use up the entire beast. But I imagine if you raise your own animals, as they did in those times, you wouldn't want to see anything go to waste.

Black pudding has seen a revival in Britain. It's back on the breakfast plate, alongside bacon, eggs, mushrooms, baked beans and hash browns as an essential ingredient of the 'full English'. It's also in gourmet dishes, transformed into croquettes (as with haggis) and as a partner to delicate seafood such as scallops, monkfish and turbot. It is back, and not just for those on the breadline, but on the menu at farm shops, Michelin-starred restaurants, and street food stalls.

Surprisingly, black pudding does have health benefits. It has relatively few kilojoules (calories), especially compared to other types of sausage, and is rich in iron and zinc, two nutrients that are frequently depleted in the average adult's body. Raw blood, however, is toxic and should not be eaten without cooking.

To try your hand at black pudding, you can purchase powdered blood from sausage supply companies, although I prefer to use my local farm and keep their pigs' blood in the freezer until needed. Whatever you do when you come to stay at my house, stay away from the ice-cream containers in my freezer that contain a raspberry-looking sorbet: it's not ice cream!

I have not used diced fat in this pudding, but you can if you like; simply cut pork back fat into small dice and add at the end when your mixture is cooling. I prefer a black pudding like the ones I grew up with. It was one of my favourite meals: black pudding with apple sauce and bread.

Makes 4 decent-size black puddings; serves 4–6

250 g (9 oz/2½ cups) rolled (porridge) oats, soaked in milk overnight, drained

100 g (3½ oz) pinhead oatmeal (steel-cut oats), soaked in milk overnight, drained

500 ml (17 fl oz/2 cups) pig's blood (thawed, if frozen)

2 egg yolks

1 small leek, thinly sliced

50 g (1¾ oz) lard

¼ teaspoon ground cinnamon

a pinch of ground ginger

3 cloves, ground

½ teaspoon ground mace

½ teaspoon black pepper

1 teaspoon chopped thyme

1 teaspoon chopped savory

1 teaspoon chopped parsley

1 teaspoon salt

sausage casing, soaked in salted water overnight (or as instructed on the pack)

butter, for frying

Black pudding

Put the drained oats into a large saucepan. Pour in the blood, then add the egg yolks, leek, lard and spices. Now bring the mixture to a boil and add the herbs and salt. Allow to cool.

Place the sausage casing over a funnel with a wide opening. You can tie the casing around the funnel if you like. I make a homemade funnel from the top of a plastic bottle; this works best to keep the sausage casing in place.

Scoop the pudding batter into a piping (icing) bag with a large plain nozzle roughly the same size as the funnel opening. Put the piping bag inside the funnel and start squeezing out the pudding mixture. It is quite runny so it will go down easily. Help the mixture along the casing by squeezing slightly with wet hands to force it down. Don't make the puddings too long: it is better to stop in time than to have filled an entire sausage only to have a hole in the middle where the mixture all pours out and makes a mess.

Make links by pushing the mixture down gently and tying a piece of kitchen string around the casing to fasten it off. Then tie another piece of string beside the first and cut between the two so you have separate sausages. Alternatively, tie the sausage casing in a knot.

Heat a large saucepan of water to just under boiling point (80°C/175°F) and place the puddings in the water. Gently simmer for 30–40 minutes, then remove them from the water and allow them to cool.

Fry the puddings whole in butter, as these black puddings are of the variety that aren't very compact.

Spread black pudding on a slice of bread and dip it in freshly made, but cooled, apple sauce.

boiled & steamed |

boiled & steamed |

If you are making a black pudding cake, why not add half a cup of melted chocolate or cacao nibs! Try it.

Black pudding in a tray

Instead of using sausage casing, line a loaf (bar) tin with baking paper, pour in the batter and bake in a preheated oven at 160°C (315°F) for 1 hour.

Makes 8–10 small pancakes

250 ml (9 fl oz/1 cup) black
  pudding mixture

1 egg

1 tablespoon plain
  (all-purpose) flour

butter, for frying

Black pudding griddle cakes

Mix the black pudding mixture with the egg and flour and
stir well to combine. Put a pancake pan or griddle iron over
medium heat and melt a knob of butter. Pour in the mixture one
generous tablespoonful at a time and fry the pancakes on both
sides. Serve with melted chocolate sauce, or stewed cherries.

White Pudding

W hite puddings and black puddings appear in English cookery books at the same time. There were two versions of white pudding: one using liver or white meat such as pork, and one that was entirely cereal in composition. The latter was called 'Ising Pudding' in early cookery books but was soon categorised under White Pudding, probably because language evolved and people forgot the name Ising.

James Joyce celebrated the white pudding in *A Portrait of the Artist as a Young Man* (1922):

White pudding and eggs and sausages and cups of tea!
How simple and beautiful was life after all!

Many recipes for Roman sausages resemble the white pudding, with Apicius: *De Re Coquinaria* listing a number of them. Spices are a very important part of this pudding, which means it wasn't a dish for the lower class but must have been meant for the elite.

In Scotland the white pudding is also known as a 'mealy pudding', but it isn't always in the shape of a sausage, which confirms the theory that people have always been looking for a way to create their favourite dishes throughout the year instead of just around hog-killing time when guts were available.

To make the best white Puddings
Take a pint of the best, thickest and sweetest Cream, and boyl it, then whilst it is hot, put thereunto a good quantity of breat sweet Oatmeal Grots very sweet, and clean pickt, and formerly steept in milk twelve hours at least, and let it soak in this Cream another night; then put thereto at least eight yolks of Eggs, a little Pepper, Cloves, Mace, Saffron, Currants, Dates, Sugar, Salt, and great store of Swines Suet, or for want thereof great store of Beef Suet, and then fill it up in the farmes according unto the order of good House-wifery; and then boyl them on a soft and gentle fire, and as they swell, prick them with a great Pin, or small Awl, to keep them that they burst not, and when you serve them to the Table, (which must not be untill they be a day old) first boyl them a little, then take them out, and roast them brown before the fire, and so serve them, trimming the edge of the dish either with Salt or Sugar.
Gervase Markham, *The English Huswife*, 1615

Be aware, this is a sweet dish, to be compared with Rice pudding in skins (see page 108).

200 g (7 oz/2 cups) rolled
(porridge) oats, soaked in
milk overnight, drained

100 g (3½ oz) pinhead
oatmeal (steel-cut oats),
soaked in milk overnight,
drained

500 ml (35 fl oz/2 cups) thick
(double) cream

a few saffron threads, added
to the cream, optional

3 egg yolks

50 g (1¾ oz) shredded suet

20 g (¾ oz) seedless dates

20 g (¾ oz) currants

3 cloves, ground

½ teaspoon ground mace

½ teaspoon salt

½ teaspoon sugar

a pinch of pepper

sausage casing, soaked in
salted water overnight (or
as instructed on the pack)

White pudding

Put all of the soaked and drained oats into a large saucepan.
Pour the cream (and saffron, if using) into the oats, then add
the egg yolks, suet, dates, currants and the combined spices.
Bring to a boil over high heat, remove from the heat and set
aside to cool.

Place the sausage casing over a funnel with a wide opening.
You can tie the casing around the funnel if you like. I make a
homemade funnel from the top of a plastic bottle; this works
best to keep the sausage casing in place.

Scoop the pudding batter into a piping (icing) bag with a
large plain nozzle roughly the same size as the funnel opening.
Put the piping bag in the funnel and start squeezing out the
pudding mixture. Help the mixture down by squeezing the
skins slightly with wet hands to force it down.

Make links by pushing the mixture down gently and tying a
piece of kitchen string around the casing to fasten it off. Then
tie another piece of string beside the first and cut between the
two so you have separate sausages. Alternatively, tie the sausage
casing in a knot.

Heat a large saucepan of water to just under boiling point
(80°C/175°F) and place the puddings in the water. Gently
simmer for 30–40 minutes, then remove them from the water
and allow them to cool.

To serve, fry the pudding whole and serve with honey, maple
syrup or golden syrup (light treacle), or a little sugar.

Hogs Pudding

Hogs pudding is connected to the West Country today, but in the olden days it used to be made nationally. There are versions using a pig's or lamb's 'pluck' – which is the heart, lungs and liver – instead of just pig's liver, giving it the name Devonshire or West Country haggis. However, I have not come across a mention of a Devonshire haggis or a West Country haggis in any of my ancient cookery books, so I believe that is a modern tale.

Hogs pudding was traditionally cut into slices and fried, and the slices were then used to decorate other plates of meat. It was eaten as a side dish, with something else. This is a nice salty pudding to have with scallops or lobster, and it is also very good for breakfast with an egg or two.

Another Sort of Hogs Puddings
To half a pound of grated bread, put half a pound of hogs liver boil'd, cold, and grated, a pound and half of suet finely shred, a handful of salt, a handful of sweet herbs, chopt small, some spice; mix all these together, with six eggs well beaten, and a little thick cream; fill your guts and boil them; when cold, cut them in round slices an inch thick; fry them in butter, and garnish your dish of fowls, hafh, or fricassee.
Eliza Smith, *The Compleat Housewife*, 1727

400 g (14 oz) pig's liver
(225 g/8 oz when cooked)

1 heaped teaspoon each
of chopped thyme, hyssop,
savory, mint and parsley

15 g (½ oz) salt

1 teaspoon black pepper

1 teaspoon ground nutmeg

225 g (8 oz/3¾ cups) fresh
breadcrumbs

50 g (1¾ oz) shredded suet

500 ml (35 fl oz/2 cups)
thick (double) cream

3 eggs, lightly whisked

sausage casings, soaked in
salted water overnight (or
as instructed on the pack)

butter, for frying

Hogs pudding

Boil the liver for 15 minutes and allow it to cool completely.

Put the liver in a food processor together with the fresh herbs, salt, pepper and nutmeg, and process to a fine grain. Taste the mixture and adjust the seasoning if needed. It should taste quite salty, but I wouldn't add more salt. Mix the finely chopped liver with the breadcrumbs, suet, cream and eggs.

Place the sausage casing over a funnel with a wide opening. You can tie the casing around the funnel if you like. I make a home-made funnel from the top of a plastic bottle; this works best to keep the sausage casing in place.

Scoop the pudding batter into a piping (icing) bag with a large plain nozzle roughly the same size as the funnel opening. Put the piping bag inside the funnel and start squeezing out the pudding mixture. It is quite runny so it will go down easily. Help the mixture along the casing by squeezing slightly with wet hands to force it down.

Make links by pushing the mixture down gently and tying a piece of kitchen string around the casing to fasten it off. Then tie another piece of string beside the first and cut between the two so you have separate sausages. Alternatively, tie the sausage casing in a knot.

Heat a large saucepan of water to just under boiling point (80°C/175°F) and place the puddings in the water. Gently simmer for 30 minutes and keep an eye on the puddings: if they seem like they are going to blow up, prick them with a sharp needle to release the pressure. Lift the puddings out of the water and allow them to cool.

When the puddings are cooled, put them in the fridge for at least 1 hour. To serve, remove the sausage casing, cut the pudding into thick slices and fry in butter. Freeze the ones you don't need.

You can also bake this pudding flat in a cake tin, placed in a deep baking dish of boiling water for 30 minutes. Leave to cool and fry to serve, cut into any shape you desire.

Serve with eggs for a hearty breakfast, or with scallops, lobster or a white fish such as cod, monkfish or turbot.

Hackin Pudding

The 'hackin' or 'hack pudding' was a pudding made in Cumbria, formerly Cumberland, in the Lake District. The custom was to eat the hackin pudding on Christmas morning and therefore it is very likely that it is the ancestor of Christmas pudding. Like plum pudding, slices of hackin were sometimes 'fired' or grilled under a rotating spit of beef or mutton, or baked just at the mouth of the oven and served before or with the meat. The following recipe is from Richard Bradley, *The Country Housewife and Lady's Director*, published in London in 1732. Mutton suet was sometimes used instead of beef.

To make a hackin. From a Gentleman in Cumberland.

Sir, There are some Counties in England, whose Customs are never to be set aside and our Friends in Cumberland, as well as some of our Neighbours in Lancashire, and else-where, keep them up. It is a Custom with us every Christmas-Day in the Morning, to have, what we call an Hackin, for the Breakfast of the young Men who work about our House; and if this Dish is not dressed by that time it is Day-light, the Maid is led through the Town, between two Men, as fast as they can run with her, up Hill and down Hill, which she accounts a great shame. But as for the Receipt to make this Hackin, which is admired so much by us, it is as follows.

Take the Bag or Paunch of a Calf, and wash it, and clean it well with Water and Salt; then take some Beef-Suet, and shred it small, and shred some Apples, after they are pared and cored, very small. Then put in some Sugar, and some Spice beaten small, a little Lemon-Peel cut very fine, and a little Salt, and a good quantity of Grots, or whole Oat-meal, steep'd a Night in Milk; then mix these all together, and add as many Currans pick'd clean from the Stalks, and rubb'd in a coarse Cloth; but let them not be wash'd. And when you have all ready, mix them together, and put them into the Calf's-Bag, and tye them up, and boil them till they are enough. You may, if you will, mix up with the whole, some Eggs beaten, which will help to bind it. This is our Custom to have ready, at the opening of the Doors, on Christmas-Day in the Morning. It is esteem'd here; but all that I can say to you of it, is, that it eats somewhat like a Christmas-Pye, or is some-what like boil'd. I had forgot to say, that with the rest of the Ingredients, there should be some Lean of tender Beef minced small.

Richard Bradley, *The Country Housewife and Lady's Director*, 1732

Makes 1 pudding in a 17 cm (6½ inch/No. 30) basin (mould); serves 4–6 people

300 g (10½ oz) lean minced (ground) beef or veal

2 eggs

100 g (3½ oz) pinhead oatmeal (steel-cut oats), soaked in milk overnight

100 g (3½ oz) shredded suet

1 apple, grated

50 g (1¾ oz) currants

1 teaspoon sugar

2 teaspoons ground mace

1 teaspoon ground allspice

1 teaspoon candied lemon peel

½ teaspoon salt

butter, for frying

Hackin pudding

Put the minced beef into a bowl with the eggs, drained oatmeal, suet, apple, currants, sugar, mace, allspice, lemon peel and salt and combine into a patty.

Layer 2 pieces of plastic wrap on a tea towel (dish towel) or pudding cloth. Shape the patty into a ball shape and place in the centre of the plastic wrap. Fold the plastic wrap around the ball, then tie into the cloth using kitchen string.

Place the pudding in a large saucepan or stock pot of boiling water, tying the pudding to the handle so the pudding doesn't touch the bottom of the pan. Alternatively, place the wrapped pudding in a pudding basin (mould) set on an inverted saucer or jam-jar lid in the bottom of the pan.

Boil for 2 hours. To serve, cut thick slices and fry in butter.

Serve on its own or with green vegetables and potatoes, or with stewed sour cherries and some bread on the side.

Cabbage Pudding

This dish was also known as a 'cabbage farce' or 'forced', meaning forcemeat, which is stuffing meat. It really is excellent and looks very pretty and rustic on your dinner table.

To make a Cabbage Pudding
Take two pounds of the lean part of a leg of veal, of beef-suet, the like quantity, chop them together, then beat them together in a stone mortar, adding to it half a little cabbage scalded, and beat that with your meat; then season it with mace and nutmeg, a little pepper and salt, some green gooseberries, grapes, or barberries in the time of the year; in the winter put in a little verjuice, then mix all well together, with the yolks of four or five eggs well beaten; wrap it up in green cabbage leaves, tie a cloth over it, boil it an hour; melt butter for sauce.
Eliza Smith, *The Compleat Housewife*, 1737

This recipe by Eliza Smith has been copied into many books after its publication; indeed, it might not even be Eliza's to begin with. I discovered the recipe after I stumbled upon it in my recently acquired first edition of *The Ladies Handmaid* compiled by Sarah Phillips in 1758, where she copies it word for word.

Richard Briggs gives a similar recipe (*The English Art of Cookery, According to the Present Practice*, 1788) that he calls 'Cabbage forced', in which he adds half a pound of bacon and leaves the veal whole in thin strips. He also adds hard-boiled eggs, nutmeg and mace, parsley and thyme, anchovies, breadcrumbs, mushrooms and raw eggs. His next recipe is a variation of this dish using the meat of a couple of plaice.

A plain green or white cabbage is what was probably used, but I prefer using a savoy cabbage because I like the flavour and the look of its bubbly leaves. I also use minced (ground) beef rather than veal, as ethically raised veal is hard to come by. The original recipe uses the same quantities of suet to beef but I'd rather not have so much suet in my pud. Sour fruits such as gooseberries, grapes or barberries can be substituted for cider vinegar and, if you can get red currants, they are quite delicious in this pudding and kind of remind me of the custom of eating paté with red currant compote.

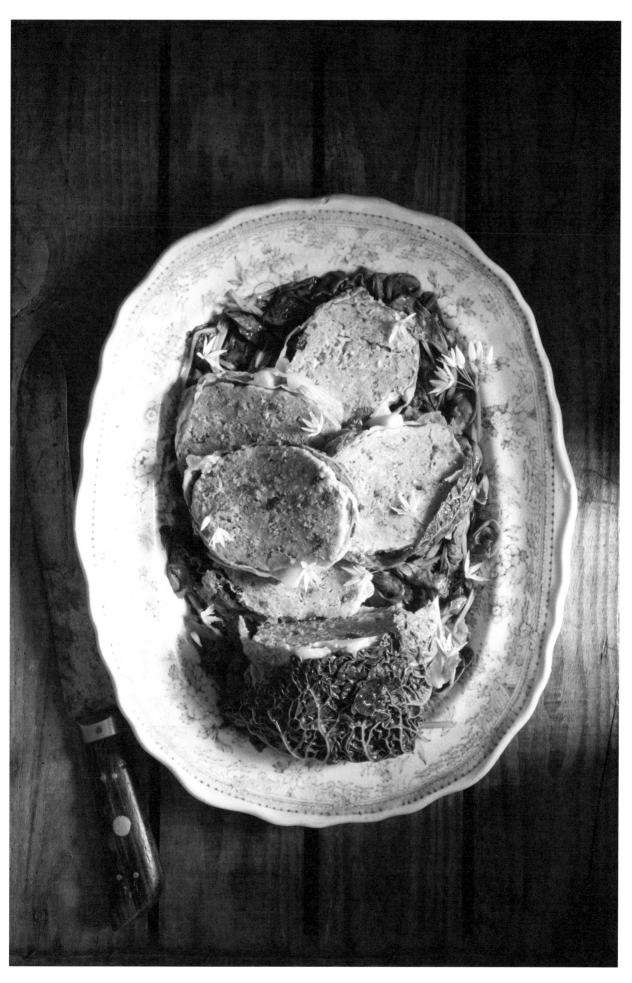

Makes 1 pudding in a 17 cm (6½ inch/No. 30) basin (mould), or make it in roly-poly style (see page 116). Serves 4–6

1 small savoy cabbage (winter cabbage)

450 g (1 lb) minced (ground) veal or pork

150 g (5½ oz) shredded suet

1 teaspoon ground nutmeg

1 teaspoon ground mace

1 teaspoon freshly ground black pepper

1 teaspoon salt

4 egg yolks, beaten

1 teaspoon apple cider vinegar, if using cranberries

20 g (¾ oz) barberries (if you can't get barberries, use cranberries)

red currant compote or extra berries, for serving

Cabbage pudding

Take off the largest and most beautiful outer leaves of the cabbage, rinse them and set aside to wrap the pudding later. Finely shred and blanch 50 g (1¾ oz) of the remaining cabbage.

Put the meat in a large bowl with the suet and the spices. Pour in the egg yolks, the apple cider vinegar, if using, and the barberries or cranberries and combine by stirring with a wooden spoon. Fold the blanched cabbage in with the meat until you get a texture as for a meat loaf.

Prepare a lightly greased pudding basin by lining it with plastic wrap. Line the basin with most of the reserved cabbage leaves, then add the meat mixture and top it off with a few more cabbage leaves. Prepare the pudding for steaming as instructed on pages 68–69, and steam for 1½ hours. Alternatively, make a roly-poly by rolling up a layer of meat mixture with the cabbage leaves.

Serve the pudding turned out on a plate, decorated with some red currant compote or fresh berries. The red colour will be very pretty with the green of the cabbage leaves. Carrot jam (see page 141) is also a nice touch. A bed of spinach and wild garlic, when in season, is a very agreeable accompaniment.

boiled & steamed

Pease Pudding

Pease pudding is an old English dish, remembered in an old nursery rhyme: 'Pease porridge hot, pease porridge cold, Pease porridge in the pot nine days old; Some like it hot, some like it cold, Some like it in the pot nine days old.' (*The Original Mother Goose's Melody*, 1889.)

It evolved from the medieval pease pottage or porridge, which was one of the main filler dishes before potatoes came to Britain. Various varieties of peas and beans were grown on a large scale throughout Britain. These legumes are one of the oldest of cultivated crops and were probably brought to England by the Romans. The pea plant is hardy and could face the often-rough weather in northern Europe. After harvest the peas were dried and kept in storage until needed. The pease pottage would be served with salted bacon when any was available, as the bacon was so salty the pea pottage would balance out the flavours nicely.

'Hot grey peas and a suck of bacon' was the cry of seventeenth century street vendors, but street sellers of peas and other foods have been documented as far back as medieval times. Similarities with the Dutch pea soup known as snert are many. To the thick snert, a salty smoked sausage – originally from the province of Gelderland – was added to provide the pottage with its much needed salty seasoning.

As soon as the pudding cloth came into use, the mixture began to be boiled in a cloth and became pease pudding; however, usage of the word pease pottage or porridge continued to be interchangeable.

While the dish does make for a perfect peasant meal, one you could imagine they would have had, it was also prepared in more noble households. *The Forme of Cury* (Samuel Pegge, ed.) mentions a 'Perrey of Pesoun' a pea purée, for the king's table in around 1390. Samuel Pepys, one of the most important diarists in history – and not a poor man – tells us: 'At noon I went home and dined with my wife on pease porridge and nothing else.' (1 February 1660)

It is very possible that Pepys's pease porridge would have looked like the one in the following contemporary recipe by Robert May:

Pease Pottage.
Take green pease being shelled and cleansed, put them in a pipkin of fair boiling water; when they be boil'd and tender, take and strain some of them, and thicken the rest, put to them a bundle of sweet herbs, or sweet herbs chopped, salt, and butter; being through boil'd dish them, and serve them in a deep clean dish with salt and sippets about them.
Robert May, *The Accomplisht Cook*, 1660

The 'sweet herbs' he mentions are named in another earlier recipe by Sir Kenelm Digby (*The Closet of the Eminently Learned Sir Kenelme Digbie Knight Opened*, 1669) as fresh mint, parsley, winter savory and sweet marjoram. Digby also adds ground coriander seeds. May instructs the cook to serve the dish with sippets, which were small pieces of toasted or fried bread.

Nineteenth century pease pudding recipes suggest boiling the pease pud in a cloth before mashing the peas, then adding butter and flavourings before boiling it again.

Today the pease pudding is often served with gammon and ham hock. But I also quite like it as a dip or a sarnie (sandwich) spread, topped with bacon. I am using the herbs Sir Kenelm Digby used in his recipe, because they give a good flavour to the peas.

Serves 4–6 people as a snack or side dish

500 g (1 lb 2 oz/2¼ cups) green or yellow dried split peas, soaked in water overnight, drained

30 g (1 oz) butter

1 tablespoon each of finely chopped mint, parsley, marjoram and savory

salt and pepper, to taste

bread, cut into triangles and toasted in clarified butter, to serve

Tip the peas into a saucepan and add fresh water to cover. Bring to the boil, skimming off any scum that rises to the surface. Lower the heat and simmer gently for an hour or until the peas are very tender.

Strain the peas and mash them, stirring in the butter and the herbs. Scoop into a nice serving dish and serve hot or warm with pork, with fish and chips, or spread on a sarnie. When served with the small pieces of toast – sippets, as instructed by Robert May – it reminds me of hummus with flatbread.

Sussex Pond Pudding

The Sussex pond pudding is still popular in Britain today. It is basically the same as the Kentish well pudding, which appears later in cookery books. The two counties share a border so it would make sense for the pudding to be popular in Kent too; however its current appearance is somewhat different from the original. Not only would this pudding have been boiled in intestine casings and later in cloth, but it had never enclosed a whole lemon until quite recently when Jane Grigson published a recipe for it in her book *English Food* (1974).

In the seventeenth century, and perhaps even earlier, this pudding was made with only a lump of butter hidden in the middle; the butter sauce running out of the pudding when it was cut would create the 'pond' that gave the pudding its name.

The oldest recipe for a Sussex pond pudding can be found in *The Queen-like Closet*, a book by Hannah Wolley, published in 1672. She calls it just a Sussex pudding. She suggests to stuff apples or gooseberries in the pudding but doesn't mention a lemon:

> Take a little cold cream, butter and flower, with some beaten spice, eggs, and a little salt. Make them into a stiff paste, then make them into a round ball, and you mold it, put in a piece of butter in the middle; and so tye it hard up in a buttered cloth, and put it into boiling water, and let it boil apace till it be enough then serve it in, and garnish your dish with barberries; when it is at the table cut it open at the top, and there will be as it were a pound [pond] of butter, then put rosewater and sugar into it and so eat it. In some of this like paste you may wrap great apples, being pared whole, in one piece of thin paste, and so close it round the apple, and through them into boiling water, and let them boil till enough, you may also put some green gooseberries into some, and when wither of these are boiled, cut them open and put in rosewater butter and sugar.
> Hannah Wolley, *The Queen-like Closet*, 1672

A century later, William Ellis, author of several books on husbandry and brewing tells us in his book *The Country Housewife's Family Companion* that on 13 June 1749 'Baitin at the Castle Inn at East-Grinstead' he watched the cook-maid prepare a Sussex pond pudding and noted the recipe. We have Ellis's observations to thank for many clues to life in eighteenth century England. In this particular case he tells us how the pudding, which he referred to as 'famous', was eaten: 'When boiled enough, they find the butter run to oil, and well soaked into the pudding, that they eat it with meat instead of bread, or without meat as a delicious pudding.'

The earliest recipe I could find for a Kentish well pudding dates back to Eliza Acton's *Modern Cookery for Private Families* from 1845. Her recipe is nearly identical in outcome to that of Wolley's Sussex pudding, but she uses suet in her recipe, which has now become the standard.

Suet crust

300 g (10½ oz/2 cups)
  self-raising flour

130 g (4½ oz) shredded suet

½ teaspoon ground cinnamon

a pinch of salt

2 teaspoons lemon juice

70 ml (2¼ fl oz) thin
  (pouring) cream, chilled

120 ml (4 fl oz) cold tap
  water

Filling

4 dessert apples, such as
  cox or jonagold (about
  440 g/15½ oz, when cored
  and peeled)

140 g (5 oz) light brown sugar

150 g (5½ oz) good-quality
  butter, cubed, chilled

*Makes 2 puddings in 14 cm (5½ inch/No. 42) basins (moulds),
or 1 large pudding in a cloth*

First prepare the pudding basins or pudding cloth following the instructions on pages 68–69.

In a large bowl, mix the flour with the suet, cinnamon and salt. Then add the lemon juice, cream and cold water to bring the dough together into a stiff paste.

Dust the work surface with flour, roll out the dough and set one quarter of the dough aside for the lids. Place the dough into the pudding basins by pressing it down. Mould it so it is roughly the same thickness all over.

Core, peel and cut the apples in large dice, mix them with the sugar so all the pieces get a good coating, then add the cubes of butter so everything is divided quite evenly.

Divide the apple mixture between the puddings and fit a lid of dough to each pudding. Make sure you crimp the edges well so the pudding remains closed.

As a variation, you can put the butter inside a cored and peeled apple and encase a whole apple in each pudding.

Steam the puddings using the method explained on page 69. These puddings need 3 hours of steaming in the oven.

boiled & steamed |

Rice Pudding in Skins

This type of rice pudding first appeared in late Elizabethan times. It is made, like white and black puddings, in sausage skins. Stuffing the sausage skins was a tedious task: at first all people had to work with was a funnel, then a large wood-and-metal sausage forcer was used in which you had to place the pudding mixture and force it through the nozzle. The recipe below is by John Murrell; I have chosen it because it uses barberries, a berry that was also frequently used to colour food, and also because I like the way Murrell writes. The recipe is, however, incomplete. He ends his recipe with the instructions to parboil – which, even back then, meant partly boil – and let the pudding cool.

Puddings were usually sliced and then fried or roasted in front of the fire, and it was no different with this rice pudding. We find the clue for that in a book from 1660, Robert May's *The Accomplisht Cook*. May gives two recipes for rice pudding: one in skins like this one, and one in a pudding cloth. At the end of the second recipe, he adds: 'If in guts, being boild, tost them before the fire in a silver dish or tosting pan.'

A Ryce Pudding.
Steep it in faire water all night: then boyle it in new Milke, and draine out the Milke through a Cullinder: mince beefe Suit handsomely, but not too small, and put it into the Rice, and parboyld Currins, yolkes of new layd Egges, Nutmeg, Sinamon, Sugar, and Barberryes: mingle all together: wash your scoured guttes, and stuffe them with the aforesaid pulp: parboyle them, and let them coole.
John Murrell, *A Newe Booke of Cookery*, 1615

The same year as John Murrell's book was published, Gervase Markham also published a recipe for rice pudding in his book *The English Huswife*. He used dates instead of barberries, added cloves and mace instead of nutmeg, and also added a pinch of salt and pepper.

Unlike a modern rice pudding, this recipe uses suet as in most boiled puddings. As we can use arborio or pudding rice today, we don't need to steep the rice overnight. I find arborio rice gives a better result if you're going to stuff the pudding into sausage skins. If you are making this as a regular rice pudding without using sausage skins, you may use pudding rice, and use a knob of butter instead of the suet. Barberries can be found in organic grocers; they are very tart but are delicious in this pudding.

boiled & steamed |

Makes 4 rice puddings

220 g (7¾ oz/1 cup)
  arborio rice

750 ml (26 fl oz/3 cups)
  milk

1 mace blade

1 cinnamon stick

a tiny pinch of salt and
  pepper

50 g (1¾ oz) shredded suet

20 g (¾ oz) sugar

25 g (1 oz) currants, soaked
  in water overnight, drained

a large handful of barberries,
  dried or fresh (if you
  can't get barberries, use
  cranberries)

2 egg yolks, beaten

sausage casing, soaked in
  salted water overnight (or
  as instructed on the pack)

butter, for frying

Boil the rice in the milk with the spices, salt and pepper in a large saucepan over low heat. When the rice is soft and the mixture is thickened, add the suet, sugar, currants, barberries and finally the egg yolks. Remove from the heat and allow to cool slightly.

Place the sausage casing over a funnel with a wide opening. You can tie the casing around the funnel if you like. I make a homemade funnel from the top of a plastic bottle; this works best to keep the sausage casing in place.

Scoop the pudding batter into a piping (icing) bag with a large plain nozzle roughly the same size as the funnel opening. Put the piping bag inside the funnel and start squeezing out the pudding mixture. It is quite runny so it will go down easily. Help the mixture along the casing by squeezing slightly with wet hands to force it down.

Make links by pushing the mixture down gently and tying a piece of kitchen string around the casing to fasten it off. Then tie another piece of string beside the first and cut between the two so you have separate sausages. Alternatively, tie the sausage casing in a knot.

Heat a large saucepan of water to boiling and place the puddings in the water. Gently simmer for 30 minutes, then lift them out of the water and allow them to cool.

To serve, cut thick slices and fry them in a frying pan with butter, or fry the puddings whole. I prefer the latter method, as it's very entertaining to serve your guests sweet sausages. Serve with raspberry vinegar, maple syrup, honey or a dusting of sugar.

Quaking Pudding

The seventeenth century diarist Samuel Pepys mentions having eaten a particularly good 'shaking pudding' in one of his many diary entries about his daily meals.

The quaking or shaking pudding is made of a custard boiled in a cloth either in water or along with the meat in the broth. It is very delicate and has a nice wobble to it when you move the plate. The pudding was usually served in a pond of melted butter, sugar and sack (a kind of sherry) or rosewater. It was then often spiked with sliced almonds or candied peel, which made it look like a hedgehog.

> To make a Quaking Pudding.
> Take a pint of cream, and boil it with nutmeg, cinnamon and mace; take out the spice, when it is boiled; then take the yolks of eight eggs, and four of the whites, beat them very well with some Sack; then mix your eggs and cream, with a little salt and sugar, and a stale half penny white-loaf, one spoonful of flour, and a quarter of a pound of almonds blanch'd and beat fine, with some rose-water; beat all tell these well together; then wet a thick cloth, flour it, and put it in when the pot boils; it must boil an hour at least; melt butter, Sack and sugar for the sauce, stick'd blanch'd almonds and candied orange-peel on the top.
>
> Eliza Smith, *The Compleat Housewife*, 1727

Makes 1 pudding in a 17 cm (6½ inch/No. 30) basin (mould)

20 g (¾ oz) sweet almonds, blanched and skinned

20 g (¾ oz) bitter almonds, blanched and skinned

1 teaspoon rosewater

550 ml (19 fl oz) thin (pouring) cream (35% fat)

½ teaspoon ground nutmeg

1 mace blade

1 cinnamon stick

50 g (1¾ oz) raw sugar

5 egg yolks

2 egg whites

½ tablespoon sherry or Madeira

45 g (1½ oz/¾ cup) fresh breadcrumbs

1 tablespoon rice flour

Prepare a pudding basin for steaming as described on pages 68–69.

Combine the sweet and bitter almonds with the rosewater and pound to a pulp with a mortar and pestle.

Put the cream in a medium saucepan with the spices, the sugar and the almond pulp, then bring to the boil. Remove from the heat and leave to infuse for 10 minutes.

Strain the warm cream. Beat the egg yolks and whites with the sherry and start adding the warm cream, whisking constantly until well combined. Fold the breadcrumbs and rice flour through the batter.

Pour the batter into the prepared pudding basin and steam for 1 hour according to the instructions on page 69.

Serve with Sack Sauce (see page 339) or raspberry vinegar (see page 340) and, if you want to go 'old school' all the way, stick some blanched almonds or candied orange peel into the pudding before serving.

Beef Pudding

Beef pudding has been a favourite meal of the British for many centuries; like other puddings it finds its origins in the old boiled meat puddings. When filled suet puddings gained popularity by the end of the eighteenth century, there appeared recipes for 'steak and kidney pudding', 'beef and baked beef steak pudding', both by Maria Eliza Rundell (*A New System of Domestic Cookery*, 1807). In the latter years of the nineteenth century, Agnes Marshall (*Mrs A.B. Marshall's Book of Cookery*, 1888) published her rather posh-sounding version, 'Beef Pudding with Anchovies', which is made by flattening out the steak, adding herbs, chopped shallots and mushrooms, then diced anchovies, before rolling it up like a small cylinder and placing the meat parcels in the suet pastry.

A few years before Marshall, in 1845, French-born Alexis Soyer gave a recipe for 'Beef Pudding' with oysters, mushrooms or kidneys in his book *A Shilling Cookery for the People*. Having a good understanding of what the upper class were eating as well as what the lower class could afford to eat, he noted the following of beef pudding:

This may truly be considered as much a national dish as roast beef and plum pudding.

234 - Beef Pudding - Take about one pound of steak, cut it lengthways in three pieces, and then slantways at each inch, instead of in lumps; but should you buy cuttings of meat from the butchers, then remove all the sinew and over fat, and cut the large pieces slantways, put them in a dish, and sprinkle over with a teaspoonful of salt, a half ditto of pepper, and a teaspoonful of flour, the same of chopped onions; mix well together, make six or eight ounces of paste as No. 319, roll it to the thickness of a quarter of an inch, or a little more, put pudding-cloth in a basin, sprinkle some flour over it, lay in your paste, and then the meat, together with a few pieces of fat; when full put in three wineglasses of water; turn the paste over the meat, so as not to form a lump, but well closed; then tie the cloth, not too close on the paste, or it will not be light; boil it fast in four quarts of water for one hour; take it out, let it stand a few minutes to cool the cloth, cut the string, turn back the cloth, place a dish on the top, and turn it over on it, remove the cloth, and serve.

235 - If you choose to add a kidney it may add to the richness of the gravy, also a few oysters, or even a mushroom. The crust should always be cut with a knife.

If you carefully follow the above instructions you will have a pudding quite perfect, the paste as light and as white as snow, and the meat tender, with a thick gravy.

236 - Observation. You will perhaps be surprised that I recommend it to be boiled fast instead of simmering. I do so, because the meat, being enclosed in the paste, and sometimes in a basin, is alone subject to the action of simmering in its own gravy. These puddings lose a less amount of nourishment in cooking than any other kind. In a large pudding a few sliced potatoes is not bad. This may truly be considered as much a national dish as roast beef and plum pudding, and being so, it is surprising that it is so often made badly, and indigestible: the pieces of meat and fat often cut two inches square, instead of smaller pieces; the pudding, sometimes left half out of this water, the crust becomes hard and black, and the meat very dry.

Alexis Soyer, *A Shilling Cookery for the People*, 1845

boiled & steamed |

Filling

500 g (1 lb 2 oz) stewing beef (I prefer chuck steak, fatty bits removed)

plain (all-purpose) flour, enough to give the meat a dusting

1 large onion

5 small mushrooms, halved

1 thyme stalk

1 bay leaf

a generous grinding of the pepper mill

125 ml (4 fl oz/½ cup) dark ale, such as porter, stout or a Belgian monastery beer (if you don't want to use alcohol, use the same quantity of beef stock)

Suet pastry

300 g (10½ oz/2 cups) plain (all-purpose) flour

130 g (4½ oz) shredded suet

1 teaspoon baking powder

juice of ½ lemon (about 2 tablespoons)

200 ml (7 fl oz) water

a pinch of salt

1 teaspoon thyme leaves or finely chopped parsley

Beef pudding

Prepare the pudding basin (see pages 68–69). Preheat the oven to 160°C (315°F).

To make the suet pastry, put the flour, suet and baking powder in a bowl and combine very well. Add the lemon juice to the water and start adding it to the mixture in small amounts, stirring constantly. Soon it will be looking like very coarse breadcrumbs. Keep adding water until you can bring the mixture together with your hands into a stiff dough.

If it is too dry, you might need another splash of water, but I have tested it several times in different weather conditions and haven't needed more water. The dough should not be sticky, make sure of that.

Keep one-third of the dough aside for the lid of the pudding. Now pad both pieces of dough into balls and lay them on a generously floured work surface. Roll each ball of dough out gently to 1 cm (⅜ inch) thickness.

Carefully place the dough for the base of the pudding over the basin and let it slide in. It is not the end of the world if it tears, you can just repair it using your fingers. Mould the dough to the basin sides, pressing down so the edges are all the same thickness. Trim off extra dough around the sides.

Now start to arrange the raw meat, vegetables and herbs in the pudding basin and season with pepper. You can first brown the meat in a frying pan over medium heat, if you like. If you have leftover cooked beef stew, you can use this instead of the meat filling.

When the basin is nearly full, pour in the beer or stock and add the lid, arranging the pastry over the rim of the basin and carefully squeezing the dough together. You might need to just lightly wet the edges of the pastry to make it stick.

Now prepare your pudding for steaming (see page 69). Steam for 2–4 hours, depending on your meat. If you've used precooked beef stew, steam for no more than 1 hour.

Why not take a leaf out of Alexis Soyer's book and use kidneys for a traditional steak and kidney pudding or oysters instead of mushrooms? You can also substitute venison and red currants for the beef and mushrooms, or try apple and pork.

Jam Roly-poly

A roly-poly is a pudding made from a flat rolled piece of suet dough, spread with jam, rolled up and, originally, boiled in a cloth. In the present day it is usually steamed or even baked to give the roll a gentle crust. The custom of boiling the roly-poly in an old shirt sleeve gave it the nickname 'Dead Man's Arm'.

No mention is made of a roly-poly before the nineteenth century and even during that period it is often called a 'jelly roll' or 'jam roll'. It is very likely that it did exist, either under a different name or in certain localities. Eliza Acton, in *Modern Cookery for Private Families* (1845), just calls it a 'Rolled Pudding' and gives a number of different options for use as flavourings. She also gives the option to use puff pastry. Henry Mayhew, in his *London Labour and the London Poor* (1851), mentions 'Rolly Polly', as if it had been around for quite some time, when he described the shapes in which a plum duff could be made. A nursery rhyme in *The Nursery Rhymes of England* (compiled by James Halliwell-Phillipps), published in 1842, already mentions the pudding: 'Rowley Powley, pudding and pie, Kissed the girls and made them cry; When the girls begin to cry, Rowley Poley [sic] runs away.' Novelist William Makepeace Thackeray, mentions 'she had the figure and complexion of a roly-poly pudding' in his 1846 *Notes on a Journey from Cornhill to Grand Cairo*.

Alexis Soyer in 1849 is the first to publish a rolled pudding recipe called 'roly-poly'. He gives the name as it is written in the nursery rhyme printed a few years earlier, which means that the term roly-poly had been around for quite some time, maybe in more rural settings, before it actually appeared in a cookery book as the name of a rolled pudding.

> 831. Rowley Powley – Roll out about two pounds of paste (No. 746), cover it with any jam or marmalade you like, roll it over and tie it loose in a cloth, well tying each end; boil one hour and serve, or cut it in slices and serve with sauce over.
>
> Alexis Soyer, *The Modern Housewife or, Ménagère*, 1849. Note: No. 746 is 'Puff Paste, with Beef Suet'

I also believe Soyer wrote the name 'Rowley Powley' as he did for his amusement, to refer exactly to the nursery rhyme, as it is clear roly-poly had already become the common way of writing it by then. Five years later, in his recipe for 'Handy Pudding' (*A Shilling Cookery for the People*), he instructs readers to 'boil the same as rolly-polly pudding'.

Just into the twentieth century our roly-poly pudding appears in Beatrix Potter's book *The Tale of Samuel Whiskers or The Roly-poly Pudding*. In this scary children's tale the roly-poly is not filled with jam but with the hero of the story! Perhaps aided by Beatrix Potter's story, the roly-poly pudding became a childhood favourite and one of the iconic puddings of mid-twentieth century British school dinners, for which it will always be remembered alongside gypsy pudding, spotted dick, treacle pudding and sticky toffee pudding. A true retro pudding, smeared with good jam and soaked in thick custard.

Although Alexis Soyer suggests using a puff pastry dough with suet, I have tried it and the dough doesn't work, so here is my version with a regular suet dough, which is most common.

boiled & steamed |

Makes 1 pudding in a medium-size loaf tin

300 g (10½ oz/2 cups) plain (all-purpose) flour

130 g (4½ oz) shredded suet

1 teaspoon baking powder

a pinch of salt

juice of ½ lemon

200 ml (7 fl oz) water

2–3 tablespoons raspberry jam, or any other preserve

Custard sauce (see page 338), to serve

Jam roly-poly

Preheat the oven to 160°C (315°F).

Combine the flour, suet, baking powder and salt in a large bowl and mix together very well.

Add the lemon juice to the water and start adding it while stirring the mixture constantly. Soon it will look like very coarse breadcrumbs. Keep adding water until you can bring the mixture together with your hands into a stiff dough.

If it is too dry, you might need another splash of water, but I have tested it several times in different weather conditions and haven't needed more water. The dough should not be sticky, make sure of that.

Roll the dough out gently to 1 cm (⅜ inch) thickness on a generously floured work surface. Try to make it as rectangular as possible, then trim the edges.

Smear the jam over the dough, leaving some space at one end to crimp the edges together and close the roll. Starting from the other end, roll up the dough into a cylinder.

Carefully place the roll on a piece of greased baking paper with a pudding cloth, tea towel (dish towel) or foil underneath. Wrap the paper and cloth around the roll and tie both ends with kitchen string: first the baking paper, then the cloth.

Place the pudding in a loaf tin, then stand the tin on a trivet or inverted saucer in a large saucepan of boiling water. The pudding should not be covered with water. Put a lid on the saucepan and steam for 1 hour.

The suet pastry shouldn't be too sweet as it will act like bread with jam. To serve, cut crossways in thick slices to expose the spiral of jam. A generous pouring of good homemade custard sauce is a must for an accompaniment.

Plum Duff

In the aftermath of a deadly outbreak of cholera in the poorest boroughs of London in the summer of 1849, Henry Mayhew, an English social researcher and journalist, started to write a full and detailed description of the industrial poor throughout England for the *Morning Chronicle*. Two years later the series of articles were compiled into a four-volume work titled *London Labour and the London Poor*.

It is one of the most beautiful works on social history ever written and transports you to the tough and often dangerous streets of Victorian London. The book is a survey of the lives of labourers in the city, from street sellers of boiled puddings to prostitutes and from watercress-sellers to pie-men. The author transcribes their words to paint a vivid picture of social behaviour: what they did for a living, what they earned, what they ate and where they slept. It is a most valuable work, giving us a number of ingredients used in street fare that are almost recipes.

One of those is for plum duff, a kind of batter pudding with raisins. 'Duff' is a former dialect pronunciation of 'dough'. Baskets of plum duff were covered with a number of cloths to keep the puddings warm. The street sellers invited custom with their cry, 'Hot plum duff, hot plum'. Mayhew notes that it was mostly children who bought their wares.

Of the Street-sellers of Plum 'Duff' or Dough
Plum dough is one of the street-eatables – though perhaps it is rather a violence to class it with the street-pastry – which is usually made by the vendors. It is simply a boiled plum, or currant, pudding, of the plainest description. It is sometimes made in the rounded form of the plum-pudding; but more frequently in the 'roly-poly' style. Hot puddings used to be of much more extensive sale in the streets. One informant told me that twenty or thirty years ago, batter, or Yorkshire pudding 'with plums in it', was a popular street business. The 'plums' as in the orthodox plum-pudding, are raisins ...
Henry Mayhew, *London Labour and the London Poor*, Vol 1, 1861

Serves 6–8

340 g (12 oz) plain
   (all-purpose) flour

2 teaspoons ground allspice

50 g (1¾ oz) lard or butter

55 g (2 oz) shredded suet

½ teaspoon treacle

200 ml (7 fl oz) water

70 g (2½ oz) raisins

Custard sauce (see page 338),
   to serve

Put the flour and allspice into a large bowl. Melt the lard or butter and the suet. Add the treacle and pour the mixture into the bowl with the flour. Add the water a little at a time, mixing well to create a stiff dough. Finally add the raisins and combine well.

Layer 2 pieces of plastic wrap on a clean tea towel (dish towel) or pudding cloth. Shape the dough into a large sausage shape and place it on the plastic wrap. Fold to close and tie both ends of the sausage with kitchen string, first of the plastic wrap, then the cloth.

Place the pudding in a large saucepan of boiling water, tying both ends of the pudding to the handle so the pudding doesn't touch the bottom of the pan. Bring to the boil, then turn down the heat and simmer for 2 hours.

Serve with custard sauce.

boiled & steamed

Castle Puddings

Steamed lemon or orange sponge puddings

Often known as 'Sutherland puddings', these are steamed sponge puddings made in smaller individual moulds and they can be flavoured with lemon, orange, orange flower water, mace or other flavourings. They should be served with either a wine sauce or a jam sauce, according to Mrs Acton and Mrs Byron, who both give recipes for these little puddings. Mrs Byron (*May Byron's Pudding Book*, 1917) specifies that the pudding is from Lancashire but the earlier recipe (below) doesn't mention a region for this pudding at all.

Sutherland or castle puddings.
Take an equal weight of eggs in the shell, of good butter, of fine dry flour, and of sifted sugar. First, whisk the eggs for ten minutes or until they appear extremely light, then throw in the sugar by degrees, and continue the whisking for four or five minutes; next, strew in the flour, also gradually, and when it appears smoothly blended with the other ingredients, pour the butter to them in small portions, each of which should be beaten in until there is no appearance of it left. It should previously be just liquefied with the least possible degree of heat: this may be effected by putting it into a well-warmed saucepan, and shaking it round until it is dissolved. A grain or two of salt should be thrown in with the flour; and the rind of half a fine lemon rasped on sugar or grated, or some pounded mace, or any other flavour can be added at choice. Pour the mixture directly it is ready into well-buttered cups, and bake the puddings from twenty to twenty-five minutes. When cold they resemble good pound cakes, and may be served as such. Wine sauce should be sent to table with them. Eggs, 4; their weight in flour, sugar, and butter; little salt; flavouring of pounded mace or lemon-rind. Obs.- Three eggs are sufficient for a small dish of these puddings. They may be varied with an ounce or two of candied citron; or with a spoonful of brandy, or a little orange-flower water. The mode we have given of making them will be found perfectly successful if our directions be followed with exactness. In a slow oven they will not be too much baked in half an hour.
Eliza Acton, *Modern Cookery for Private Families*, 1845

The recipe resembles that of a pound cake, using equal weights of flour, butter, sugar and eggs. The best-known version of this pudding today is usually referred to as a 'lemon sponge pudding' and uses baking powder for a lighter result.

The secret to a good castle pudding is in the mixing; you have to take your time to whisk the butter with the sugar and then the eggs with the sugar and butter and so on, otherwise you will get a different result. How lucky we are to have electric mixers!

butter, for greasing

200 g (7 oz) butter, softened

200 g (7 oz) raw sugar

4 eggs

200 g (7 oz/1⅓ cups)
   self-raising flour

Lemon flavouring

zest of 1 small lemon

a jar of lemon curd

Orange flavouring

zest of ½ small orange

thinly sliced orange rounds

sugar, for sprinkling

Castle puddings

Preheat the oven to 180°C (350°F). Prepare individual mini basins by greasing them generously with butter, then cut a disc of baking paper to fit inside the base of each basin and press it into the mould.

Using an electric mixer fitted with the whisk attachment, whisk the butter with the sugar until pale and creamy. This is an important step so whisk thoroughly. Grate in the lemon or orange zest for the flavouring of your choice. Start adding the eggs one at a time, whisking until each egg is fully incorporated. Finally, fold in the flour and combine well.

Put one teaspoon of lemon curd or a thin slice of orange sprinkled with sugar in each mini pudding basin, before adding the batter. Divide the batter between the basins until they are about two-thirds full.

Place the puddings in a deep baking dish. Carefully pour hot water into the dish to come halfway up the sides of the basins. Cover the dish with foil and bake in the centre of the oven for 50 minutes, checking after 40 minutes by inserting a toothpick into the pudding to see if it comes out clean.

Allow the puddings to cool in the basins. (If not needed directly, freeze them in the basins and reheat in the microwave after defrosting.)

When you are ready to serve, loosen the pudding from the mould with the tip of a knife and turn the pudding out like a cake. Serve with an accompaniment of custard or ice cream; my favourite is clotted cream (see page 336).

Cabinet Pudding

This pudding is also sometimes called 'Newcastle pudding', 'diplomat pudding' or 'Chancellor's pudding', though the connection with politics isn't clear. Recipes also vary. Most recipes are tipsy puddings – much like a trifle – with pieces of sponge cake or sometimes even plain buttered bread or biscuits soaked in booze layered with dried fruits and custard. These are placed in a fancy mould and the pudding is then steamed.

Alexis Soyer gives a recipe for an 'Iced Cabinet Pudding', basically placing the pudding into ice for two hours until the custard has frozen. I tried and failed; however, preparing the same pudding by steaming rather than placing over ice makes for an excellent cabinet pudding.

Iced Cabinet Pudding

Have ready prepared, and rather stale, a sponge-cake as directed (No. 859), which cut into slices half an inch thick, and rather smaller than the mould you intend making the pudding in, soak them well with noyeau brandy; then lay some preserved dry cherries at the bottom of the mould, with a few whole ratafias, lay one of the slices over, then more cherries and ratafias, proceeding thus until the mould is three parts full; have ready a quart of the custard (No. 804), omitting half the quantity of isinglass, pour it lukewarm into your mould, which close hermetically, and bury in ice and salt, where let it remain at least two hours.

Alexis Soyer, *The Modern Housewife or, Ménagère*, 1849

Makes 1 pudding in a 1 litre (35 fl oz/4 cup) fancy mould

190 g (6¾ oz) stale sponge cake

10–15 ratafia biscuits (see page 346) or amaretti biscuits

cognac or dark rum, to taste

half quantity of custard sauce (see page 338)

10–15 glacé cherries

Preheat the oven to 180°C (350°F).

Slice the sponge cake in 1 cm (⅜ inch) thick pieces and arrange in a deep dish with the biscuits. Drizzle with a generous amount of cognac or rum and let it soak.

Lightly grease the mould (if you don't want to take any risks getting the pudding out later, line it with plastic wrap – the sort that doesn't melt in the oven – sticking it to the butter).

Make the custard and let it cool slightly while you fill the mould. Place a few cherries in the base of the mould, then add a layer of sponge cake and one of biscuits, then add a few more cherries and another layer of sponge and biscuits. Repeat until the mould is three-quarters full.

Pour in the lukewarm custard then place the mould on top of a trivet or inverted saucer in a deep ovenproof pot that can completely cover the mould. Fill the pot with boiling water halfway up the sides of the mould, place a saucer on top of the mould and put the lid on the pot.

Carefully put the pot in your oven. Leave to steam for 1 hour, then allow the pudding to cool for 5 minutes in the mould before attempting to turn it out on a plate.

Serve with Sack sauce (see page 339) or just on its own, as it shouldn't be dry.

Spotted Dick

Mentioning this pudding to people unfamiliar with British food always generates great amusement. Its etymology is the culprit, though an entirely innocent explanation can be provided. 'Dick' is simply an old dialect pronunciation of 'dough', just like 'duff' in plum duff.

The first documented recipe for spotted dick appeared in *A Shilling Cookery for The People* in 1854:

> 339. Spotted Dick.- Put three-quarters of a pound of flour into a basin, half a pound of beef suet, half ditto of currants, two ounces of sugar, a little cinnamon, mix with two eggs and two gills of milk; boil in either mould or cloth for one hour and a half; serve with melted butter, and a little sugar over.
>
> Alexis Soyer, *A Shilling Cookery for the People*, 1854

A few years earlier, in 1849, the same author had published another recipe for spotted dick in his book *The Modern Housewife or, Ménagère*. Then he called it a 'Plum Bolster, or 'Spotted Dick' – this recipe, however, was for a rolled suet pudding like a roly-poly. His recipe for roly-poly is printed just above the spotted dick in the book.

Nowadays the pudding is sold in tins, a reminder of how the English searched for a way to have their puddings without having to spend the time making them! Spotted dick was also a popular school-dinner pudding; many people who were young in the sixties and seventies will remember them well, all covered in custard. Well prepared, it is a treat and a pudding so iconic, especially because of its most peculiar name, that it could not be omitted from this book.

Makes 1 pudding in a 17 cm (6½ inch/No. 30) basin (mould)

300 g (10½ oz/2 cups) plain (all-purpose) flour

130 g (4½ oz) shredded suet

50 g (1¾ oz) raw sugar

a pinch of ground cinnamon

1 teaspoon baking powder

1 egg

200 ml (7 fl oz) milk

150 g (5½ oz) currants, soaked in water, brandy or rum

Preheat the oven to 160°C (315°F). Prepare the pudding basin for steaming (see pages 68–69).

Combine the flour, suet, sugar, cinnamon and baking powder together in a large bowl and mix well.

Add the egg and a little of the milk while constantly stirring the mixture. Soon it will be looking like very coarse breadcrumbs. Keep adding milk until you can bring the mixture together with your hands into a stiff dough. If it is too dry, you might need another splash of milk, although the dough should not be wet or sticky.

Finally work in the currants.

Roll the dough into a ball and press into the prepared pudding basin. Steam the pudding in the oven, as described on page 69, for 4 hours. Serve with custard sauce (see page 338).

Treacle Sponge Pudding

There is a tale that tells of the secret treacle mines in England, and everyone knows about them, but no-one knows exactly where they are. There are old folk who remember talking to a treacle miner back in the day, or so they tell their grandchildren …

Treacle, called molasses in America, began to be mass-produced in 1950 by the British manufacturer, Lyle's. Treacle pudding, like treacle tart, began to be made with golden syrup (light treacle) after it was invented in the 1880s by Lyle's, which still exclusively produces Golden Syrup and Black Treacle today. Both thick sweet syrups are a byproduct of the sugar cane refining process, but have a completely different taste.

Many Brits will think of their schooldays when a steamed treacle pudding is presented to them. It was one of those classic school-dinner puds, like spotted dick.

The earliest recipe for treacle pudding that I could find dates from 1852, but it doesn't look like the pudding we know today.

A Treacle Pudding.
Ingredients, two pounds of flour, twelve ounces of treacle, six ounces of suet or dripping fat, a quarter of an ounce of baking-powder, a pinch of allspice, a little salt, one pint of milk, or water. Mix the whole of the above-named ingredients in a pan, into a firm compact paste; tie it up in a well-greased and floured pudding-cloth; boil the pudding for at least two hours and a-half, and when done, cut it in slices, and pour a little sweetened melted butter over it.
Charles Elme Francatelli, *A Plain Cookery Book for the Working Classes*, 1852

It is hard to tell how the treacle in Francatelli's recipe would have tasted. Lyle's Black Treacle is quite bitter, while some other brands of molasses are softer in flavour. The first treacle puds were made with a suet dough like that of the spotted dick: it was only at the start of the twentieth century that a sponge cake batter became more popular.

Mrs C F Leyel's book, *Puddings* (1927), gives a recipe for boiled treacle pudding. It is made by making layers of suet dough in a pudding basin, covering each layer with syrup and a squeeze of lemon, then boiling it by wrapping the basin in a cloth. In the same book she also gives a recipe for a treacle sponge, in which she instructs the cook to create a sponge cake mixture using golden syrup and adds ground ginger as a flavouring. Other cookery books of the early twentieth century also use golden syrup and a sponge batter becomes standard.

Beware, this pudding will give you a sugar rush: don't say I didn't warn you!

*Makes 1 large pudding in
a 16 cm (6 inch/No. 36)
basin (mould)*

150 g (5½ oz/1 cup) plain
(all-purpose) flour

1 teaspoon baking soda

60 g (2¼ oz) shredded suet

50 g (1¾ oz) dark brown
sugar

40 g (1½ oz) golden syrup
(light treacle)

a super-tiny pinch of salt

¼ teaspoon ground allspice

1 egg

100 ml (3½ fl oz) buttermilk

3 tablespoons golden syrup,
extra, for the basin

Treacle sponge pudding

Preheat the oven to 180°C (350°F). Prepare the pudding basin
for steaming, as explained on pages 68–69.

Combine the flour, baking soda, suet and sugar together in
a large bowl, then add the golden syrup, salt and allspice
followed by the egg and the buttermilk. Mix well to combine.

Pour the extra 3 tablespoons of golden syrup into the prepared
basin. Pour the batter into the basin and prepare for steaming,
as explained on page 69. Cook for 1½ hours, checking after
1 hour and 15 minutes by inserting a toothpick into the
pudding to see if it comes out clean.

When ready to serve, open the foil and loosen the side of the
pudding with the tip of a knife, then turn the pudding out like
a cake. Be careful, as hot water could have seeped into the foil
and could run out, so wear oven mittens.

If it is not needed directly, freeze it in the basin and reheat it in
the microwave after defrosting.

Serve with custard sauce (see page 338), icy cream (see page 320)
or clotted cream (page 336).

Plain Suet Dumplings

As puddings were boiled along with the meat for centuries out of necessity, this suet dumpling was put in with the meat without being contained by a cloth or gut, to stew along with it and be eaten with it just as its big brother pudding was eaten. However, this way of eating pudding with your meal has survived until the present day. The Hungarians and the Czechs have dumplings in their stews; the Italians have their potato gnocchi; and the Swedes, Germans and most other countries of the world have their favourite dumpling.

A Simple Suet Dumpling – One pound of flour, half a pound of chopped suet, a teaspoonful of salt, quarter ditto of pepper; moisten with water until a stiff paste: use where required. They may be rolled in small balls, and may be used in savoury pies, hash, or stews.

Alexis Soyer, *A Shilling Cookery for the People*, 1854

The recipe on the following page is easy, and based on the nineteenth century recipe of Alexis Soyer, as published in his book *A Shilling Cookery for the People* (1854), a book written to help the poor cook on a very tight budget. He also wrote *Soyer's Charitable Cookery* and gave the proceeds of the book to various charities. But this was only a small part of what Soyer – who was chef at the prestigious Reform Club and regarded by many as Britain's first celebrity chef – did for the poor. He established one of the first soup kitchens and also worked with Florence Nightingale, improving the diet of wounded soldiers.

The *Morning Chronicle* said about Soyer, 'he saved as many lives through his kitchens as Florence Nightingale did through her wards.'

I am using self-raising flour instead of regular flour in my dumplings. This makes them less stodgy and more palatable to our tastes today. To make the original recipe, just use plain (all-purpose) flour and double the suet.

Makes 8–10 dumplings

230 g (8¼ oz) self-raising flour

50 g (1¾ oz) shredded suet

1 teaspoon salt

a pinch of black pepper

1 teaspoon thyme leaves or finely chopped parsley, optional

170 ml (5½ fl oz/⅔ cup) milk

meat stew, such as goulash or ragout, or oxtail soup (below)

Plain suet dumplings

Combine the flour, suet and the salt and pepper – and the herbs if you are using them – in a bowl. Make a well in the centre and start adding the milk in small portions, to make sure you don't use too much and end up with sticky dough. Use a blunt knife to stir as you do this so your hands don't get covered in gooey dough.

When the dough comes together you can use your hands to knead it into a paste. Roll into dumplings the size of ping-pong balls and set them aside on a tray.

When the meat stew is at its last 15 minutes of stewing, add the dumplings and allow them to stew together with the meat, or add to a vegetarian stew using vegetable suet.

Serve together.

1 carrot

1 turnip

3 onions

1 celery stalk

butter, for frying

800 g (1 lb 12 oz) oxtail

2 bay leaves

a few sprigs of thyme

a few sprigs of parsley

1 teaspoon peppercorns (about 15)

1 teaspoon salt

Oxtail soup

Preheat the oven to 140°C (275°F).

Chop the vegetables into small dice, about 5 mm–1 cm (¼–⅜ inch).

Put a generous knob of butter into a cast-iron casserole and melt it, then add the vegetables and fry until golden. Remove the vegetables from the casserole.

Add another knob of butter and gently brown the oxtail on both sides. When the juices are starting to stick to the pan, return the vegetables to the casserole and add about 600 ml (21 fl oz) of water to deglaze the pan and submerge the oxtail. Make sure the meat is completely covered in water.

Now add the herbs, peppercorns and salt and bring to the boil, uncovered. When the water boils, cover the casserole with the lid and cook in the oven for 3–4 hours, or until the meat falls from the bone and the fat is nearly all melted away.

Remove the oxtail from the casserole, pull the meat off the bone and return the meat to the soup. Add the dumplings and simmer for 15 minutes on the stove top.

War & Peace Pudding

During wartime, ingredients for plum pudding were hard to come by so the Ministry of Food produced a recipe for a 'War and Peace Pudding' made of carrots, potatoes and suet. The recipe also appeared as a 'Wartime Christmas Pudding'. Carrots and potato were both promoted by the Ministry of Food because they grew easily and were plentiful, and therefore they were important to keep people healthy. Potato was often used as an alternative to other ingredients in dishes and carrots were used because of their sweet flavour. At some point 'carrots on sticks' were sold to children instead of ice cream – which was banned – and 'toffee carrots' replaced toffee apples.

This pudding was made in Canada during the last war, and since then many people have never bothered with a rich Christmas pudding.
Mix together 1 cupful of flour; 1 cupful of breadcrumbs, half a cupful of suet, half a cupful of mixed dried fruit, and, if you like, a teaspoonful of mixed sweet spice. Then add a cupful of raw potato, a cupful of grated raw carrot and finally a level teaspoonful of bicarbonate of soda dissolved in two tablespoonful of hot water. Mix all together, turn into a well-greased pudding bowl. The bowl should not be more then two-thirds full. Boil or steam for at least 2 hours.
Ministry of Food, War cookery leaflet no. 4, *Carrots*, WW2

Getting children to eat carrots was such a big deal that carrot cartoon figures were created: first Doctor Carrot, then Carrot George and his friends, created by Walt Disney.

Makes 1 pudding in a 14 cm (5½ inch/No. 42) diameter basin (mould)

75 g (2¾ oz) carrots, grated

100 g (3½ oz) potatoes, grated

85 g (3 oz) plain (all-purpose) flour

30 g (1 oz/½ cup) fresh breadcrumbs

30 g (1 oz) shredded suet

1 teaspoon ground allspice or mixed spice

1 teaspoon bicarbonate of soda (baking soda)

2 tablespoons warm water

1 tablespoon mixed dried fruit, soaked in water, rum or brandy

Preheat the oven to 160°C (315°F). Prepare the pudding basins for steaming as instructed on pages 68–69.

In a large bowl, combine the carrot, potato, flour, breadcrumbs, suet and allspice. Dissolve the bicarbonate of soda in the water and add to the mixture. On a lightly floured work surface, knead into a ball. Don't be alarmed if the mixture seems dry, it will come together after kneading it for a few minutes.

Work through the mixed dried fruit and roll the dough into a ball. Put the ball into the prepared pudding basin and push it down. Prepare the pudding for steaming as instructed on page 69. Steam for 2 hours.

Serve with carrot jam (see recipe opposite).

Carrot Jam

Carrot jam was a wartime recipe but it had also appeared in Mrs Beeton's *Book of Household Management* in 1861 as 'Carrot jam to imitate apricot preserve'. It is delicious served with war and peace pudding, but also with the cabbage pudding (see page 96) or hackin pudding (see page 92).

500 g (1 lb 2 oz) carrot purée, made from boiled carrots

500 g (1 lb 2 oz) raw sugar

juice of 1 lemon

zest of ½ lemon, grated or cut into fine strips

5 apricot kernels

2 tablespoons brandy

Put the carrot purée in a large saucepan and bring to the boil. Add the sugar, lemon juice and zest and apricot kernels. Boil until the mixture has thickened and gels quickly when spooned onto a cold plate.

Remove from the heat and take out the apricot kernels if you can spot them. Stir the brandy through the jam and decant into sterilised jars. Close the jars and turn them upside down to cool.

The jam has a hint of apricot; it was marketed as mock apricot jam.

This jam doesn't keep long and must be stored in the fridge.

Sticky Toffee Pudding

Many puddings are surrounded by legends and this is one of them. It is said that the sticky toffee pudding was invented in the 1960s by Francis Coulson of the Sharrow Bay Hotel by the majestic Ullswater in the Lake District. He called it an 'icky sticky toffee sponge'. I have pondered this legend and the original recipe – which is said to be locked away in the hotel's vault – while I was enjoying the first spring sun on the Victorian steamer on Ullswater. We passed the hotel and, of course, the voice on the boat mentioned that the sticky toffee pudding was invented there. But it wouldn't be a pudding without other counties competing over its origins. Yorkshire claims that sticky toffee pudding was invented in 1907 by the landlady of the Gait Inn in Millington; and of course the Scots claim it as their own, insisting it was first served in the Udny Arms Hotel in Newburgh, Aberdeenshire, in 1967.

Many have tried to trace the original recipe so I share with you my own. This pudding is made with prunes instead of the traditional dates. But feel free to use dates; I just don't care for them. As with all my personal recipes, I try to reduce the sugar content because I find that sugar can take over the flavour and I do not enjoy a sugar headache.

In this delightful pudding, which has won many of my friends over to the idea of British food, I use a very more-ish apple butter (appelstroop) from Belgium. The syrup is very thick, like treacle, and although sweet, it has some acidity too which works very nicely with the sweetness of the pudding.

The pudding has a sour hint on the tip of your tongue that cuts through the sticky sweetness. This is the apple butter's doing. This little sweet is very enjoyable with a traditional Belgian sour beer. I cooked it for my exams in beer school and only saw happy indulging faces staring back at me after the first bite.

Makes 8 small puddings in 7–8 cm (2¾–3¼ inch/mini) basins (moulds); alternatively, use a muffin tray, which will give a slightly different result as the holes are shallower.

225 g (8 oz) pitted prunes

85 g (3 oz) unsalted butter, softened

100 g (3½ oz) muscovado (dark brown) sugar

2 eggs

2 tablespoons apple butter, or add an extra tablespoon of sugar

a pinch of salt

175 g (6 oz) self-raising flour

thick (double) cream or clotted cream (see page 334), to serve

Toffee sauce

50 g (1¾ oz) unsalted butter

175 g (6 oz) muscovado (dark brown) sugar

200 ml (7 oz) thick (double) cream

1 tablespoon apple butter

Preheat the oven to 180°C (350°F). Prepare the individual pudding basins for steaming as explained on pages 68–69.

Put the pitted prunes in a heatproof bowl and pour boiling water over them to cover. Allow to stand for about 15 minutes, then drain and use a blender to reduce the prunes to a purée.

In a clean bowl, combine the butter with the muscovado sugar and beat until pale and creamy. Add the eggs and whisk to create a light batter. Fold in the apple butter and the prune purée and a super-tiny pinch of salt. Sift in the flour and mix well to combine.

Pour the batter into the prepared pudding basins and place in a baking dish or deep tray, adding boiling water to come halfway up the sides of the basins. Cover the dish with foil and steam in the middle of the oven for 40–50 minutes, checking after 30 minutes by inserting a toothpick into the pudding to see if it comes out clean.

Allow the puddings to cool slightly in the basins. (If not needed immediately, freeze them in the basins and reheat in the microwave after defrosting.) When you are ready to serve, loosen the pudding from the basin with the tip of a knife and turn it out like a cake.

Prepare the toffee sauce by melting the butter in a saucepan over medium heat, then add the other ingredients and simmer until the sugar is dissolved. Dip hot puddings in the sauce and pour cream over to serve.

Brown bread ice cream (see page 323) or icy cream (see page 320) are also big hits with this pud. But double cream or clotted cream will do the trick just fine and are equally more-ish.

CHAPTER 2

BAKED PUDDINGS

Baked puddings

Although John Murrell, in his early seventeenth century tome *A Newe Booke of Cookerie*, gives a recipe 'To make a Pudding in a Frying-panne', and mentions that his 'A Fierced Pudding' can either be boiled or baked, it would take a while before people would actually start baking proper puddings in the oven. Pastry ovens were constructed in a few important kitchens in the early sixteenth century but they would be used solely for more delicate pastry. Florentines and other tarts were often made into elaborate shapes, resembling a stained-glass window, and beautifully decorated with elaborately cut pastry covers, an ancestor of the lattice tart top. They could be made as part of the tart, but often were made separately to act as a beautifully crafted lid that could be taken off before serving, and sometimes reused for another tart.

I believe that as Robert May gives designs for each of these tarts or pies in his book, *The Accomplisht Cook* (1660), dinner guests would know by looking at the design of the tart which filling it enclosed. These 'Cut–Laid' covers, as they were called, appear in one of my favourite still-life paintings, painted by Clara Peeters from my hometown of Antwerp in 1611. Recipes for these covers, however, are exclusively found in English cookery texts. Historian Ivan Day has discovered that it would not be until the eighteenth century that these kind of recipes appeared outside of England; in Austria in Conrad Hagger's *Neues Saltzburgisches Kochbuch* in 1719.

How were puddings baked if ovens were only available to the elite households? Earthenware dishes or cast-iron skillets containing a pudding mixture could be placed close by the fire or in the embers to bake. Cast-iron pots could be used as ovens when placed on the embers or by the fire, much like a Dutch oven, and were often also covered in embers. When the peasants wanted to bake a more delicate pie, they had to go to the baker's oven, where it would be baked along with the pies of other people from the village. This communal baking is something that is seen all over Europe.

Tray-baked black pudding was made in England when animals were bled and guts weren't available. Blood was also made into small cakes and baked on a griddle iron. This shows that people were constantly looking for ways to prepare puddings without the need for animal intestines as a vessel, or even a pudding bag or cloth. But pastry was time consuming and called for a skilful hand, so it made sense that earthenware dishes were produced to be used instead of pastry. Some of these even mimicked the look of a pastry casing, featuring the same pinched rims. The pie dishes we know today are descendants of those early earthenware pie dishes.

Another popular vessel to make baked puddings in was the pie plate. These plates were made of silver or pewter and appeared in various sizes. A Bakewell-style pudding, for example, is traditionally baked on a plate, as were many similar puddings and pies before it. The vessel that ought to be used was not usually specified in ancient recipes. One was supposed to know that one type of pudding was made in a plate, a fruit tart or florentine was made in a shortcrust or paste-royal casing, and the large variety of ancient custard tarts were made with a hot water pastry. The chef was supposed to know, and the recipes weren't meant as clear instructions.

It is only at the very beginning of the 1700s that recipes for baked puddings start to appear along with the boiled version in cookery books. And even then most households would not have been able to bake them as the kitchen range only came into use by the general public by the end of the nineteenth century.

As soon as kitchen ranges were introduced into many homes, more baked pudding recipes appeared as people began to experiment. Dumplings, previously boiled, would now also be baked, which explains two postcards I found from around 1910, depicting a 'Devonshire Dumpling' which was clearly baked rather than boiled, with a pastry more like a puff pastry or shortcrust pastry instead of the more stodgy suet and bread dough it was made with before.

Soon the technique for steaming a pudding in the oven became popular and so most of the boiled puddings were prepared in a pudding mould, which would allow the cook to create various shaped puddings. In Victorian cookery books, pictures of shaped plum puddings appeared and decorative moulds became extremely popular. One mould could be used for a baked pudding, a jelly or an ice cream; they were expensive and therefore people would have wanted to use them as much as they could. Even teacups were used for baking small puddings.

It seems to me that a baked pudding always added an extra bit of festivity to a meal, as it wasn't as straightforward to cook as a boiled pudding. Far more things can go wrong with baking a pudding than with boiling, so it also called for a more skilled cook. That cook was also often expected to create lavishly decorated versions of baked puddings or tarts. Flour used for pastry had to be finely milled and was therefore expensive, so I believe that puddings and tarts in a pastry casing would have been the privilege of the upper class rather than the peasant home.

Puddings made with breadcrumbs tell us that either there was surplus bread that wasn't eaten or there was enough bread to use fresh breadcrumbs, meaning that these kitchens had plenty of food. In the peasant home you would probably have to scrape the crumbs from the table and floor to be able to find a scrap of bread that wasn't eaten. And I am sure the mother of the house would have beaten you to it and already collected the crumbs to keep in a jar for pudding or thickening soup.

We can also not forget that the bread of the peasantry wasn't as refined as the white manchet bread that the rich had been eating for centuries. It was gritty and dark, and you could break your teeth on it. Hardly a good base for a delightful pudding. Bread puddings would often be baked, although not all bread puddings are baked puddings; that is why those puddings that have bread as their main ingredient, such as bread-and-butter pudding (see page 240), are in a separate chapter in this book.

It is safe to say that baked puddings have graced the elite dinner table for far longer than the tables of the humble working class. But I believe that inventive cooks, however poor they were, would always have tried to bake them. Recipes for these poor man's baked puddings are virtually unknown, but that doesn't mean they weren't put by the fire, or in a communal oven somewhere at some time.

Sambocade

T he 'Sambocade' is a form of cheese-curd tart flavoured with elderflowers. The recipe first appears in the book of the Master Cooks of King Richard II, *The Forme of Cury* (1390). It is called sambocade after the Latin word for elderflower, sambucus. It may be one of the earliest cheesecakes of Britain, although we know that cheesecakes have been around since Ancient Greek times.

Constance Hieatt and Sharon Butler, authors of 'Curye on Inglish' – a scholarly essay on medieval manuscripts including *The Forme of Cury* – mention that sambocade does not appear in any fourteenth century French source. They believe the tart was brought to England by Anglo–Norman crusaders returning from the Middle East and was most probably from Italy.

> Take and make a crust in a trap & take cruddes and wryng out þe wheyze and drawe hem þurgh a straynour and put hit in þe crust. Do þerto sugar the þridde part, & somdel whyte of ayren, & shake þerin blomes of elren; & bake it vp with eurose, & messe it forth.
> *The Forme of Cury* c. 1390

This recipe tells us to make a crust in a 'trap': trap being the word for the earthenware dish that supported the pastry crust. The kind of pastry is not specified as it was assumed the chef would know. Historians have determined that the pastry for this tart should be a hot-water crust without any addition of fats such as butter, lard or suet; however, a puff pastry or shortcrust pastry could also be used. The hot-water pastry is quite hard, but I still like it.

It was the custom in medieval times to sometimes remove the sides of a pastry or pie casing, only leaving the bottom part. It was common enough that removing the sides and even the tops of pies and tarts need not be mentioned in these medieval recipes. After some time, but who knows how long, it became accepted that the pastry would be left on. Today we can't imagine removing the pastry from our pies and tarts, as it is often the best part, but in the old times when cooking vessels weren't plenty and ovens less precise, the pastry would provide not only a vessel for cooking, but also a protective layer for delicate foods, and it had the ability to act as a closed casserole dish. The notion, however, that the pastry was never eaten in those days is nonsense. It was eaten, it just depended on the dish.

Makes a 20 cm (8 inch) diameter pie in a 4–5 cm (1½–2 inch) deep plain tart dish. For a medieval-style tall pie, double the quantities below and use a high-sided tin.

1 litre (35 fl oz/4 cups) milk, yields about 220–240 g (7¾–8¾ oz) cheese curd

1 tablespoon buttermilk or fresh lemon juice

2 teaspoons vegetable rennet

1 quantity hot-water pastry (see page 343), or use shortcrust pastry (see page 342) if you prefer

3 tablespoons fresh or dried elderflowers

40 g (1½ oz) raw sugar

½ teaspoon rosewater

1 tablespoon plain (all-purpose) flour

3 egg whites

Sambocade

Make the cheese curd by pouring the milk into a clean saucepan and heat to 37°C (98°F), otherwise known as body temperature or blood heat.

Turn down the heat and stir in the buttermilk or lemon juice, then the rennet in one large movement to spread it through the milk. Remove from the heat and allow to stand in the pan for 15–30 minutes until it has set, then transfer to a bowl lined with muslin (cheesecloth), tie the cloth at the top, and hang it up to drain for 5 hours. You can do this the day before, and keep the curds in the fridge.

Preheat the oven to 180°C (350°F). Lightly grease the pie dish and sprinkle with flour. Make the pastry and place it in the pie dish, crimping the edges for an authentic look. Pick the elderflowers from their delicate stems.

Pass the cheese curds through a large sieve and combine with the sugar, rosewater and elderflowers. Sift in the flour and combine. Beat the egg whites to stiff peaks, then fold into the cheese mixture. Fold gently with a spatula or wooden spoon until combined well, then pour into the prepared pie case.

Bake in the lower part of the oven for 1 hour or until nicely risen and golden.

If you cannot get the elderflowers, you can also make this tart with orange flower water: use 1½ teaspoons for a half recipe and double for a large tart.

Hot-water pastry is traditional but might not be to modern taste: if you are unsure, you can use shortcrust pastry

Instead of making your own cheese curds, substitute 240 g (8¾ oz) of unsalted fresh ricotta cheese, drained.

Daryols

Daryols are small custard tarts made in 5 cm (2 inch) deep tins with the same name (darioles). Originally there were no tins, and the tart crust was hand-raised to look narrow and tall like the moulds that were later made for them. Other custard tarts were 'doucets'; they were wider and less high, like individual custard tarts are today. The reason these tarts were so small, was because the filling was expensive and the smaller the pastry case, the better the filling would bake.

The name 'daryol' or 'dariole' is probably Anglo–Norman French and appears also in old French from the period around 1350 to 1400. In old French 'dariole' could come from 'doriole' – meaning 'dorer' – which means to gild. This could be referring to the fact that the pastry cases, which were baked without the help of dariole tins in the early days, were baked golden in the oven.

The tart filling could be made with vegetables, fish, cheese curd, custard or an almond filling. Cream and eggs were used to set the dish but often recipes also call for broth. Spices could be saffron, ginger, mace, cloves, cinnamon and pepper. Dried fruit, such as dates and prunes, is mentioned and also fresh strawberries when they were in season. To sweeten, honey was used most commonly, but sugar was used in the kitchens of the most noble households. Whether the dish contained fish or fruit, it was always spiced as a sweet dish.

Daryols - Take Creme of Cowe mylke. oþer of Almandes. do þerto ayren with sugur, safroun, and salt, medle it yfere. do it in a coffyn. of II. ynche depe. bake it wel and serue it forth
The Forme of Cury, c. 1390

Makes enough for five 3.5 cm (1⅜ inch) dariole moulds, or 6 cm (2½ inch) tart tins

1 quantity hot-water pastry (see page 343) or use shortcrust pastry (see page 342) in a shallow tart tin

500 ml (17 fl oz/2 cups) thick (double) cream

20 g (¾ oz) blanched almonds, pounded to a pulp

30 g (1 oz) raw sugar

a tiny pinch of salt

a few saffron threads

8 egg yolks

Preheat the oven to 160°C (315°F).

Make the hot-water pastry according to the instructions. Roll out the pastry as thin as you can manage without breaking it, then divide it into smaller pieces for the individual moulds. Let the pastry sink into the tins and mould it with your fingers, pressing it so you don't have an uneven thickness. Trim the extra pastry and use your fingers to crimp the edges.

Blind bake for 5 minutes as instructed (or for 25 minutes if using shortcrust pastry).

Put the cream and almond pulp into a saucepan with the sugar, salt and saffron. Bring to a simmer then remove from the heat.

Beat the egg yolks in a bowl, strain the cream mixture and start adding the cream to the eggs in small batches. Whisk constantly until you get a smooth custard. For fruit daryols, drop currants, chopped dates or chopped fresh strawberries into the pastry case before adding the custard mixture. Pour the mixture into the pie crusts. Bake for 25–30 minutes until the filling is just set and the pastry is golden.

Prune Tart

Prune tarts have always been my favourite. They are traditionally eaten in my hometown of Antwerp on Ash Wednesday, though nobody knows exactly why. I haven't been able to find out why this is a tradition unique to Antwerp. On Ash Wednesday the shopfronts of the bakeries showcase prune tarts – some open, some with a lattice top. I prefer as little pastry as possible, as the bakeries often use a lot of sugar in their pastry.

This recipe by Gervase Markham instructs the cook to stew the prunes in the oven while they bake bread. I do that too, but rather with a pot of stew bubbling away slowly so that the prunes give off their maximum flavour, and they do have a beautiful flavour; I can only describe it as dark and luxurious. Markham tells us to make templates of all kinds of shapes for the tart pastry. He then instructs us to cut out the shapes in the prepared pastry and pinch the sides up to make a pastry case, which you can bake in advance. After baking you can use the case when you need it and fill them with this thick, rich, gloriously dark prune jam.

Take of the fairest Damask Prunes you can get, and put them in a clean Pipkin, with fair water, Sugar unbruised Cinnamon, and a branch or two of Rosemary, and if you have bread to bake, stew them in the Oven with your bread: if otherwise, stew them on the fire. When they are stewed, then bruise them all to mash in their syrup, and strain them into a clean dish; then boil it over again with Sugar, Cinnamon and Rose-water, till it be as thick as Marmalade: then set it to cool, then make a reasonable tough paste with fine flower, Water, and a little butter, and roll it out very thin: then having patterns of paper cut into divers proportions, as Beasts, Birds, Arms, Knots, Flowers, and such like. Lay the patterns on the paste, and so cut them accordingly: then with your fingers pinch up the edges of the paste, and set the work in good proportion: then prick it well all over for rising, and set it on a clean sheet of large Paper, and so set it into the Oven, and bake it hard: then draw it, and set it by to cool: and thus you may do by a whole Oven full at one time, as your occasion of expense is: then against the time of Service come, take of the Confections of Prunes before rehearsed, and with your Knife or a spoon fill the Coffin according to the thickness of the Verge, then strew it over with Caraway Comfits, and prick long Comfits upright in it, and so taking the Paper from the bottom, serve it on a Plate or in a Dish or Charger according to the bigness of the Tart, and at the second course; and this Tart carrieth the colour black.

Gervase Markham, *The English Huswife*, 1615

450 g (1 lb) prunes

1 teaspoon lemon juice

1 cinnamon stick

1 rosemary sprig

1 tablespoon dark
brown sugar

1 quantity shortcrust
pastry (see page 342),
doubling the recipe if
you want to make a
lattice lid

1 egg yolk, for egg
washing

Prune tart

If the prunes have stones, remove them and try to remove some of
the kernels using a nutcracker. The stones are hard to crack so never
mind if you can't get them out. Soak the prunes in water overnight
with the lemon juice, cinnamon and rosemary.

Strain the prunes and reserve 250 ml (9 fl oz/1 cup) of the soaking
water. In a medium saucepan, bring the prunes and reserved water
to a simmer over low heat with the brown sugar. Simmer for about
30–45 minutes or until the liquid has reduced and is as thick as jam.

Allow the prunes to cool, then purée them in a blender or food
processor. If the purée is too runny at this point, you can put it
back in the saucepan over low heat to reduce it a bit further. If you
do this, let it cool again before further use. It will become more
solid when it has cooled. The consistency should be very thick, not
runny; when stirring through the prunes, the base of the saucepan
should be visible.

Preheat the oven to 160°C (315°F).

While the prune purée cools completely, make the shortcrust pastry
case as instructed. If you plan to make a lid, cut the dough in half
and return the second half to the fridge until ready to make the lid.

Pat the pastry down on a lightly floured work surface using a
rolling pin and then start rolling. If the pastry cracks, knead it a bit
to make it more elastic, then shape it into a ball and roll out to
about 2 mm (1⁄16 inch) thickness.

Gently turn the pastry over the tart tin or pie plate and allow it
to sink in. Trim off the excess pastry.

If you are not using a pastry lid or lattice top, you may blind bake
the pastry for 25 minutes, and then fill it with the prunes.

When ready to fill, spread the prune purée into the pastry casing
and then egg wash the rim to attach the lid, if you are making one.

Roll out the remaining pastry and cut a round the same size as the
pie plate or tart tin. With the pastry laid on baking paper, you can
cut out fancy shapes or make ribbons for a lattice top if you prefer.

Carefully, yet swiftly, lift the pastry lid off the baking paper, laying
it over the tart. Trim off any excess pastry when needed, then crimp
the edges either with your fingers, or with a pastry jigger or stamp.

Bake the tart in the middle of the oven for 40–50 minutes or
until nicely golden brown. If you have not added a lid, bake it for
20–25 minutes only. Let the tart cool completely before serving.

Quince Tart

Quince was a favoured fruit from as early as we can know from contemporary cookery books. Recipes for quince tart and preserving quince are plenty. In fact, it appears there are more recipes using quince than any other fruit.

'Chardequince' and 'Chardewarden' were sweet fruit pastes made from quince or warden pears, thickened with eggs, that appear in medieval English cookery manuscripts. Little sweetmeats were imported from Portugal, Genoa, Spain and France and were known as 'marmalades', from the Portuguese 'marmelo' meaning quince. Later, quince were cooked down to a paste which was then moulded by a seal-like wooden stamp. 'Paste of Genua' was one of the recipes, similar to the modern Spanish 'membrillo' which came to be known as quince cheese. Eventually, 'marmalade' became the name for the orange preserve we know today rather than quince preserve, but early recipes are very much more like a fruit cheese or 'cutting marmalade' (quince cheese) which would be stored in boxes.

To keep the quince's nice red colour they were cooked with the lid on the pot for a long time, but sometimes the juice of red barberries, grapes or the colouring agent cochineal – made from crushed beetles – was added to enhance the colour.

In the recipe below the author instructs to use close or cut covers: these cut covers were early lattice tops, with shapes cut out of the pastry lid to create a design for which templates were often provided in old books.

> Boil your Quinces in Water, sweetened with Sugar, till they be soft, then skin them and take out the Cores; after that boil the Water with a little more Sugar, Cloves, Cinnamon and Lemon peel till it becomes of the thickness of a Syrup; when cold lay your Quinces in Halves or Quarters, scattering Sugar between each Layer; put a pint of the Syrup, or more according to the Biggness of your Pye or Tart, make the Coffin round with close or cut Covers, and bake it pretty well. And thus you may do with Pippins and Pearmains, or with Winter-Fruit, and also with green Codlings.
> *The Whole Duty of a Woman*, 1707

1 quantity shortcrust pastry
(see page 342); doubling the
recipe if you want to make
a lid

2 large quinces, 400 g (14 oz)
each

1 cinnamon stick

2 cloves

peel of 1 lemon

350 g (12 oz) raw sugar

70 g (2½ oz) raw sugar, extra

1 egg, beaten, for egg washing

Quince tart

Prepare the shortcrust pastry as instructed. If you are using a
pastry lid, don't blind bake the pastry base. Line the pie dish
with the pastry, leaving enough pastry on the rim to fasten the
lid to.

Preheat the oven to 160°C (315°F).

In a large saucepan cover the quinces with water and boil until
tender. Remove the quinces from the saucepan, reserving the
water. Core, peel and cut them into thin slices. Reserve the
cores and the skin.

Measure out 500 ml (17 fl oz/2 cups) of the reserved cooking
water and toss the reserved quince cores and skin back into the
cooking water with the spices and lemon peel. Add the sugar
and simmer on low heat until reduced to a syrup.

Neatly arrange the quince slices in the pastry case, strewing
some of the extra sugar in between each layer, then strain and
pour the syrup over until the fruit is covered but not drowned.
Any leftover syrup will keep for a week or two in the fridge
when transferred to an airtight container.

If using a pastry lid, cut a circle of pastry the same size as the
pie dish and carefully place it over the filling. Crimp the edges,
or create a nice pattern using a pastry jigger if you have one.
Egg wash the pastry lid.

Bake in the middle of the oven for 50 minutes.

*This tart is very good made with quince purée: it might even be
more appealing to modern palates. Boil 3 quinces whole with
the same flavourings as the recipe above, then peel and cut them
into chunks. Weigh the quince and add the same weight in sugar.
Proceed as for making jam, being careful, as quince jam tends
to spit. When ready, pour the purée into the pastry and bake for
50 minutes.*

Tort de Moy

To the ear, 'tort de moy' sounds more French than English; indeed, the word 'moy' is derived from the French word 'moelle', for bone marrow. Early mentions of the tart give it the name 'Turt de moil'. It might have been popular in France at one time but it was in England that it continued to be favoured. The tart uses bone marrow as one of its prime ingredients and was served at the coronation of King James II in 1685. We know this because of Francis Sandford's *History of the Coronation* (1687), a most interesting record of the festivities. 'Turt de moil' appears at number 98 on Sandford's list of dishes and a plan of the king and queen's banqueting table even shows us alongside which other dishes it was served: five partridge pies, cold marinated smelts and three soused pigs.

The early tort de moy was made with the white meat of a capon, while later versions are made solely with marrow, candied peel, cream, eggs, spices and grated or crumbled sponge biscuits, omitting any meat. I have here a recipe from a manuscript referred to as *The Cookbook of Unknown Ladies* (c. 1690), which is held at Westminster City Archives. The oldest recipes in this manuscript are believed to date back even earlier. This recipe uses the white meat of a chicken, while later recipes use almonds beaten to a purée.

Mrs Gibbs' Tort de Moy
Pound a quarter of a pound of almonds with sack, and beat the white part of a young pullet that is very tender & half boiled. Skin it and pound it very small. 4 naple biscuits grated, some pounded cinnamon, half a pint of sack, 6 spoonfuls of rose water, some pounded mace, half a nutmeg, some sugar to your taste, sliced citron & candied lemon peel. Then beat 4 eggs, two whites and mix it with half a pint of cream. When you have beaten your eggs and cream well together, put your other ingredients to it and mix them well together and put them in a skillet over the fire and keep continually stirring [it] one way till it is as thick as a tansy. Your fire must be slow. Then have a dish with puff pastry at the bottom and sides, and when it is pretty cool, put half of [the mixture] in your dish and then a layer of whole marrow and the juice of a lemon over it. Then put the other half in, then cross bar it with pastry [on the] top and bake it in a very slow oven. 3 quarters of an hour bakes it. You can leave out the marrow if you like.
The Cookbook of Unknown Ladies, c. 1690

Makes a 25 cm (10 inch) tart

85 g (3 oz) beef marrow

500 ml (17 fl oz/2 cups) thick
(double) cream

25 g (1 oz) raw sugar

1 cinnamon stick

1 mace blade

a pinch of ground nutmeg

6 egg yolks

1 quantity shortcrust pastry
(see page 342)

25 g (1 oz) candied orange
peel

25 g (1 oz) candied lemon
peel

85 g (3 oz) sponge cake
(see page 349)

1 tablespoon rosewater
(or, if you dislike the flavour,
orange flower water)

Tort de moy

For the bone marrow: ask your butcher to cut pieces of bone
in short chunks so you can easily get out the marrow using the
back of a spoon or a marrow spoon if you have one. The bones
should be at room temperature to extract the marrow with
ease. Have a bowl of cold water ready when you do this and
toss the bits of marrow in it. Leave the marrow in the water for
2 hours. Any impurities such as bone splinters will sink to the
bottom and the blood washes away.

Preheat the oven to 160°C (315°F).

Make the custard by bringing the cream to a gentle simmer
in a medium saucepan with the sugar, cinnamon, mace and
nutmeg. Beat the egg yolks in a bowl, pour in a small amount
of the warm cream and whisk thoroughly. This prepares the
yolks for the hot liquid and will prevent it from curdling. Now
gradually add the rest of the cream, whisking until it is all
incorporated. Allow to cool, then strain out the spices.

Meanwhile prepare the shortcrust pastry as instructed and
blind bake it in the tart tin. Let it cool.

Chop up the candied peel and arrange it over the base of
the pastry case, cover this with 1 cm (⅜ inch) diced pieces
of sponge and then sprinkle it with the rosewater. Place little
pieces of marrow in between the pieces of sponge cake and
then gently ladle the cold custard over it.

Bake in the middle of the oven for 25 minutes or until the
custard has set. Let the tart cool before serving.

*This tart is also delicious if you add 50 g (1¾ oz) of almonds,
crushed with a little rosewater to prevent them from producing
oil. Add this to the cream with the spices and sugar, then strain
out with the spices.*

Chestnut Tart

Chestnut pudding or 'chestnut tarts' appear often in eighteenth century cookery books. Usually they are made by making a purée of cooked chestnuts, flavoured with orange flower water or rosewater. Eggs are added, and cream too, making it into a batter, which is then usually poured into puff pastry.

In the eighteenth century book *The Ladies Companion* (1743), I found a recipe that is very different from other chestnut puddings. It uses whole roasted chestnuts, bone marrow, candied peel and is then covered in custard. The recipe reminds me of a tort de moy (see page 166).

Chestnut tart
First roast your Chestnuts, and peel them, then sheet a dish with Puff-paste, and between every two Chestnuts put a Lump of Marrow, rolled in Eggs, and some Orange and Lemon-Peel cut small, then make a Custard and put all over it, and garnish with roasted Chestnuts all over.
The Ladies Companion, 1743

*Makes a 22–24 cm
(8½–9½ inch) pie*

30 g (1 oz) beef marrow

250 ml (9 fl oz/1 cup) thick
  (double) cream

1 tablespoon sugar

1 mace blade

1 cinnamon stick

3 egg yolks

½ quantity puff pastry
  (see page 344)

18–20 chestnuts

10 g (⅜ oz) candied
  lemon peel

10 g (⅜ oz) candied
  orange peel

Prepare the bone marrow as instructed on page 168 (for Tort de moy). Preheat the oven to 180°C (350°F).

Make the custard by putting the cream in a medium saucepan and bringing it to a gentle simmer with the sugar, mace and cinnamon. Beat the egg yolks in a bowl, pour a small amount of warm cream into the egg yolks and whisk thoroughly. This prepares your yolks for the hot liquid and will prevent it from curdling. Gradually add the rest of the cream, whisking until it is all incorporated. Allow to cool, then strain out the spices.

Meanwhile prepare the puff pastry as instructed on page 344.

Roast fresh chestnuts in a cast-iron frying pan over medium heat. They are ready when the skins have blackened. Peel and remove any threads. Alternatively, use chestnuts from a jar, which are already roasted and peeled.

Blind bake the pie case as instructed. Chop up the candied peel and arrange over the base of the pastry case. Neatly arrange the whole chestnuts over the base of the pie dish. Put a small chunk of bone marrow in between each chestnut. Now scoop the custard in and transfer to the lower part of the oven for 15 minutes. After 15 minutes place the pie in the middle of the oven and bake for another 15–20 minutes until the pastry is nicely golden brown.

Allow to cool completely before serving.

baked puddings |

Bakewell Pudding

Imagine a pub in a quintessentially English village: you enter with an appetite and the special on the menu is a pudding named after that village. You just have to try it, don't you? And so the Bakewell pudding rose to fame. Even though *Wonders of the Peak*, the first travel guide to the Peak District, was written by Charles Cotton in 1681, tourism reached a high in Victorian times, helped by the development of the railway and an increasing interest in geology. Victorians also came to 'take the waters' in the spa towns of Buxton, Matlock Bath and Bakewell.

Today, when visiting the Derbyshire village to which this pudding owes its name, you can't ignore the many quaint-looking bakeries claiming to present the one true Bakewell pudding. Its heritage has intrigued me for years, so naturally when I first visited Bakewell, I needed to explore and also ask some questions in those Bakewell bakeries.

Recipes for this type of pudding pop up in cookery books and manuscripts as early as the 1830s, but there are a number of versions of this pud and it is not clear who first linked it with the little Peak District town. Most probably it was one of the inn landlords of which the legend speaks: it is said that the pudding was invented in the White Horse Inn (now the Rutland Arms) by a waitress called Ann Wheeldon who made a mistake while preparing a pudding from the recipe book of mistress Ann Greaves. Mrs Greaves's great-great-great-grandson believes the pudding must have been created in the 1850s. This is, however, quite a few years later than other Bakewell pudding recipes and about the date of a manuscript recipe I have in my possession by a person from Oxfordshire, which is not at all in the north. This means that by the 1850s the pudding was already quite well known and so was the recipe. The Bakewell pudding also appears in American cookery books before the 1850s, but it seems the earliest in print comes from a book called *The Magazine of Domestic Economy*, printed in London in 1836.

One of the earliest manuscript recipes of a Bakewell pudding I could find is in the possession of food historian Ivan Day. It is written down as one of three Bakewell pudding recipes at around 1830. The author of the manuscript credits the recipe to a Mrs Anthony, Castle Hotel, Bakewell. The plot thickened when I found out, with the help of Mr Day's research, that there were three recipes in a book called *Traditional Fare of England and Wales*, of which one had a note: 'A Mr Stephen Blair gave £5 for this recipe at the hotel at Bakewell about 1835.' I looked for the book, and found it, and the recipes are indeed there. It is nearly identical to Ivan Day's recipe from Mrs Anthony, only Mr Blair gives the option of flavouring the filling with bitter almonds, which is still such a recognisable flavour in the Bakewell pud today.

Bakewell pudding
Line a dish with fine puff paste and spread over it a variety of preserves with strips of candied lemon peel. Then fill the dish with the following mixture – ½ lb. butter (clarified) ½ lb. castor sugar 10 yolks and 2 whites of eggs. Flavour with either bitter almonds, lemon, nutmeg or cinnamon. (These ingredients to be well mixed, but not beaten up). Bake in a moderate oven. When cold grate white sugar over pudding.
A Mr. Stephen Blair gave £5 for this recipe at the hotel at Bakewell about 1835.
Traditional Fare of England and Wales, 1948

All of the 1830s recipes for Bakewell pudding are quite different in character, which makes it hard to define the 'real' Bakewell pudding. There are also very strong similarities with a Sweet-meat Pudding from Eliza Smith's book *The Compleat Housewife* (1737). Some Bakewell puddings have a layer of jam, others have a layer of candied peel and preserves as in the sweet-meat pudding. Some use bitter almonds, others do not. It leads me to believe that the Bakewell pudding wasn't a pudding invented in an inn in Bakewell, as the popular myth likes people to believe; it was an existing pudding that was renamed thus to attract customers in the nineteenth century. And because it became famous in that locality, it disappeared in the rest of the country, making it a regional dish.

The version with just a layer of jam is the one that the Bakewell bakeries adopted as the true recipe. But if you would like to taste the earlier sweet-meat pudding version, here it is. I use powdered raw sugar, as early recipes often ask for loaf sugar, powdered, and it works better indeed. If you have a heatproof plate that will go into your oven, use that instead of a pie dish, as I believe this was the original vessel used to bake this pudding.

Makes 2 puddings in 23 cm (9 inch) shallow plates

25 g (1 oz) bitter apricot kernels

1 teaspoon rosewater

110 g (3¾ oz) clarified butter, melted

110 g (3¾ oz) raw sugar, powdered in a food processor

5 egg yolks

1 egg white

1 quantity puff pastry (see page 344)

2 tablespoons raspberry jam

50 g (1¾ oz) candied lemon peel, cut into strips

Bakewell pudding

Preheat the oven to 180°C (350°F).

Blanch and skin the apricot kernels by pouring boiling water over them to make the skins come off. Rinse under cold water and dry them using a clean tea towel (dish towel) to rub off the last of the skins.

Using a mortar and pestle, pound up the blanched apricot kernels with the rosewater. This will prevent the apricot kernels from producing oil and also will add a heavenly scent. Transfer to a bowl and whisk in the clarified butter and the sugar, whisking until creamy. Add the eggs and whisk to combine. Don't be alarmed if the filling seems runny to you, it is normal.

Line a pie dish or plate with the puff pastry rolled out as thin as you can manage and spread the raspberry jam over it, leaving a 2 cm (¾ inch) border that will become the rim. Neatly arrange strips of candied lemon peel over the jam, then gently pour in the filling mixture.

Bake in the bottom of the oven for 15 minutes, then move to the middle of the oven and bake for a further 15 minutes, or until the pastry is puffed and golden brown.

Serve on its own or with fresh raspberries and maybe a little whipped cream.

baked puddings |

General Satisfaction

I chose this pudding for its name, because I love these peculiar pudding names. The recipe was published by a woman named Mary Jewry and it appeared in both books she compiled for her publisher, Warne. She doesn't note her source, but I haven't been able to find this recipe in any other books of the same period, except in a handwritten recipe book I bought at an auction. The result looks a little like a queen of puddings, which does appear in a pudding book around this time, but this is more like a pie as it has a puff-pastry crust. Unlike the queen of puddings, which is topped with meringue, this pudding is finished off with a layer of egg whites beaten to a froth.

General Satisfaction
Some preserve; finger spongecakes; a gill of milk; an ounce of butter; a spoonful of flour; the peel of a lemon; yolk of an egg; a little nutmeg, and sugar to taste; whites of three eggs; puff paste
Line a pie-dish with rich puff paste. Put a layer of raspberry or strawberry preserve at the bottom, then a layer of the finger spongecakes, then a layer of the following mixture: Take a gill of milk, one ounce of butter, a spoonful of flour, and the peel of a lemon grated, and boil it until it thickens.
When cold, add the yolk of a beaten egg, a little nutmeg, and sugar to your taste. Cover the edge of the paste to prevent its burning, and bake it in a moderate oven. Whisk the whites of three eggs to a stiff froth, lay it on the pudding when baked, and put it again into the oven for a few minutes before serving.
Mary Jewry, *Warne's Model Cookery and Housekeeping Book*, 1868

Makes a 20 cm (8 inch) pie

145 ml (4¾ fl oz) thin (pouring) cream

30 g (1 oz) unsalted butter

1 teaspoon sugar

grated zest of 1 lemon

a pinch of ground nutmeg

1 teaspoon rice flour

2 egg yolks

½ quantity sponge cake (see page 349) or lady fingers (see page 350)

½ quantity puff pastry (see page 344)

1 tablespoon raspberry preserve

3 egg whites, 1 teaspoon sugar added (optional)

Preheat the oven to 180°C (350°F).

Bring the cream to a simmer in a saucepan with the butter, sugar, lemon zest and nutmeg, adding the rice flour when it boils. Stir constantly until the mixture thickens, remove from the heat and set aside to cool slightly.

Beat the egg yolks in a bowl and add a small amount of the warm cream mixture, whisk until incorporated, then gradually add the rest of the cream mixture, whisking constantly.

Cut the sponge cake into 1 cm (⅜ inch) strips, or use whole lady fingers.

Line the pie pan with puff pastry as instructed and spread the raspberry preserve all over the base. Now add a layer of sponge strips, then pour the cream mixture over the top.

Bake in the bottom part of the oven for 15 minutes, then move to the middle of the oven and bake for a further 15 minutes. or until the pastry is puffed and golden brown.

When the pie is baked, whisk the egg whites to a froth and spread them over the pie, then return it to the oven until cooked: it will look a bit marshmallowy and wrinkled. I find a teaspoon of sugar added to the egg whites improves the topping.

Why not try it with fresh raspberries?

Eve's Pudding

When mentioning Eve's pudding I immediately think of apples, and indeed the earliest recipe does contain apples, as does the modern pudding. But in the mid-nineteenth century other fruits were used as well and the pudding is called a soufflé pudding. The recipe below, and those in later books, requires the cook to boil the pudding and there are no visible layers, but the version we know today is made with a layer of chopped apples and a layer of sponge cake. This is a completely different pudding, one that doesn't appear under the name 'Eve's pudding' in any of the nineteenth century books, nor in the early twentieth century. It is not clear when the 'modern' Eve's pudding made with sponge cake became the fashion but it's still a favourite today, and really very good on a winter's day.

> Eve's pudding.
> Grate three-quarters of a pound of bread; mix it with the same quantity of shred suet, the same of apples and also of currants; mix with these the whole of four eggs, and the rind of half a lemon shred fine. Put it into a shape; boil three hours, and serve with pudding sauce, the juice of half a lemon, and a little nutmeg.
> Maria Eliza Ketelby Rundell, *A New System of Domestic Cookery*, 1807

Although the modern recipe requires you to make a simple sponge cake, I prefer using fresh breadcrumbs for a more authentic pudding. Breadcrumbs were used when raising agents weren't yet common. Use the best bread you can afford, which will define your pudding. Whatever you do, do not use ready-made dried breadcrumbs because that is an entirely different product.

Makes enough for an 18–20 cm (7–8 inch) cake tin or pie dish

3 cooking apples, such as bramley or cox

50 g (1¾ oz) currants

1 tablespoon light brown sugar

200 g (7 oz) butter

2 teaspoons finely grated lemon zest

50 g (1¾ oz) light brown sugar, extra

4 eggs

200 g (7 oz/3⅓ cups) fresh breadcrumbs

Preheat the oven to 180°C (350°F).

Peel, core and chop the apples into large but elegant chunks. Generously butter the pie dish or cake tin. Toss in the apples and the currants, and add the light brown sugar.

Prepare the batter by creaming the butter, lemon zest and the extra sugar in a separate bowl, add the eggs one at a time, stirring constantly, and then gradually add the breadcrumbs. When everything is well combined, pour or spoon the batter evenly over the apple.

Bake in the middle of the oven for 50–60 minutes, until nicely golden brown.

Serve with clotted cream (see page 336) or custard sauce (see page 338), or vanilla ice cream.

Some stewed rhubarb added to the apples instead of the currants makes for another wonderfully comforting pudding. If you want to make this pudding with flour, use 200 g (7 oz/1⅓ cups) of plain (all-purpose) flour instead of the breadcrumbs.

Queen of Puddings

A pudding with such a regal name must be of royal origin. Except it isn't. Some claim it was invented in honour of Queen Victoria, but it wasn't. Puddings using milk-soaked bread, custard and jam were plenty in historical cookery books. The first time one appears under the name queen of puddings is in *Massey and Son's Comprehensive Pudding Book*, where it is named 'A queen's pudding'. The pudding is made of a layer of custard thickened with breadcrumbs, on which a layer of jam is spread followed by a layer of pretty meringue swirls.

> Add one pound of bread crumbs to one quart of milk, a quarter of a pound of sugar, the zest of a lemon, No.986, two ounces of butter, and four eggs; bake in a buttered pie dish; when done, spread the top of the pudding with apricot jam, and mask with meringue, No.979; set in the hot closet, and serve cold with whipt cream in a boat.
> *Massey and Son's Comprehensive Pudding Book*, 1865

The modern recipe usually uses raspberry jam (it appears the Brits have a love for raspberry jam). Alan Davidson, author of the formidable *Oxford Companion to Food* (3rd edition, 2006) notes that this pudding, in its modern form, is one of the best British puddings.

Makes 6 individual puddings, or use one 18 cm (7 inch) ovenproof dish

butter, for greasing

4 egg yolks

600 ml (21 fl oz) milk

20 g (¾ oz) raw sugar

zest of 1 lemon

25 g (1 oz) unsalted butter

80 g (2¾ oz/1⅓ cups) fresh breadcrumbs

2 tablespoons raspberry jam

Meringue

4 egg whites

225 g (8 oz) caster (superfine) sugar

Preheat the oven to 180°C (350°F). Generously grease the ovenproof dish or individual basins (moulds) with butter.

Whisk the egg yolks in a large bowl. Bring the milk, sugar and lemon zest to a simmer in a saucepan. Now add the butter and melt it, making sure the mixture doesn't boil.

Pour a little of the hot milk mixture into the egg yolks and whisk thoroughly. Continue to add the hot milk in batches, stirring until fully incorporated and you get a smooth custard sauce.

Make a layer of breadcrumbs in the buttered dish, or divide them between the individual moulds, then pour the custard sauce over and let it rest for 15 minutes.

Prepare a deep baking dish with boiling water and place the dish or small pots in it. Carefully place the baking dish with the pudding(s) into the oven and bake for 35 minutes.

Towards the end of the baking time, make the meringue topping. Whisk the egg whites using an electric mixer until you get soft peaks when removing the whisk. Add the sugar a tablespoon at a time, still whisking, until the meringue is stiff and glossy.

Remove the pudding from the oven and spread the raspberry jam over the custard layer making sure you don't break the custard layer. Now either scoop the meringue onto the hot pudding, or scoop into a piping (icing) bag and make fancy swirls or peaks.

Return the pudding to the oven until the meringue is slightly coloured, which will take 15–20 minutes. Serve warm or cold.

Semolina Pudding

Shaped semolina puddings have been appearing in English cookery books since the beginning of the nineteenth century. The puddings are either prepared in a pastry shell like a pie, or baked or steamed in a mould. The soft porridge-like semolina pudding that is more common today was popularised during the Second World War, when packaged versions (the same brand as custard powder) were sold and ingredients have rarely been added since then.

Victorian semolina puddings, often meant for the nursery, were made in many ways. Some used almond milk, others used currants or fruit preserve. The recipe below from *Massey and Son's Comprehensive Pudding Book* uses broken up ratafia, a biscuit made with sweet and bitter almonds that has a distinctive marzipan flavour. They are also known as 'amaretti' in Italy.

Semolina pudding baked
Three-quarters of a pound of semolina, six ounces of sugar, half a pound of butter, eight eggs, a pint of cream, one tablespoonful of orange flower water, and two ounces of ratafias; mix the semolina with the sugar, orange flower water, half the butter, two eggs, the cream and salt, in a stewpan; stir this over the fire until it boils, then continue stirring until it is smooth and detaches from the sides, withdraw it from the fire, and gradually mix in the remainder of the eggs, butter, and bruised ratafias; put this into a mould, No. 973, put the mould into a deep saucepan half full of hot water, place in the oven and bake for one hour and a quarter, and serve with sauce
Massey and Son's Comprehensive Pudding Book, 1865

Makes enough for two 600–800 ml (21–28 fl oz) basins (moulds)

600 ml (21 fl oz) thick (double) cream

70 g (2½ oz) raw sugar

15 g (½ oz) butter

145 g (5¼ oz) semolina

a pinch of salt

1 tablespoon orange flower water

2 eggs

40 g (1½ oz) ratafia biscuits (see page 346), broken, or use store-bought amaretti biscuits

butter for greasing

Preheat the oven to 160°C (315°F).

In a medium saucepan, bring the cream to a gentle simmer with the sugar and butter. Pour in the semolina, salt and orange flower water and stir until it starts to boil, turn down the heat completely, then add the eggs one at a time and continue to stir until the mixture is smooth. Now fold in the crushed biscuits.

Lightly grease the basins and pour in the pudding mixture. Place the basins in a baking dish or large ovenproof pot and pour hot water into it to come halfway up the sides of the pudding basins.

Bake for 40 minutes and then remove from the oven and allow to rest for about 10 minutes. Loosen the puddings at the sides by pushing gently with your fingers, then unmould by placing a plate on top of each basin and turning them over.

Serve with stewed soft fruits, such as apricots, peaches or raspberries. A drizzle with raspberry vinegar (see page 340) gives the dish a punch and looks very pretty. For decoration you can add some candied orange peel.

College Puddings

J ames Woodforde, the diarist who has told us much about food of the eighteenth century, entertained six guests at 'New College' Oxford on 27 July 1774: 'We were very merry and pushed the Bottle very briskly. I gave my Company for dinner, some green Pea Soup, a chine of Mutton, some New College Puddings, a goose, some Peas and a Codlin Tart with Cream.' (*The Diary of a Country Parson*, 1758–1802.) The 'New College Puddings' he mentions are very possibly those Eliza Smith gave a recipe for:

> To make New-College Puddings.
> Grate a penny stale Loaf, and put to it a like quantity of Beef-suet finely shred, and a Nutmeg grated, a little Salt, some Currants, and then beat some Eggs in a little Sack, and some Sugar, and mix all together, and knead it as stiff as for Manchet, and make it up in the form and size of a Turkey-Egg, but a little flatter; then take a pound of Butter, and put it in a Dish, and set the Dish over a clear fire in a Chafing-dish, and rub your Butter about the dish till 'tis melted; put your Puddings in, and cover the Dish, but often turn your Puddings, until they are brown alike, and when they are enough, scrape Sugar over them and serve them up hot for a side Dish. You must let the Paste lie a quarter of an hour before you make up your puddings.
> Eliza Smith, *The Compleat Housewife*, 1737

After this recipe, history remains silent until 1822, when William Kitchiner published his recipe explaining to us that although this pudding is usually fried, he prefers them baked in patty pans (shallow muffin tins) in the oven. He also adds ginger and candied orange or citron peel to the batter and serves the pudding with white wine sauce.

Makes 10

100 g (3½ oz/1⅔ cups) fresh breadcrumbs

50 g (1¾ oz) shredded suet

50 g (1¾ oz) raw sugar

½ teaspoon ground nutmeg

a pinch of salt

2 eggs, lightly beaten

2 teaspoons sherry or Madeira

10 g (⅜ oz) currants, soaked in brandy, drained

1 teaspoon candied lemon peel

clarified butter, to fry

icing (confectioners') sugar, for dusting

In a bowl combine the breadcrumbs, suet, sugar, nutmeg and salt. Add the eggs and sherry and knead into a thick dough. Don't be alarmed if it seems too dry at first: when you knead it the dough will come together.

Let the dough rest for 15 minutes.

Fold in the currants and candied lemon peel and shape the dough into balls the size of a golf ball, then flatten slightly like little burgers.

Melt a knob of clarified butter in a cast iron frying pan, and fry the flattened dough balls in the butter until browned.

Serve as a side dish, or as a snack dusted with icing sugar.

baked puddings |

Carrot Pudding

Most eighteenth century recipes for this pudding require you to boil the carrots, while Rebecca Price's seventeenth century recipe, below, uses raw grated carrots. I find the texture of the raw carrot far more agreeable and rustic.

Carrot pudding my Lady Howe's recipe
Take a twopenny lofe grated; and the same quantity of raw caret grated very small; mix them together; and put to it the yolks of eight eggs, and the whites of 3 beat them well and put them in, then stir in a quarter of a pounde of butter being melted, and a little sack; and grated nutmeg; put in milk enough to make it of a good thickness, about a pinte I believe will be enough; sweeten it pretty sweet to yr tast, mingle all well together; and bake it in a dish, half an hour will do it; when you draw it, poure a little melted butter with Sack in it; one ye top of it.
Rebecca Price, *The Compleat Cook*, 1681

Henry Howard, in *England's Newest Way in Cookery* (1703) also uses boiled carrot but lines his dish with puff pastry and gives the option of using orange flower water instead of sack. Eliza Smith, in 1737 (*The Compleat Housewife*), gives a recipe for carrot pudding with puff pastry crust and uses raw carrots; her recipe is very similar to that of Price but uses double the amount of bread and includes cinnamon as well as nutmeg to spice the pudding.

The recipe below uses the filling from Rebecca Price's recipe in combination with a puff pastry base. I also added a tiny pinch of cinnamon, as in Eliza Smith's recipe. It is equally as good when baked in a dish without the puff pastry.

Makes a 22 cm (8½ inch) pie

4 egg yolks

2 egg whites

½ teaspoon ground nutmeg

½ teaspoon ground cinnamon

50 g (1¾ oz) raw sugar

170 g (6 oz) carrots, grated

2 tablespoons sherry

150 ml (5 fl oz) thick (double) cream

120 g (4¼ oz/2 cups) fresh breadcrumbs

100 g (3½ oz) butter, melted

½ quantity puff pastry (see page 344)

Preheat the oven to 190°C (375°F).

Beat the eggs in a bowl with the spices and the sugar, then add the grated carrots, the sherry and the cream. Now fold in the breadcrumbs and melted butter and combine well with a wooden spoon to make a thick batter.

Line the pie dish with the puff pastry as instructed, pour in the batter and bake in the bottom part of the oven for 30–40 minutes until the pastry is nice and golden.

Trinity Burnt Cream

Trinity burnt cream is a pudding that, according to legend, first appeared in 1617 at Trinity College in Cambridge; however, even the college can't trace the pudding as far back as 1617. The first recipe for a 'burnt cream' – or 'crème brûlée', as it is known in France – appeared in the French book *Nouveau Cuisinier Royal et Bourgeois* (Francoise Massialot) in 1691. Yet by the 1731 edition of this book the name had changed to 'Crème Anglaise'. Maybe this dish was most popular in England, or maybe it originated in England after all. The earliest recipe for a burnt cream in an English cookery book I have found is from *The Cooks and Confectioners Dictionary* written in 1723 by John Nott. However, Jane Grigson, in *English Food* (1974) tells us that she had found a recipe for a burnt cream in a seventeenth century manuscript, but unfortunately she doesn't name the recipe book.

Burnt Cream
Take yolks of four or five Eggs, beat them well in a Stew-pan with a little Flour; pouring on Milk by degrees to the quantity of a Quart; then put in a small Stick of Cinnamon, some candy'd and green Lemon-peel cut small. Set the Cream on the Furnace, stir it continually, that it do not stick to the Bottom. When it is boil'd, set a dish upon the Furnace, and pour the Cream into it, and let it boil again, 'till it sticks to the side of the Dish; then set it aside, and sugar it well on the top; heat the Fire-shovel red hot, and brown the Cream with it to give it a fine golden Colour.
John Nott, *The Cooks and Confectioners Dictionary*, 1723

It is unclear where the dish originated, as recipes for Crema Catalana go back centuries as well. We will perhaps never know, or we can assume that it is only natural for any cook to try out burning some sugar on top of the custard with a red hot salamander – a shovel-like instrument made hot in the fire and used to give dishes a fried top.

Although we associate a crème brûlée or burnt cream with vanilla, these early recipes never use it. In these recipes the cream is flavoured with candied peel and sometimes orange flower water.

Makes enough for six 150 ml (5 fl oz) ramekins

6 egg yolks

1 teaspoon plain (all-purpose) flour or rice flour

800 ml (28 fl oz) milk

1 cinnamon stick

1 teaspoon chopped candied lemon peel

Preheat the oven to 180°C (350°F).

Whisk the egg yolks thoroughly in a large bowl and stir in the flour. Boil water in a kettle or saucepan so you have hot water at hand.

Put the milk in a saucepan over low heat with the cinnamon and chopped lemon peel. Bring to a simmer, then when the milk starts to bubble, remove the saucepan from the heat.

Take out the cinnamon stick. You can strain out the candied peel too, if you like, but I never do and quite enjoy a bit of peel here and there.

Pour a small amount of warm milk into the egg yolks and whisk thoroughly. This prepares the yolk for the hot liquid and will prevent it from curdling. Gradually add the rest of the milk, whisking constantly until it is all incorporated.

baked puddings

Place the ramekins in a large baking dish and pour in enough hot water to come about 1.5 cm (⅝ inch) up the sides. Now pour or spoon the warm custard mixture into the ramekins, filling them up right to the top. If a foam develops, skim it off with a spoon.

Bake in the middle of the oven for 50 minutes or until the mixture is set but still has a gentle wobble. Carefully and cautiously lift the ramekins out of the baking dish and place them on a wire rack to cool.

Transfer them to the fridge when cooled, until you need them. When you are ready to serve, gently spread a teaspoon of sugar over each custard and then get out your kitchen blowtorch. Gently burn the sugar by holding the flame just above it and moving the torch around until the sugar is caramelised.

Black Caps

I have the best possible memory of this simple pudding on a rather chilly day in May in an old Cumbrian longhouse owned by food historian Ivan Day. The apples were baked in an authentic wood-fired stove and filled the house with that comforting scent apples can give to a breeze in the air. They came out of the oven, black as if they'd been to hell and back, and were eaten for pudding after a most memorable meal and in the company of the most diverse food history enthusiasts.

I was told by my host that this is the original toffee apple. Recipes for toffee apples only appeared around the end of Victorian times, when venerable publications such as the *Yorkshire Evening Post*, on 14 July 1896, warned of the 'dangers' of this new craze among the young.

For Black Caps, a few recipes can be found in the eighteenth century; each writer has their own way of creating this dish, so I would say make it your own by altering it to your taste.

> Take six large apples, and cut a slice off the bottom end, put them in a tin, and set them in a quick oven till they are brown, then wet them with rose water, and grate a little sugar over them, and set them in the oven again till they look bright, and very black, then take them out, and put them into a deep china dish or plate, and pour round them thick cream custard, or white wine and sugar. It is a pretty corner dish for either dinner or supper.
> Elizabeth Raffald, *The Experienced English Housekeeper*, 1782

6 dessert apples, such as jonagold or orange cox

about 2 tablespoons sugar, to sprinkle

1 tablespoon orange flower water or rosewater

a naughty drizzle of Grand Marnier (orange-flavoured liqueur) or brandy (optional)

Preheat the oven to 200°C (400°F).

Wash the apples and slice off a strip of the skin around the middle to prevent the apples from popping. Sprinkle the apples with sugar. Arrange them in a baking tray and drizzle the rosewater or orange flower water over so each apple has some splashes.

Bake in the oven for 30 minutes.

After 30 minutes have passed, remove from the oven, sprinkle with a little more sugar and add Grand Marnier or brandy, if you like, before the apples go back in the oven. Makes for a rather festive dish, but is no must.

Put the apples back into the oven for a further 30 minutes, until quite tender but not reduced to pulp. The apples should be blackened, hence the name 'Black Caps'.

Fabulous with custard sauce (see page 338), clotted cream (see page 336) and ice cream, I mostly enjoy them with a thick strained yoghurt for breakfast or an afternoon nibble.

Cooking over a fire? Use the Dutch oven method: Rest a heatproof dish holding the apples on a trivet in a Dutch oven. Fire the coals and let them go grey, then stand the pot over the coals on a trivet and place some of the coals on the Dutch oven's lid. As fire is unpredictable I can't give you an exact cooking time, but check after 30 minutes; if they aren't already well on their way, the coals aren't hot enough.

CHAPTER 3

BATTER PUDDINGS

Batter puddings

In early kitchens with open fires, large dripping pans were used to catch the fat dripping from a rotating spit of meat. This was so the dripping could be used to baste the meat, or kept in store to use for other cooking. One side of the pan usually had a spout to pour the dripping into another receptacle. 'Dripping', 'fired' or 'batter' puddings were made by placing batter in a 'toss-pan', which was then placed under the spit where the dripping pan would usually sit. Often, these dripping puddings would be made out of a pancake batter, but some puddings were also made with potatoes.

The first printed recipe for a dripping pudding can be found in *The Whole Duty of a Woman* in 1737. The anonymous author instructs the cook to place the pudding under a shoulder of mutton instead of the dripping pan. As with most recipes, these dripping puddings must have been around for quite some time before they appeared in print.

> Make a good Batter as for Pancakes, put it in a hot Toss-pan over the Fire with a Bit of Butter to fry the Bottom a little, then put the Pan and Batter under a Shoulder of Mutton instead of a Dripping-pan, keeping frequently shaking it by the Handle and it will be light and savoury, and fit to take up when your Mutton is enough; then turn it in a Dish, and serve it hot.
> *The Whole Duty of a Woman*, 1737

The plain dripping pudding, made of a pancake batter, was later renamed a 'Yorkshire Pudding' in Hannah Glasse's 1747 book, *The Art of Cookery*. Today it is no longer made under the dripping of a roasting joint, but with oil, in which the batter is poured.

As mentioned in the recipe above, pancakes were also batter puddings. In the Roman book Apicius: *De Re Cocinaria*, the pancakes are made of eggs and milk with a little flour and are served with honey and pepper. Although recipes for pancakes do not appear often in early cookery books, they are mentioned in the Austin manuscripts from around 1430 as if they had been around with that name for quite some time. Pancakes became most popular in the seventeenth century, when they were made with cream, eggs (quite a lot of eggs) and often fortified with sack (sherry) or brandy.

Batter puddings were also made with meat baked into the batter: small game birds were used, as well as pigeon, rabbit, hare, pork and beef. The iconic British dish 'Toad-in-the-hole' – sausages baked into a batter – was being made as far back as the mid-1700s and probably earlier.

Fritters, which sound quite modern, have been around since before medieval times. They are basically small batter puddings fried in oil or butter. They were made of a dough to which ale or cider barm (froth) was added to give it a lift. The Romans called them 'scriblita' and we find a recipe for 'cryspej' in the fifteenth century Austin manuscripts. 'Smoutebollen' and 'poffertjes' in Belgium and Holland descend from these fritters, as do the Spanish churros, as well as doughnuts, choux and beignets. We find a recipe for churro-type fritters in Robert May's seveneenth century book *The Accomplisht Cook*. He titles it, 'To fry Paste out of a Syringe or Butter-squirt'. A later manuscript written by Elizabeth Jacob (*Physicall and Chyrurgicall Receipts*, 1654) includes a detailed recipe 'To Make A Snake', which sounds even more impressive.

Another type of fritter with the fifteenth century name of 'froyse' was made with pork or veal and beaten eggs, and trout on 'fish days' when the consuming of meat was forbidden by the church. Fritters could contain fruits, like the hasty fritters on page 212, or green herbs, and even cheese curd. Recipes are plenty in old texts, and they must have been a festive food, as they still are today.

batter puddings |

Yorkshire Pudding

I t is near impossible to re-create the original Yorkshire or dripping pudding of times gone by. We would need a hearth and a large joint of meat suspended on a turning spit jack or bottle jack in front of a roaring fire. The radiant heat and seasoning of the fire in combination with the animal fats give the pudding a unique flavour and texture that is not possible to re-create in a modern electric or gas oven.

You could use lard or tallow instead of sunflower oil to get a slightly more meaty result. It is popular to use cupcake tins to create whimsical individual Yorkshire puds, but I must advise you to try a whole one to share, as it was intended centuries ago. Another great way of serving it is to make a large Yorkshire pudding and to serve the meat and gravy in it as if it were a bowl. The pudding can then suck up all the nice flavours.

I'm sharing with you, below, the original recipe for a Yorkshire pudding; the first time this dripping pudding was named as such. It was, in fact, not a pudding exclusive to the northern region of Yorkshire, as these dripping puddings were being made in many locations throughout Britain.

A Yorkshire Pudding.
Take a Quart of Milk, four Eggs, and a little Salt, make it up into a thick Batter with flour, like a Pancake Batter. You must have a good Piece of Meat at the fire, take a Stew-pan and put some Dripping in, set it on the Fire, when it boils, pour in your Pudding, let it bake on the Fire till you think it is high enough, then turn a plate upside-down in the Dripping-pan, that the Dripping may not be blacked; set your Stew-pan on it under your Meat, and let the Dripping drop on the Pudding, and the Heat of the Fire come to it, to make it of a fine brown. When your Meat is done and set to Table, drain all the Fat from your Pudding, and set it on the Fire again to dry a little; then slide it as dry as you can into a Dish, melt some butter, and pour into a Cup, and set in the Middle of the Pudding. It is an exceeding good pudding, the Gravy of the Meat eats well with it.
Hannah Glasse, *The Art of Cookery, Made Plain and Easy*, 1747

The pudding serves 4–6 people

110 g (3¾ oz/¾ cup) plain
   (all-purpose) flour

a pinch of salt

280 ml (9¾ fl oz) milk

3 eggs

sunflower oil, clarified butter,
   lard or tallow, for frying

Proceed by creating the batter as you would for a pancake batter, adding the flour and pinch of salt to the milk and eggs, making sure there are no lumps. I find that the pudding improves if you leave the batter to rest for 30 minutes or so before cooking.

Preheat the oven to 250°C (500°F).

Pour 1 cm (⅜ inch) of sunflower oil, clarified butter, lard or tallow into a baking dish or cake tin and set it in the middle of the hot oven. Place a larger tray underneath in case the oil drips; you don't want extra cleaning and a smoky kitchen afterwards.

When the oil is hot (you will see it spitting), carefully but swiftly pour the batter into the hot oil and close the oven door. Bake for 20–25 minutes without opening the oven until the pudding is puffed up and nicely coloured.

Wood-fired oven?
Melt some lard or tallow in a baking tray and place on one side in the oven just after you have moved the fire to one side. When the fat is hot, remove from the oven, carefully pour in the batter and place back in the oven. Keep an eye on the pudding at all times, as cooking time depends on the heat of the oven, but the pudding should be ready in minutes if the oven is very hot.

Dripping Pudding

For those eager to try a dripping pudding made under the dripping of the meat, this is a method in the oven. It is not quite like the original, which was prepared under a dripping, spit-roasting joint of meat in front of the radiant heat of the fireplace, but the flavour comes close.

The batter recipe stays the same, you just need a piece of rib eye on the bone, or if you are lucky enough to have a proper joint of beef, that would work very well too.

The pudding serves 4–6 people

1 piece of rib eye on the bone, fat not trimmed

110 g (3¾ oz/¾ cup) plain (all-purpose) flour

a pinch of salt

280 ml (9¾ fl oz) milk

3 eggs

Preheat the oven to 50°C (120°F). Put the meat into a tray just large enough to hold it and roast in the middle of the oven for 50 minutes.

After 50 minutes, remove the tray of meat and turn the oven up to 220–250°C (425–500°F).

While the oven temperature rises, proceed by creating the batter as you would for a pancake batter, adding the flour and pinch of salt to the milk and eggs, making sure there are no lumps. I find that the pudding improves if you leave the batter to rest for 30 minutes or so before cooking.

Prepare the oven by putting a large baking dish on the bottom: make sure it is large enough so you can place the pan or tray for the batter inside it.

When the oven is ready, transfer the meat to the rack above the baking dish, put the pan for the batter underneath and wait – looking through the oven window if you like – until the fat starts dripping down into the pan.

When you have a little fat in the pan or tray, take it out of the oven, carefully. Pour in the batter and return it to the tray under the meat, until the meat is done to your liking.

If you happen to have a fireplace with a spit, you can proceed by placing the dripping pudding under the meat when it is nearly done. The fat and juices need to run clear before you place it under the meat, and you want them roughly to be ready at the same time.

Serve with the meat. This is very rich.

Toad-in-the-hole

Hannah Glasse, who came up with the term 'Yorkshire pudding' in 1747, also had a recipe in her book *The Art of Cookery* for 'Pigeons in a Hole'. It was basically a toad-in-the-hole using whole pigeons rather than bangers (sausages).

Fifty years later the novelist Fanny Burney mentions the trend for 'putting a noble sirloin of beef into a poor, paltry batter-pudding!' (*Diary and Letters of Madame D'Arblay*, December 1797). Sausages were being used in this manner as well; in the mid-eighteenth century the diarist Thomas Turner mentions that he 'dined on a sausage batter pudding' (9 February 1765). Richard Briggs, in *The English Art of Cookery* (1788), is the first instance I can find that actually names the dish Toad-in-the-hole, although his version uses beef.

Alexis Soyer gives not one but eleven versions of a toad-in-the-hole in *A Shilling Cookery for the People* (1854), his book aimed at the working classes. The first uses 'trimmings of either beef, mutton, veal, or lamb, not too fat'; then there is a plain version with potatoes, and one with peas. Further, he suggests to use calves' brains; larks or sparrows; ox cheek or sheep's head; a rabbit; the remains of a previously cooked hare; a blade-bone of pork; and finally the remains of salt pork.

The next mention I wish to share with you comes from the Italian Pelegrino Artusi. He mentions a recipe for toad-in-the-hole in *La Scienza in Cucina e l'Arte di Mangiare Bene* (1891). The recipe is called 'twice-cooked meat English style' (lesso rifatto all'inglese) and in his description he mentions that 'toad-in-the-hole' is the name of this twice-cooked meat. He also goes on to explain that it is a delicious dish and it would be an insult to call it a toad. Artusi had a great sense of humour and that is something you can see in his introductions to his recipes. However, the toad-in-the-hole he mentions is not for a sausage cooked in batter, but uses meat for boiling, sliced and browned on both sides.

What becomes clear is that the toad-in-the-hole is a popular dish to use up leftovers at this period in time. Mary Jewry gives three recipes for toad-in-the-hole in her book, *Warne's Every Day Cookery*: one for a batter pudding with a veal-stuffed chicken, one with rump steak and one to use up cold roast mutton.

During the war years, people were instructed to cook toad-in-the-hole using Spam rather than the (by then) more commonly used sausage. Today the dish has become so connected with British food culture it is no wonder references can be found as early as the mid-1700s.

Toad-in-the-hole is now a favourite dish of small and tall: every child loves a banger, and every grown-up likes to be transported back to his or her childhood. It now features on the menus of laid-back pubs and restaurants that prepare it with posh locally sourced bangers. And a festive Bonfire Night, too, wouldn't be the same without it.

batter puddings |

Serves 3–4

3 or 4 good-quality pork
sausages

sunflower oil or clarified
butter, for frying

a few sprigs of rosemary
(optional)

1 quantity Yorkshire pudding
batter (see page 197)

Toad-in-the-hole

Preheat the oven to 250°C (500°F).

Fry the sausages in sunflower oil or clarified butter in a frying
pan until nearly cooked through.

Pour 1 cm (⅜ inch) of sunflower oil, clarified butter, lard or
tallow into a baking tray or cake tin and set it in the middle of
the hot oven. Place a larger tray underneath in case the oil drips;
you don't want extra cleaning and a smoky kitchen afterwards.

When the oil is hot (you will see it spitting), arrange the
sausages in the tray along with any oil or butter remaining in
the frying pan. Carefully but swiftly pour the batter into the
hot oil, stick in the rosemary sprigs, if using, and close the
oven door. Bake for 20–25 minutes without opening the oven
until the pudding is puffed up and nicely coloured.

Serve with mustard, braised red cabbage, jacket potatoes or
mashed potato and caramelised onions, if you like.

batter puddings |

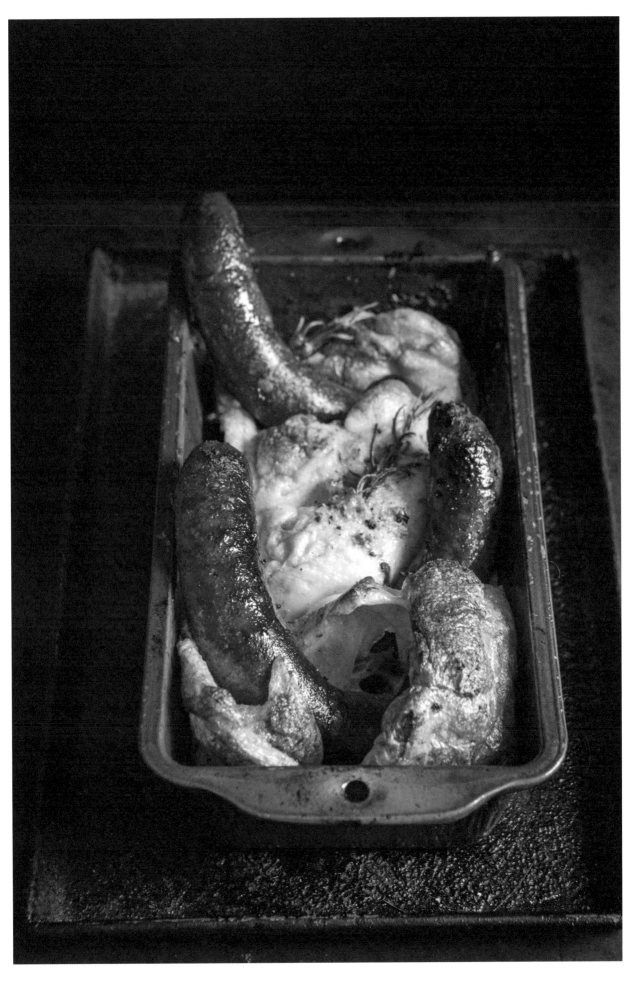

Kentish Cherry Batter Pudding

A cherry batter pudding is a variation on a Yorkshire pudding or a toad-in-the-hole, only with fruit. It is often, these days, called a 'Kentish cherry batter pudding', because Kent is the cherry-growing county of England. Recipes for batter puddings with fruit are plentiful in the historic cookery books; however, none use the name cherry batter pudding until it appears in a domestic column in a Warwickshire newspaper.

> Cherry batter pudding is nice for a change, and is generally liked by those who are unable to eat boiled suet crust. Mix one pint of milk and three tablespoonful of flour to a smooth paste, add 1oz. of butter (melted), a little salt, three well-beaten eggs, and stir in 1 lb. cherries (stoned). Boil for two hours, and serve with wine sauce.
> *Leamington Spa Courier*, Saturday 15 August 1891, by 'A Lady'

The modern version of a cherry batter pudding is often made like a clafoutis, but also as a Yorkshire pudding batter with cherries. I prefer the latter and give the recipe for it below.

Makes 8–10 small puddings or one large

110 g (3¾ oz/¾ cup) plain (all-purpose) flour

a pinch of salt

280 ml (9¾ fl oz) milk

3 eggs

sunflower oil, clarified butter, lard or tallow, for frying

Braised cherries

300 g (10½ oz) fresh cherries

150 ml (5 fl oz) unsweetened apple juice or water

20 g (¾ oz) raw sugar

If you have cherries in brandy, these cherries will work too for a more boozy pudding. Remove the stones from the cherries first if you are using these. For a variation, why not use peaches, plums or even gooseberries?

Proceed by creating the batter as you would for a pancake batter, adding the flour and salt to the milk and eggs, making sure there are no lumps. I find that the pudding improves if you leave the batter to rest for 30 minutes or so before cooking.

Preheat the oven to 250°C (500°F).

To make the cherry sauce, remove the stones from the cherries by halving them or use a fancy tool to get the stone out. Put them in a small saucepan with the apple juice or water and bring to a simmer.

Add the sugar and let it dissolve, simmering until you get a dark-coloured sauce. I like not to cook it too long so the cherries aren't reduced to jam. If you like a thicker sauce, add cornstarch according to the packet instructions. Set aside until ready to serve.

Pour 1 cm (⅜ inch) of sunflower oil, clarified butter, lard or tallow into a baking dish or cake tin and set it in the middle of the hot oven. Place a larger tray underneath in case the oil drips; you don't want extra cleaning and a smoky kitchen afterwards.

When the oil is hot, quickly but safely remove the tray from the oven – don't spill the hot fat! – scoop the batter into the dish and then add a couple of the braised cherries.

Return the dish to the oven and don't touch the oven door until the puddings have risen and are golden brown: this should take about 25–30 minutes.

Serve with the braised cherries and sauce, a spoonful of clotted cream (see page 336) or Greek-style natural yoghurt.

batter puddings |

Apple Tansy

A tansy is a medieval egg bake using the bitter herb tansy. It would have been a dish made exclusively in spring when the tansy herb isn't poisonous. Because of this seasonal link, the dish became associated with Easter and Lent. It would indeed be a perfect dish to use up the last eggs before fasting. Intriguing is the fact that in Flanders we have a pancake called 'kruidkoek' which is also made using tansy. It is a pancake that is now only eaten around the town of Diest, but it used to be a national dish.

Recipes for the English tansy first appear in 1430; of course, it would have been around for some time by then, but cookery manuscripts from that period are scarce. In early cookery books and manuscripts there was usually just the one recipe for a tansy, but soon we find recipes for an apple tansy, a damson tansy, and other variations often even omitting the bitter herb that gives its name to this dish. It is a possibility that this is because the herb is poisonous when picked at any other time than spring, and people still wanted to cook up a tansy at other times of the year when they had eggs to use up. By the seventeenth century, cream is added, along with spices such as nutmeg, ginger, cinnamon and probably mace. Breadcrumbs are also added sometimes.

To make an Apple-Tansey
Pare your Apples and cut them in thin round slices, then fry them in good sweet Butter, then take ten Eggs, sweet Cream, Nutmeg, Cinamon, Ginger, Sugar, with a little Rose-water, beat all these together, and poure it upon your Apples and fry it.
WM, *The Compleat Cook*, 1658

At some point in the eighteenth century the tansy recipes are renamed 'tansy puddings'. Although tansies are usually prepared in a pan, over a fire, the Scottish Elizabeth Cleland in *A New and Easy Method of Cookery* in 1755 also gives a recipe for a 'plain tansy' cooked in the dripping pan under roasting meat, just like dripping puddings. Tansies are still cooked in Britain today, but now it is a name for a kind of pudding of which there are many variations.

batter puddings

Makes a 25 cm (10 inch) pancake; serves 4–6

1–2 dessert apples, such as jonagold

butter, for frying

3 eggs

50 ml (1¾ fl oz) thin (pouring) cream

1 teaspoon rosewater

a pinch each of ground nutmeg, cinnamon and ginger

1 teaspoon sugar

Core the apples and slice them thinly.

Make a batter by whisking the eggs with the cream, rosewater and the spices.

Melt some butter in a large frying pan. Arrange the apple slices neatly in the pan and fry them lightly. When they start to color, turn them over and pour the egg mixture over the top. Fry over low heat until the mixture has set, as you would an omelette.

Serve with the sugar strewn over.

Why not try with plums, peaches or (in spring only) with some actual fresh-picked tansy, finely chopped?

Snake Fritters

Many European dishes appear at the same time in contemporary writings, which makes it difficult to determine whether or not they have been inspired by or copied from each other. Recipes for syringed fritters can be found in cookery books in Italy, Spain, France, England, Portugal and Germany by the seventeenth century. Medieval Arabic recipes for piped fritters are also common, which makes you think that maybe the Moors are the originators of the Spanish churros we still know today. The Spanish word for a syringe is a 'churrera', which explains the etymology of the name; however, Arabic recipes do not use the choux-like pastry that the churros and other syringed fritters do. So perhaps it is a whole different dish after all.

A recipe for 'Fruta de siringa' appears in the Portuguese book *Arte de Cozinha* (Domingos Rodrigues) in 1758, while a Spanish recipe in *Arte de Cocina* (Francisco Montiño) in 1763 only instructs to use the dough for syringed fritters in a recipe for 'Otros buñuelos de viento' (other fritters).

The first printed recipe in English for these fritters can be found in Robert May's *The Accomplisht Cook* from 1660. He mentions a 'butter-squirt', a syringe used for making decorative butter swirls. He flavours the fritters with saffron and sugar and fries them in clarified butter:

> To fry Paste out of a Syringe or Butter-squirt.
> Take a quart of fine flower, & a litle leven, dissolve it in warm water, & put to it the flour, with some white wine, salt, saffron, a quarter of butter, and two ounces of sugar; boil the aforesaid things in a skillet as thick as a hasty pudding, and in the boiling stir it continually, being cold beat it in a mortar, fry it in clarified butter, and run it into the butter through a butter-squirt.
>
> Robert May, *The Accomplisht Cook*, 1660

Elizabeth Jacob's manuscript recipe of the same period (*Physicall and Chyrurgicall Receipts*, 1654–1685) gives a much longer and detailed recipe and the author names the dish a 'snake'. She instructs that when the dough is pressed through the syringe 'it must be done quick, and with great Strength'. As flavouring, she uses a little salt, nutmeg and rosewater. While most fritter recipes call for butter to fry, she instructs to use 'Beasts lard'. To serve she suggests brushing the curls with some butter and rosewater melted together, and then to 'scrape' some sugar on them.

a few saffron threads

100 ml (3½ fl oz) white wine

125 g (4½ oz) butter

50 g (1¾ oz) raw sugar

225 g (8 oz/1½ cups) plain
(all-purpose) flour

1 teaspoon baking powder

lard, tallow or oil, to fry

extra sugar, to sprinkle
(optional)

Snake fritters

Soak the saffron in the wine until the wine is nicely coloured.

In a saucepan, heat the wine, butter and sugar gently and simmer until the butter is melted and the sugar has dissolved.

Take the saucepan off the heat and add the flour and baking powder. Combine well with a spatula until the mixture comes away from the pan and forms a ball, just like choux pastry. When the dough looks silky smooth, it is done.

Scoop the dough into a piping (icing) bag fitted with a large star nozzle. Heat the lard in a deep-fryer or large heavy-based saucepan until it reaches 160°C (315°F), or until a tiny bit of dough dropped in the oil turns golden brown in 30–35 seconds.

Carefully but swiftly pipe a long snake of the pastry into the hot fat. Fry until golden and transfer to sheets of paper towel to absorb some of the fat. Sprinkle with sugar just before serving, or leave plain.

Some historical recipes call for extra flavourings, such as nutmeg or rosewater. I like to add a generous pinch of nutmeg to the batter when melting the butter.

Hasty Fritters

Recipes for apple fritters can be found in many eighteenth century books and are very similar: some require you to slice the apples in discs and some in chunks. This fritter is called a hasty fritter because the batter is done quickly, and the apples are coarsely chopped up. You can try using other fruits; the recipe below from 1747, for example, gives you the option of using currants instead. The dish takes only minutes from start to finish. You can also make these fritters without any fruit: they are nice dipped in a sauce.

To make hasty fritters
Take a stew-pan, put in some butter, and let it be hot: in the mean time take half a pint of all-ale not bitter, and stir in some flour by degrees in a little of the ale; put in a few currants or chopped apples, beat them up quick, and drop a large spoonful at a time all over the pan. Take care they don't stick together, turn them with an egg-slice, and when they are of a fine brown, lay them in a dish, and throw some sugar over them. Garnish with orange cut into quarters.
Hannah Glasse, *The Art of Cookery*, 1747

The ale in this recipe acts as a leavening agent and will puff up the dough while it fries. You can also use cider if you don't like the flavour of ale. You don't need to use butter to fry these in, as lard or vegetable oil works just as well.

Makes about 12–14 fritters

330 ml (11¼ fl oz/1⅓ cups) apple cider, without added sugar, or use unhopped ale

300 g (10½ oz/2 cups) plain (all-purpose) flour

3 small dessert apples, such as jonagold, cut in 12 mm (½ inch) pieces, or 6 tablespoons currants, or use both apple and currants

icing (confectioners') sugar, to dust

lard, tallow or oil, for frying

Pour the cider into a large bowl, sift in the flour and make it into a smooth dough. Fold in the apple and/or currants. If the apples are very juicy, it works better to dust them with icing sugar so they don't make the batter too soggy.

Carefully heat up the fat or oil in a deep-fryer or heavy-based frying pan to 160°C (315°F) or until a cube of bread or a little of the batter dropped into the oil turns golden brown in 30–35 seconds. Carefully drop small dollops of the batter into the pan using two tablespoons. It is better to take your time and fry the fritters in small batches rather than to rush and have them stick together in lumps.

Fry until they are golden and drain on paper towel to absorb some of the fat.

Serve with a dusting of icing sugar.

A Quire of Paper

The word 'quire' comes from the Latin 'quaterni' which means a set of four. It is a term used by printers and bookbinders, meaning a stack of paper that is bound into a book. This recipe is not for a stack of paper but for a pile of rich cream pancakes, thin as paper, served layered as a cake instead of individually. The pancake pile is cut into wedges and served with a dusting of fine sugar and a rich sauce.

The earliest recipe for this 'quire of paper' I found in a book from 1714. It is not a dish that often appears, either in the books of the period or those published later, but the author in this early work mentions the dish is 'call'd a Quire of Paper' which means it must have been known in this manner for some time. It was, however, a dish privileged for the gentry, as use of eggs makes it too expensive for normal folk.

Thin Cream pan-cakes, call'd a Quire of Paper
Take to a Pint of Cream, eight eggs, leaving out two whites, three Spoonfuls of fine Flour, three Spoonfuls of Sack, and one Spoonful of Orange-flower Water, a little Sugar, a grated Nutmeg, and a quarter of a Pound of Butter, melted in the Cream; mingle all well together, mixing the flour with a little Cream at firft, that it may be fmooth : Butter your Pan for the firft Pan-cake, and let them run as thin as you can poffibly, to be whole; when one Side is clour'd, 'tis enough; take them carefully out of the Pan, and ftrew some fine-sifted-sugar between each; lay them as even on each other as you can : This Quantity will make twenty
Mary Kettleby, *A Collection of Above Three Hundred Receipts in Cookery, Physick and Surgery*, 1714

Makes a stack of 12

490 g (1 lb 1½ oz) plain (all-purpose) flour

1½ teaspoons grated nutmeg

2 teaspoons of sugar

300 ml (10½ fl oz) thick (double) cream

6 eggs plus 2 egg yolks, extra

2 teaspoons orange flower water

120 ml (4 fl oz) sherry

200 g (7 oz) butter, plus extra for frying

caster (superfine) sugar, to sprinkle in between layers

Combine the dry ingredients in a bowl and gradually add the cream and then the eggs, one at a time, including the extra yolks. When thoroughly combined, add the orange flower water and the sherry and whisk until smooth. Warm the butter until just melted, pour into the batter and whisk until it is well incorporated.

Put a frying pan or pancake pan on the stovetop and let it get very hot. Add a little butter, pour in a spoonful of batter and let it spread as you turn the pan to guide the batter into shape. Let it colour golden on one side, and place on a plate with the fried side down. Sprinkle with a little caster sugar. Repeat to make the rest of the pancakes, stacking each one on top of the first and sprinkling a little sugar before adding the next layer. If you bake them thin enough, you should get 12 pancakes out of this batter. For a higher cake of 24 layers, simply double the recipe.

Place the last pancake on the stack with the fried side up. Serve with sack sauce (see page 339). A squeeze of lemon won't hurt either and will cut through the rich flavour.

These pancakes are also delicious fried on both sides, as we have our normal pancakes, although they have a slightly more savoury note than regular pancakes today.

batter puddings

Curd Fritters

As I enjoy making cheese curd and using it in various dishes, curd fritters could not be missing from this book. The recipe below is from Eliza Smith and has been copied by Hannah Glasse in *The Art of Cookery* in 1747, along with many other of Eliza's recipes. It must have been good for Glasse to include it.

To make Curd Fritters.
Take a handful of curds, a handful of flour, ten eggs well beaten and strained, some sugar, some cloves, mace, nutmeg, and a little saffron; stir all well together, and fry them in very hot beef-dripping; drop them in the pan by spoonfuls; stir them about till they are of a fine yellow brown; drain them from the suet, and scrape sugar on them when you serve.
Eliza Smith, *The Compleat Housewife*, 1727

Serves 2 (makes 20–22 fritters)

1 litre (35 fl oz/4 cups) milk, yields about 220–240 g (7¾–8¾ oz) cheese curd

1 tablespoon buttermilk or lemon juice

2 teaspoons vegetable rennet

5 eggs

a pinch each of sugar, ground cloves, mace, grated nutmeg and saffron threads

20 g (¾ oz) plain (all-purpose) flour

butter or lard, for frying

Make the cheese curd by pouring the milk into a clean saucepan and heat to 37°C (98°F), otherwise known as body temperature or blood heat.

Turn down the heat and stir in the buttermilk or lemon juice, then the rennet in one large movement to spread it through the milk. Remove from the heat and allow to stand in the pan for 15–30 minutes until it has set, then transfer to a bowl lined with muslin (cheesecloth), tie the cloth at the top, and hang it up to drain for 5 hours. You can do this the day before, and keep the curds in the fridge.

To make the fritters, combine the cheese curd with the eggs and the spices and stir well. Now sift in the flour and whisk into a batter as for pancakes, yet slightly thicker.

Melt a generous knob of butter or lard in a heavy-based frying pan and scoop in the batter in small batches. Fry on both sides until golden.

Serve with fine sugar for a traditional flavour, with lemon juice, honey, or fresh or stewed fruit. A little raspberry vinegar (see page 338) would be very good too.

Instead of making your own cheese curds, substitute 240 g (8¾ oz) of unsalted ricotta cheese.

Jersey Wonders

Jersey wonders are not really wonders, but rather a traditional pudding from the island of Jersey made of twisted dough browned in lard. The housewives of Jersey would fry their wonders as the tide was going out. They believed that if they fried them on an incoming tide, the fat would overflow the pan. Today it is a favourite at Jersey's country fairs and many people on the island have recipes going back generations, all apparently similar.

This recipe is very easy; the only difficulty is turning the dough into the traditional twist without tearing it. Mary Jewry in her book *Warne's Model Cookery and Housekeeping Book* of 1868 gives us the recipe and explains how to turn the dough. It is, however, easier if you see someone do it rather than read Jewry's instructions.

> Work the sugar and butter together till quite soft, throw in the eggs that have been previously well beaten, and then add the flour and a little nutmeg, knead twenty minutes and let it rise; then roll it between your hands into round balls the size of a small potato, but do not add any more flour; flour your pasteboard lightly and roll out each ball into a thin oval the size of the hand, cut with a knife three slits like bars in the centre of the oval, cross the two centre ones with your fingers, and draw up the two sides between, put your finger through and drop into it boiling lard, which must be ready in a small stewpan. Turn them as they rise, and when a nice brown, take them up with a fork and lay them on a tray with paper underneath them.
> Mary Jewry, *Warne's Model Cookery and Housekeeping Book*, 1868

Modern recipes often use double the amount of sugar that is used in the traditional recipes; this doesn't surprise me but I have chosen to stay true to the traditional measurements Mary Jewry gives in her book, using a little less butter to make the dough easier to handle. Apparently it isn't traditional to dust sugar over these fritters, but I do think a light dusting improves them and makes them look very festive.

110 g (3¾ oz) raw caster
    (superfine) sugar

200 g (7 oz) unsalted butter,
    softened

3 large eggs

a pinch of ground nutmeg

450 g (1 lb/3 cups) plain
    (all-purpose) flour

lard, tallow or oil, for frying

Jersey wonders

Beat the sugar and butter together thoroughly until pale and fluffy, then add the eggs one at a time and combine well. Stir in the nutmeg.

Add the flour bit by bit and, once the dough becomes stiff, turn it out on a lightly floured work surface and knead for about 20 minutes. Wrap the dough in plastic wrap and chill in the fridge for at least 30 minutes.

Cut off a 40 g (1½ oz) piece of dough or, as Jewry states, the size of a small potato. (Jersey is famous for its Jersey Royal potatoes, after all.)

Roll the piece of dough into a ball and then use a rolling pin to flatten it into an oval shape about 4 mm (³⁄₁₆ inch) thick. To make the knots, use a small sharp knife to cut 3 even slits lengthways in the centre of the disc, and twist the top end of the oval through the middle slit.

When you are ready to fry the wonders out of these Jerseys, melt some lard, tallow or oil in a deep-fryer or heavy-based frying pan, making sure you have enough to cover the dough.

Have a tray ready, lined with paper towel to absorb the fat from frying. When the fat or oil is hot – 190°C (375°F) or when a cube of bread dropped into the oil turns golden brown in 10 seconds is good – carefully place a wonder in the lard and fry until browned but still blushing golden. You can fry a couple of wonders at the same time, but make sure they don't stick together, or stick to the frying basket, if you are using one.

I like to dust them with icing (confectioners') sugar, but traditionally they should be served plain.

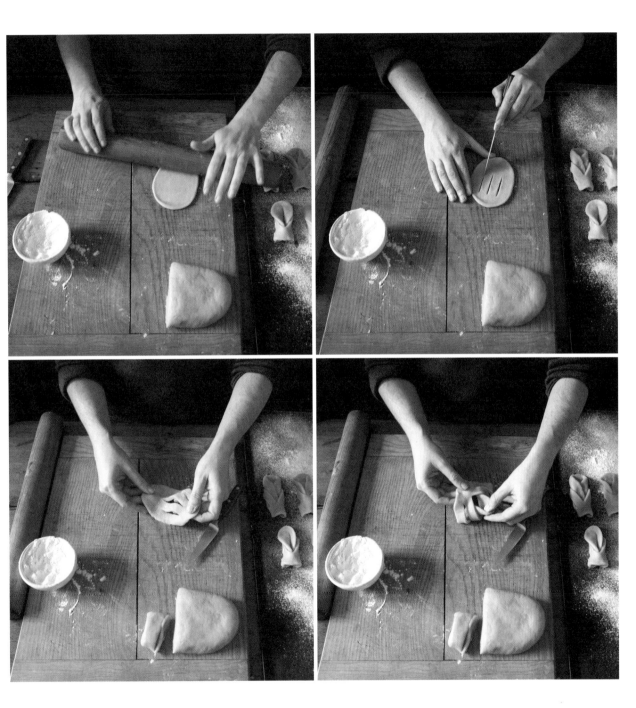

CHAPTER 4

BREAD PUDDINGS

Bread puddings

They are versatile, our bread puddings. Bread-and-butter style puddings are baked, eggy bread puddings are fried, charlottes are either baked in a mould layered with bread, or left to set in a bread or sponge-cake casing. Summer pudding, for example, is made by putting berries – or other juicy fruits if you like – into a mould lined with thick slices of white bread. It is left to rest to soak up all the wonderful juices and is one of those puddings that used to be a popular dish to serve to those who were poorly.

As I mentioned in the introduction to the chapter on baked puddings, many bread puddings are baked, but not all of them are. That is why they get their very own chapter. I've chosen not to include puddings containing breadcrumbs in the bread pudding category, although they have been in the past. I do not believe that, for example, a carrot pudding – despite containing a large quantity of breadcrumbs – is a bread pudding. That pudding fits in much better with the baked pudding category.

To argue that bread puddings are called thus because they are a way to use stale bread is also not a requirement. Some puddings call for fresh bread or day-old bread rather than stale. When making bread puddings, the quality of the bread is paramount. I'm not being snobby here; if you make these puddings your bread shouldn't contain any nasty additives. Flour, water, yeast and salt; that is all. If using brioche you are allowed some milk and sugar.

Back home in Flanders we only have one bread pudding, so if you speak of bread pudding, it always refers to that particular pudding. It is usually made by bakeries from their leftover bread. Raisins and spices are added, and the bread pudding gets a topping of chocolate or plain sugar icing. I used to love the bread pudding from our local market vendor; he made his bread pudding from leftover raisin buns and to this day I have never found any other bread pudding that can rival it.

The city of Aalst in Belgium also has a pudding that they call 'vlaai', which is in essence another word for pudding. They make this Aalster vlaai from old 'mastellen' (cinnamon buns), broken up and soaked in spiced milk, then baked. There is no bread involved, but one could argue that the peperkoek, which is a spiced cake similar to gingerbread, could in fact be categorised as a type of bread.

As with baked puddings, the oldest bread puddings were often prepared in a Dutch oven in the embers of a fire. The Devonshire white-pot (see page 232) is a prime example of that. Today and in the last century, the pudding was and is prepared in a regular oven. The result is scrumptious but I implore you to try placing the pudding in a Dutch oven on top of the embers of a barbecue. If you have a deep lid, you can place some of the embers on top of the oven so there is heat on top of the pudding too. The pudding that comes out of that cast-iron pot is the same, yet the fire and its unpredictable heat will caramelise sugars and maybe even slightly burn bits to give the pudding a rustic and primitive identity. In the oven it will bake nice and evenly, but

bread puddings |

in the fire it will get sudden kicks of heat and the dough will spring in the butter or fat making it look rather interesting and anything but uniform when you open the lid. As always, be careful with fire, but do give it a go to taste how this pudding might have tasted hundreds of years ago when we didn't have the luxury of fancy ovens with thermostats.

Pain Pur-dew

Pain pur-dew (pain perdu), or 'lost bread', is also known as 'eggy bread' in Britain. Its French name has led many to assume it is a French dish; it is, in fact, a dish that appears simultaneously in many European cookery books in medieval times.

In the fourteenth century a recipe 'pour faire tostees dorees' (to make golden toast) appears in the French book *Le Viandier de Taillevent*. Around 1450 a virtually identical recipe appears in the Italian *Libro de Arte Coquinaria* (by Martino de Rossi), adding rosewater and saffron to the mixture. The earliest recipe I could find for pain pur-dew in an English manuscript dates from around 1420 and can be found in Thomas Austin's collection (*Two Fifteenth-century Cookery-books*, 1964): it is identical in mode of preparation but, like the French version, omits the rosewater and saffron. This is not to say these flavourings weren't added. They might just have been in such common usage that they were not mentioned in the instructions.

> Payn pur-dew. – Take fayre jolkys of Eyroun, & trye hem fro þe whyte, & draw hem þorw a straynoure, & take Salt and caste þer-to; þan take fayre brede, & kytte it as troundej rounde; þan take fayre Boter þat is claryfiyd, or ellys fayre Freysshe grece, & putte it on a potte, & make it hote; þan take & wete wyl þin troundej in þe jolkys, & putte hem in þe panne, an so frye hem vppe; but ware of cleuyng to þe panne; & whan it is fryid, ley hem on a dysshe, & ley Sugre y-nowe þer-on, & þanne serue it forht.
> Thomas Austin, ed., *Two Fifteenth-century Cookery-books*

For the earliest recipe known to man, we have to go back to around the fourth century CE. In the Roman cookery book Apicius: *De Re Coquinaria* we find a recipe that is simply named 'another sweet dish'. The only difference is that the bread is soaked in milk and fried in olive oil. Eggs aren't mentioned, but scholars know that often in Apicius, as in other manuscripts, recipes weren't complete because things were left out that were common knowledge or because they were badly copied from earlier texts.

Serves 2

four 1 cm (⅜ inch) thick
   slices of day-old white bread
   or brioche, not stale

50 g (1¾ oz) clarified butter

4 egg yolks, beaten

1 teaspoon rosewater
   (optional)

sugar or honey, to serve

Remove the crusts from the bread if you like, although I prefer to leave them on. Heat a frying pan that is large enough to hold the pieces of bread over medium heat.

Use a pastry brush to brush the bread all over with the clarified butter, then put it in the pan and fry on both sides until golden.

Put the beaten egg yolks into a deep plate and add rosewater if you want to use it. Dip the fried bread in the egg so that it is nicely coated. Return the bread to the pan and fry until the egg is cooked.

Serve with sugar strewn over it, or with a drizzle of honey as the Romans would have done.

You can use whole eggs, which I tend to do. Otherwise I end up with containers and freezer bags full of egg whites I forget to use. Simply use 2 large eggs instead of 4 egg yolks.

bread puddings |

Poor Knights of Windsor

Although this seems like a pain perdu, 'Poor knights of Windsor' is a different dish that evolved from the same Roman recipe. Poor knights has sweet spices, such as nutmeg, added to the pudding. White bread is soaked in cream then fried until golden with eggs and nutmeg, and served sprinkled with fine sugar and cream.

The origin of the name is a bit of a mystery: similar dishes throughout northern Europe have the name 'poor knights', such as the dish 'köyhät ritarit' in Finland, or 'Arme Ritter' in Germany, which is a pain pur-dew today but in *Das Buch von guter Speise* from the fourteenth century, however, the dish is not titled 'Arme Ritter' but 'a good dish'. It was a pie made with layers of chicken and fried and battered bread – which the book calls 'armeritlere' (from which the name Arme Ritter is derived) – and slices of apple and spices.

The earliest English recipe in *The Compleat Cook* (by W.M., 1658) suggests to serve the pudding with rosewater, sugar and butter. The recipe remains unchanged until at least 1723, as John Nott's recipe (*The Cooks and Confectioners Dictionary*) is virtually identical. By the mid-nineteenth century the same dish is served with a wine sauce by J.H. Walsh in *The English Cookery Book*. Strangely enough, the pudding doesn't appear in any of my Victorian pudding books.

> To make poore knights.
> Cut two penny loaves in round slices, dip them in half a pint of Cream or faire water, then lay them abroad in a dish, and beat three Eggs and grated Nutmegs and sugar, beat them with the Cream then melt some butter in a frying pan, and wet the sides of the toasts and lay them in on the wet side, then pour in the rest upon them, and so fry them, serve them in with Rosewater, sugar and butter.
> W.M., *The Compleat Cook*, 1658

The Scottish Mrs Frazer is the first person I can find to call the pudding 'poor knights of Windsor', in her book *The Practice of Cookery* (1791). She was a cookery teacher in Edinburgh and successor to Mrs MacIver who also left us an interesting book (*Mrs MacIver's Cookery*, 1773) to read. Frazer soaks her slices of bread first in white wine and sugar before dipping them in egg yolk and frying them. She serves the pudding with sugar and cinnamon strewn over it.

The Poor Knights of Windsor, established in 1352, were originally a number of mendicant military veterans attached to the Order of the Garter, who were fed and housed at Windsor Castle in return for saying daily prayers for the sovereign and his successors, and for the Knights of the Order of the Garter. The Military Knights of Windsor still exist as military pensioners and participate in the pageantry of the Order of the Garter today.

Ambrose Heath, in *Good Sweets*, 1937 soaked the bread of his poor knights of Windsor in sherry, and served the fried bread with a butter, sherry and sugar sauce, which has been a favourite pudding sauce for centuries (see Sack sauce, page 339). His pudding was clearly inspired by Mrs Frazer's recipe.

The next change to the recipe for this pudding was made by one of the most-loved modern English food writers, Jane Grigson, in her *English Food* in 1974. She added fresh raspberries and whipping cream, but leaves out the eggs.

As I said in my recipe for pain pur-dew, the quality of the bread is very important and should be the best you can afford. I suggest using day-old bread, but when it is two days old it will work even better. When bread goes dry, it keeps its shape better when soaking and frying.

I like to serve this dish with a sack sauce, as Heath suggests, and add raspberries, as in Jane Grigson's book. It truly makes this a very luxurious and festive breakfast dish.

Poor knights of Windsor

Serves 2

175 ml (5½ fl oz/⅔ cup) thick (double) cream

1 tablespoon caster (superfine) sugar

four 1 cm (⅜ inch) thick slices of day-old white bread or brioche, not stale

50 g (1¾ oz) clarified butter

4 egg yolks, beaten

1 quantity Sack sauce (see page 339)

Raspberry compote

500 g (1 lb 2 oz/4 cups) raspberries

125 g (4½ oz) raw sugar, processed to a fine powder in a food processor

¼ teaspoon ground cinnamon

To make the compote, sprinkle the raspberries with the sugar and cinnamon. Allow to stand until they produce some liquid and look like a slightly runny whole-fruit jam. Taste and add more cinnamon and sugar if necessary, but you want to keep some of the tartness of the fruit.

Meanwhile, whip the cream and add caster sugar to taste, but no more than 1 tablespoon or it becomes too sweet.

Remove the crusts from the bread if you like, I prefer to leave them on. Heat a frying pan that is large enough to hold the pieces of bread over medium heat. Use a pastry brush to brush the bread all over with the clarified butter, then fry on both sides until golden.

Whisk the egg yolks and dip the fried bread in them before returning the bread to the pan to fry briefly until the egg has set.

Meanwhile, reheat the sack sauce.

Place 2 slices of fried bread on a plate, pour the sack sauce over, then scoop on some of the raspberry compote and finally the whipped cream. Enjoy with a smile, as your day is bound to be great with a breakfast like this.

If you want to try Mrs Frazer's and Ambrose Heath's version of this dish, simply add some sherry or white wine to the egg yolks and proceed. If you prefer to use whole eggs rather than only the yolks, use 2 whole eggs.

Devonshire White-pot

Recipes for white-pots appear in most seventeenth and eighteenth century cookery books. 'Pot' meant pudding in Devon dialect but, after a while, the pudding became connected to Devon in name too. Gervase Markham mentions, in his early seventeenth century book *The English Huswife*, that pots are puddings in the West Country. A Devonshire white-pot is a sweet, buttery bread pudding – though sometimes rice is used – set with custard and layered with raisins or other dried fruits. It is usually flavoured with sugar and lightly spiced with nutmeg and sometimes mace. The bread was either used in slices, or as breadcrumbs. Some recipes call for soaking the bread then whisking it with the egg and cream mixture while others say to lay the bread in the basin and pour the egg and cream mixture over it. Yet another version is made by making layers of bread, fruit and spices, and then covering it with the egg and cream mixture.

> To make a Devonshire White-pot.
> Take a pint of Cream and straine four Eggs into it, and put a little Salt and a little sliced Nutmeg, and season it with Sugar somewhat sweet; then take almost a penny Loaf of fine bread sliced very thin, and put it into a Dish that will hold it, the Cream and the Eggs being put to it; then take a handfull of Raisins of the Sun being boyled, and a little sweet Butter, so bake it.
> W.M., *The Compleat Cook*, 1658

The eighteenth century book, *The Ladies Companion* (1743), has a chapter on white-pots: it is tiny, with just two recipes, but apparently the author found it important enough to place these two recipes under a separate heading. One white-pot is made in a puff pastry base, while the other is made with rice.

Another white-pot version comes from Yorkshire. Place a layer of bread in the basin, then add thinly cut slices of apple, a layer of spices and raisins, then the bread again until your basin is full, then pour the egg and cream mixture over. This was a recipe originally from 1769, given by May Byron in her fabulous book, *Pot-luck* (1932), a collection of regional recipes of Britain. Sadly, she does not mention the sources of her recipes, only that they come from family manuscript books, so it is hard to track down the originals.

This pudding is best with day-old bread, not stale but not super-fresh.

 Cooking over a fire? Use the Dutch oven method:
Place the pudding basin on a trivet in the base of the Dutch oven and cover with the lid. Fire the coals and let them go grey, then stand the oven on a trivet over the coals and place some of the coals on the Dutch oven lid. You can use a barbecue for this: just place the grill plate close to the coals and set the Dutch oven on top. As fire is unpredictable I can't give you an exact cooking time, but check after 30 minutes: if the pudding isn't already well on its way, the coals aren't hot enough and you will have to add some new ones. Use your intuition for this.

Makes 1 pudding in a 16 cm (6¼ inch/No. 36) basin (mould)

butter, softened, for spreading and greasing

500 ml (17 fl oz/2 cups) thick (double) cream

½ teaspoon freshly grated nutmeg

a pinch of salt

2 large eggs

1 large egg yolk

40 g (1½ oz) raw sugar

1 loaf of white bread (stale brioche works well), sliced

100 g (3½ oz) raisins or currants, soaked in water or rum overnight

Preheat the oven to 140°C (275°F). Generously grease the pudding basin with butter.

Put the cream in a medium saucepan with the nutmeg and salt and bring to a simmer, then remove from the heat and allow to stand for a minute or two. In a bowl, whisk the eggs and egg yolk with the sugar and gradually add the warm cream a little at a time, whisking constantly, to make a custard. Let the custard cool slightly, while you take the crusts off the slices of bread, and butter them on one side only.

Begin the layering of the pudding by placing the first piece of bread, butter side down, in the basin, then adding a layer of currants or raisins, followed by a layer of bread until the basin is filled halfway.

Now pour in half the custard and continue making layers of bread and fruit until the basin is almost filled, with room for one more layer of bread. Pour in the remaining custard.

Finally place the last layer of bread, leaving a small hole for the steam to get out. Place the pudding basin on a trivet in a Dutch oven or cast-iron ovenproof pot and cover with the lid.

Bake in the middle of the oven for 30–40 minutes until the bread is a beautiful golden brown.

Serve with vanilla ice cream, or icy cream (see page 320), or clotted cream (see page 336), which is always a winner.

bread puddings

Apple Charlotte

The apple charlotte is a relative of the summer pudding (see page 242). Both are puddings made in a mould lined with slices of bread, and both hold some kind of fruit. It is said that the apple charlotte is named after Queen Charlotte, the wife of King George III, who might have been the patron of the apple growers.

Some have claimed this pudding was invented by the French chef Carême in 1802, and that he published a recipe for 'charlotte a la parisienne' and later changed it to 'charlotte russe' when he worked for Tsar Alexander of Russia; however, in that same year a recipe for charlotte of apples was published by John Mollard (*The Art of Cookery Made Easy and Refined*, 1802). Moreover, Carême only published his first book in 1815, not 1802, and as far as I know the pudding does not appear in it. In 1802 Carême was an 18-year-old apprentice, working for a pastry chef who encouraged him to learn to read and write. Hardly a time at which he would write a book.

Although the earliest recipe in print I could find is John Mollard's, it is very possible this pudding did appear earlier in manuscript recipe books. What we do know is that it is more likely that the apple charlotte is an English invention after all.

> Charlotte of apples.
> Stew some apples with a bit of fresh butter, a little syrup of quinces, half a pound of apricot jam, and half a gill of brandy; rub all through a hair-sieve, add a few dried cherries, and put into a mould lined with bread cut in diamonds of four inches square and half an inch thick, and previously dipped in oiled butter. Cover with slices of bread, likewise dipped in butter, bake of a light colour, and sift sugar over.
> John Mollard, *The Art of Cookery Made Easy and Refined*, 1802

John Mollard instructs the cook to make a pulp of apples, stewed with brandy, a little quince syrup, apricot jam and dried cherries. Mary Eaton, in *The Cook and Housekeeper's Dictionary* (1822), uses thinly sliced apples, layered with butter and a little sugar until the mould is full. Mollard tells us to dip the bread in butter, while Eaton omits that step.

bread puddings |

*Makes enough for 1 charlotte
mould or 16 x 10 x 7.5 cm
(6¼ x 4 x 3 inch) loaf (bar) tin*

3 cooking apples, such as
granny smith or bramley,
about 500 g (1 lb 2 oz),
peeled and cored

5 tablespoons apricot jam

60 ml (2 fl oz/¼ cup) brandy
or dark rum

1 loaf of stale plain white
bread, about 550 g
(1 lb 4 oz)

50 g (1¾ oz) butter, melted

sugar, for sprinkling

Preheat the oven to 190°C (375°F). Generously grease the
mould or loaf tin with butter and place a disc or strip of baking
paper in the bottom.

Chop up the apples and put them in a saucepan with the
apricot jam and brandy. Cook until soft and pulpy. You might
need a splash of water to prevent the apples from burning.
Allow to cool in the pan.

Cut thick slices of bread in 5 cm (2 inch) wide rectangles the
same height as the side of the mould and use a pastry brush to
generously coat them with the melted butter.

Place the bread in the mould, overlapping the edges a little so
there are no gaps. Finally put a disc or strip of bread onto the
bottom of the mould, making sure there are no gaps.

Scoop the apple mixture into the bread-lined mould, then
close the top with a final few slices of buttered bread and
sprinkle some sugar on top.

Bake in the middle of the oven for 30–40 minutes until golden
brown, as you prefer your toast. When ready to serve, turn the
mould onto a plate and allow to stand for 5 minutes before
attempting to remove the mould.

Serve with clotted cream (see page 336), brown bread ice
cream (see page 323), vanilla ice cream, or custard sauce (see
page 338) for the custard lovers.

Bread-and-butter Pudding

Recipes for bread-and-butter pudding are plenty in vintage cookbooks, and all very similar. This is one of my favourites to make with leftover buns. You can use hot cross buns, bath buns, Sally Lunns, cinnamon buns, all kinds of buns. If the bun doesn't contain spices or currants, I'd recommend you add some to the custard. Currants, dates, raisins and cranberries all work well. You can also go classic and use regular stale bread, or leftover raisin bread, or panettone.

Makes enough for two 20 cm (8 inch) enamel pie dishes, or one large one

butter, for greasing and spreading

2–3 stale, but not rock-hard, hot cross buns, or 2 slices of bread cut unto small triangles

25 g (1 oz) currants, soaked in water or rum overnight (optional)

350 ml (12 fl oz) milk

50 ml (1¾ fl oz) thick (double) cream

1 mace blade

2 tablespoons light brown sugar

4 egg yolks or 2 whole eggs

2 teaspoons sugar, to sprinkle

Preheat the oven to 180°C (350°F). Grease the pie dishes generously with butter.

Cut the buns into 1 cm (⅜ inch) thick slices and butter each slice on one side. Or, for a more rustic pud, just halve the buns if they are not that big.

Arrange a layer of bun slices, or bread, buttered side up, in the bottom of the dishes. If using currants, scatter them over the top of the buns.

To make the custard, gently warm the milk, cream, mace and light brown sugar in a small saucepan over low heat. Whisk the eggs in a bowl, add a little of the warm milk mixture to the eggs and whisk well, before gradually adding the rest of the milk mixture, whisking constantly.

Pour the custard over the prepared bun or bread layer and sprinkle with the sugar.

Bake in the middle of the oven for 20–25 minutes until the custard has set and the tops are nicely golden brown.

Serve with brown bread ice cream (see page 323) or vanilla ice cream, or clotted cream (see page 336).

Summer Pudding

A summer pudding is a delightfully light pudding which is made by lining a pudding basin or charlotte mould with stale white bread slices, then filling it up with lightly stewed summer fruits and topping it off with a juice-soaked bread lid. I always enjoy unmoulding this pudding, to see how the blank white slices of bread have been tinted by the deep crimson juice. It looks like a fresh red wine stain on a crisp white tablecloth. When ready to indulge, serve with cream, or ice cream, whichever you prefer.

This pudding was also known as a 'hydropathic pudding' and was all the rage in the health spas of the nineteenth century. Its light bread casing instead of pastry or a suet crust made it the perfect treat for the health-conscious ladies.

By the end of the nineteenth century the pudding began to be known as a summer pudding, although it doesn't appear in any of my pudding books of that period. I did, however, come across two recipes for summer pudding in newspapers from 1893.

In the only printed recipe I have been able to find for a hydropathic pudding, it suggested serving it with a custard, which doesn't sound very light and spa-approved at all. But the booklet was sponsored by the classic brand Bird's Custard, so we might have our answer there!

Hydropathic Pudding.
Line a greased pint basin with bread. Stew 1lb. of juice fruit with a little water, sweeten it, and while still very hot, put carefully into the basin. Cover the top entirely with bread, lay a plate on the pudding, and put a weight on the plate. Any juice that overflows should be kept to serve with the pudding. When perfectly cold and stiff, turn out, and serve with custard over.
The Liverpool Training School of Cookery, *Plain Cookery Recipes*, 1902

The most important factor in making this pudding excellent is to use the best-quality white bread you can get your hands on. Cheap bread full of unnecessary additives will turn slimy and your pudding will certainly collapse. When the best products are used, the outcome is always outstanding. Any kind of summer fruit should do: raspberries and redcurrants are traditional, blackberries can mix it up a little, but strawberries should be avoided as they do not remain pleasant enough to enjoy after a couple of hours or a night of soaking.

*Makes enough for a 17 cm
(6½ inch/No. 30) basin
(mould); you could also use
a rectangular cake tin or
a charlotte mould*

650 g (1 lb 7 oz) raspberries

150 g (5½ oz) blackberries

100 g (3½ oz) redcurrants, or
  blueberries or frozen mixed
  berries

50 g (1¾ oz) raw sugar

1 loaf of plain white bread

Lightly grease the pudding basin and line with plastic wrap
so that the pudding will be easier to remove when soaked all
the way through. Leave enough plastic wrap overhanging the
edges of the basin to cover the pudding.

Toss all the berries into a saucepan and heat gently with
the sugar to get the crimson juices running, no longer than
2–3 minutes. When using frozen berries – which is fine and
far more economical – do the same, but they will need a little
longer to stew. Let the berries cool in the pan.

Cut a round out of a slice of your bread to fit the bottom of
the basin. Now cut the rest of the bread in 1 cm (⅜ inch)
thick slices – about 6 slices or as many as you need – and trim
them into a slight trapezium shape to fit the sloping edges of
the bowl. If your bowl is straight or you are using a cake tin or
charlotte mould, you don't need to fuss with cutting shapes,
just remove the crusts. On this occasion you really do need to
remove the crusts.

Line the basin or mould with the bread, making sure there
are no gaps, so the filling will stay in. Now spoon the cooled
berries into the bread-lined basin, reserving as much of the
juice in the saucepan as you can manage.

Cover the pudding with another slice or slices of bread and
pour over some of the reserved juice so the bottom is nicely
covered, nothing more. Reserve the remaining juice for serving.

Cover the pudding with the overhanging plastic wrap, then
place a plate or a lid on it and put a weight on top. A tin of
tomatoes is what I use.

Refrigerate overnight so the bread can soak up the juices nicely.
When ready to serve, open the plastic wrap, place a plate on
top of the basin or mould and invert.

Pour over the reserved juice and serve with more fresh berries,
vanilla ice cream, icy cream (see page 320) or whipped cream.

CHAPTER 5

JELLIES, MILK PUDDINGS & ICES

The pleasure of deception

Jellies are delicately set liquids, forced into a shape because they are otherwise shapeless. They can be beautifully transparent, or mystically opaque. They can be created in one or many colours, look dramatically majestic, entertainingly funny or romantic. Jellies can be embedded with, and display, fresh, preserved or candied fruits, or even a whole fish for theatrical effect. Flavour is entirely up to the creator and can be used to mislead the receiver. The card of deception has been played well, with cooks making jellies look like castles, scallops, or even bacon and eggs. And just like early puddings, jellies started as savoury dishes.

In medieval times, jellies were only the privilege of kings, queens and nobles because they demanded great skill and time. They were called 'gelé', or 'gelee' in Middle English and usually served with the 'pottage course'. Pigs' ears or feet, and later calves' feet, were used as a gelling agent. On the many fish days when the eating of meat was prohibited by the church, certain fish parts such as skin and bones were utilised. A strong fish stock was used to stew eels, plaice, stockfish and cod, which would be cooked until gelatinous. The stock, either from fish or meat, was then clarified using a woollen, probably flannel, jelly bag or 'jelly-poke'. *The Durham Manorial Accounts* (edited by J.T. Fowler, 1898) mention a jelly bag like this in 1516–17.

These earliest medieval jellies, however, did not have the ability to stand upright or be moulded into a shape, nice and wobbly, as we know them today. They were more like stews, or brawns when more set. By the fifteenth century jellies were made into shapes and a spectacular specimen was made for the installation feast of the Bishop Clifford in 1407, as reported in *A Noble Boke off Cookry* (ed. A. Napier, 1882). It featured a jelly-filled castle in the midst of a custard moat with a demon and a priest on it. Together with the sugar 'subtleties' made to look like temples and castles, these feasting tables must have been a testament to great splendour.

Clear jelly was also used to encase vegetables, meat and fish. I believe this is where the aspics of the eighteenth century had their beginning. Another type of jelly was made with almond milk, sweeteners and flavourings such as rosewater. These opaque jellies were called 'leach' or 'leche' and made to slice into shapes to create a design. Gervase Markham, in *The English Huswife* (1596), instructs us to cut the 'white leach' in squares and lay gold upon them. A gilded leach like this was also served at Henry VIII's Garter feast at Windsor in 1520, as reported by Elias Ashmole in *Institution, Laws, and Ceremonies of the Order of the Garter* (1672).

Recipes for 'leach' can, however, be found earlier. In fourteenth century manuscripts they still contained meat. *The Forme of Cury* (edited by Samuel Pegge, c. 1390) gives a recipe for 'Leche Lumbard': though not resembling a jelly at all, this dish is a meat loaf made to look like peas in a pod and served with a spiced raisin and almond milk sauce. Thomas Awkbarow's fifteenth century manuscript has a 'Leche Lumbard' that fits the name 'leach' better. The author instructs the cook to create layers of different-coloured mousses made of minced chicken or pork and almonds, mixed with eggs and white wine. A leach jelly like this would later be known as a 'ribbon jelly'.

jellies, milk puddings & ices

The invention of the gelling agent 'isinglass' in Russia is where we can place the birth of jelly as we know it today. Isinglass is derived from the swimming bladder of the sturgeon and was extremely expensive. By 1590 it was commonly used in elite kitchens; a contemporary recipe treats it as if it was common knowledge and doesn't include instructions. With the usage of isinglass it became possible to shape jellies using more elaborate moulds. The term jelly was now mostly used for sweet concoctions, although jellies incorporating savoury ingredients continued to exist. Sadly, no jelly moulds survive from the Tudor period, but we know they existed because contemporary writings describe moulded jellies. A Spanish priest named Francesco Chieregati was particularly impressed with the jellies served to him and his party at a great feast hosted by Henry VIII in 1517: 'but the jellies, of some twenty sorts perhaps, surpassed everything; they were made in the shape of castles and animals of various descriptions, as beautiful as can be imagined'. Luckily we always have contemporary diarists, letter writers and book authors to thank for lifting the veil of the sometimes foggy history of feasting tables long gone.

Not only animal-derived setting agents were used. Starches and gums were also commonplace to set jellies, leaches, flummeries and blancmanges. Arrowroot, semolina, tapioca, sago, rice, cornflour (cornstarch), bran, crushed biscuits and even bread were among the starches used. Rice and later cornflour were the usual ingredients for setting blancmange, while crushed bread and biscuits were often used for sickroom dishes.

Flummery was an opaque jelly made by steeping oats or bran in water overnight and then boiling the strained liquid with flavourings such as orange flower water or rosewater. The flummery was then transferred to a wooden or earthenware mould and left to set. Gervase Markham is one of the first to mention it in his 1615 book, *The English Huswife*: 'From this small Oat-meale, by oft steeping it in water and clensing it, and then boyling it to a thicke and stiffe jelly, is made that excellent dish of meat which is so esteemed in the West parts of this Kingdome, which they call Wash-brew, and in Chesheire and Lankasheire they call it Flamerie or Flumerie.' In Scotland and some northern regions of England this same dish was known as 'sowens'.

By the mid-seventeenth century, isinglass, hartshorn and ivory were sometimes added to give a firmer set to enable shaping of the flummery into even more novelty shapes. Hartshorn, which were the antlers of a young male deer, and ivory – elephant tusks – were both scraped and the dust used to set jellies and flummeries. Hartshorn jellies were thought to be restorative and were often made for the sickroom but were also eaten as an aphrodisiac and to strengthen male potency!

Another method of jelly-making can be found in William Rabisha's 1661 book, *The Whole Body of Cookery Dissected*, in which he gives instructions to create a tart of jelly and leach. He also provides a template in his book to create a pastry case that looks a lot like a stained-glass window. Templates for tarts and pies were often added to the books of that period and the century after.

Ribbon jellies, popular in the eighteenth century, are directly related to the medieval leach dish. They were either composed into chequered designs, as Charles Carter illustrates in *The Complete Practical Cook* in 1730, or made into layers in the dainty jelly glasses of the period. Shops were founded where people could order ready-made jellies and ice creams for their special occasion.

Jellies made into astronomical subjects or temples, as well as jellies made to look like something they were not, were very popular in Georgian England. The art of deception and imitation continues to impress dinner guests centuries after the medieval cockatrice and other fantastical creations. Mrs Raffald shares recipes in her book (*The Experienced English Housekeeper*, 1782) for flummery made to look like playing cards, a hen's nest with flummery eggs, fish ponds and an impressive Solomon's temple. As in the early days, counterfeit eggs were made to be eaten on fish days, although in Georgian times they were made just for the pleasure of dramatic effect.

During the nineteenth century, jellies were still reserved for the wealthiest households. The upper class would more often buy great splendid jellies for dinner parties and balls from the same shops as they would buy ice-cream puddings and ornamental cakes. Jelly moulds, previously produced in earthenware, were now also manufactured in tin-lined copper and tin and became much bigger than the ones produced in the eighteenth century. The moulds also became more elaborate in shape; or there were core moulds that were in the shape of an obelisk or pyramid in which an insert decorated with painted flowers or landscapes could be placed, which could be seen through the jelly to dazzle the guests. The higher the jelly, the better the wobble effect, which would always be entertaining at a dinner party.

Jellies remained labour-intensive and tedious to make from raw ingredients. Mass-produced gelatine was the answer and was advertised from the 1840s onwards. Cookery books aimed at the lower and lower–middle classes start to give instructions including their usage too. From the moment Mrs Beeton published her writings in the 1860s, the use of prepared isinglass and gelatine had become common. She gives 26 recipes for jellies in her book, but notes that jellies made with homemade gelling agents were far more delicate and much better in flavour than the prepared alternative, which often tasted like glue.

Eliza Acton, known and loved for hanging on to the days of splendour in the kitchen, still gives several recipes for jelly in her book (*Modern Cookery for Private Families*, 1845) that are worthy of any nobleman's table. Her instructions are always clear and her recipes illustrated with pen-and-ink drawings of different moulds. One particularly interesting jelly is her basket with oranges filled with jelly, garnished with aromatic myrtle leaves. The jellies were often eaten with savoy cakes or sponge cakes (see page 349).

Twentieth century jellies still took on fine shapes and the nineteenth century creamware moulds remained in production. Some are still made today, although on a smaller scale. It is true that after the two world wars, jellies and other foods were massively adulterated with chemical flavourings and stabilisers; powdered mixes were sold and in recent decades a children's party wouldn't be complete without frightfully coloured store-bought jellies. However, the classic jelly has seen a revival, with chefs using tiny jellies as flavour sensations in their dishes.

Much as you could order a novelty jelly from a jelly shop in the eighteenth century, today a company is again offering bespoke theatrical jellies for special occasions, movies and events. As with so many things, the circle is complete: we've gone from chemical-looking jellies in supermarkets back to elaborate and elegant looking temples, castles and domes made with quality products. Are you a brave enough cook to try your hand at unmoulding a jelly?

Blancmange

Mentioned in the prologue to Geoffrey Chaucer's *Canterbury Tales* (1475), this dish – the name of which means 'white food' – is one of the most international early dishes of European cuisine. From the Middle Ages onwards the name of this dish in its various forms – blanc mange, blanc manger, blamange, manjar branco, biancomangiare – can be found in most European cookery books.

Blancmange was a dish for the elite in the Middle Ages; its ingredients of rice, almonds, flavourings such as saffron and garnishes such as pomegranate were exotic and luxurious and only available to those with deep pockets. By the fifteenth century, however, many of these exotic goods, including rice, were being cultivated in Europe, making them more widely available – though still only among the higher tiers of society – rather than exclusively for the king's table.

It is believed by many food historians that the earliest recipe for blancmange dates back to the twelfth century. The first written recipe for it was found in a Danish cookbook possibly written by Henrik Harpestræng (*Libellus De Arte Coquinaria*), who died in 1244. A recipe for blancmange also features in one manuscript version of *The Forme of Cury* and in the edited version by Samuel Pegge (1390), there were two. By 1395, two recipes for blancmange can be found in the *Viandier* manuscripts, the first French cookbook: one is a dish for the sick, the other is a multicoloured dish, which is at odds with the name's literal meaning. Historian Terrence Scully (*The Art of Cookery in the Middle Ages*, 1995) believes the name might have meant 'bland food' instead of 'white food', which could also explain why the dish often pops up in the chapters for food for the sick. Scully also believes that the humoral properties of the main ingredients – chicken, capon or fish, almonds and rice – were thought by medieval physicians to be beneficial to health.

The different blancmange recipes of the Middle Ages feature the basic dish made with minced chicken or capon meat, and the Lenten blancmange which substitutes white fish for the meat. Then there was the fancy decorative blancmange, made in different colours and garnished with pomegranate seeds or flowers to become a decoration for the table.

A Catalan-style blancmange is recorded in 1475 in Bartolomeo Platina's *De Honesta Voluptate*, which is considered the first printed cookbook. However, for the recipe to be recorded in a book means that it most probably had been around for years before. This Catalan version was made with rice rather than rice flour, which made it more of a porridge-like pudding, similar to a rice pudding perhaps. Blancmange was a very popular dish in Italy and featured on a lot of feast menus.

Blancmange tarts

In seventeenth century recipes, cooks start using egg whites and breadcrumbs, but the traditional recipes appear alongside them. Robert May, in 1660 (*The Accomplisht Cook*), even suggests to pour the blancmange mixture into pastry casings so they look like tarts. He gives two templates for the design.

jellies, milk puddings & ices

CORN FLOUR BLANC-MANGE
BROWN & POLSON'S.

2½ozs. (5 level tablespoonfuls) Corn Flour "Patent" quality. 2 pints good sweet milk. Mix Corn Flour well with a little of the milk. Heat the rest of the milk to boiling point. Pour Corn Flour into heated milk, stirring well. Add a teaspoonful of butter and pinch of salt; Boil and stir well for 10 minutes (by the clock) Sugar and flavour, if desired, but served with stewed fruit, jam or marmalade is better. Pour into this mould, and cool. Re-heat gently in mould, if desired, before the fire or in oven. Then turn out and serve, cold or hot.

The end of the original

From the eighteenth century, the dish was usually set with hartshorn or isinglass, from the bladder of a sturgeon, instead of using rice or rice flour. This method was also used for making flummery and so blancmange and flummery became more or less the same dish. The puddings were now being moulded into shapes thanks to the increasing availability of ceramic moulds that were being produced by English potteries. Previously they had more often been served in shallow dishes, or turned out of those dishes onto a plate and decorated.

A blancmange that was made by adding egg yolks to the mixture, along with white wine and the juice of seville oranges, appeared in an eighteenth century cookery book. The dish was called a 'jaune mange' (yellow food). Despite its French name, it hasn't been spotted in French recipe collections and I know food historian Ivan Day has been looking for one for some time now. In the nineteenth century the blancmange was made with cornflour and the brand Brown & Polson created moulds with their 'Corn Flour Blanc-Mange' recipe printed on them.

School dinners

The latest version of the blancmange is the sweet dish that evolved in the nineteenth century. From this time, cornflour (cornstarch) or gelatine was added and, as food manufacturing progressed, blancmange powder was born. Artificial colouring and flavours made it so that the dish that once graced the tables of kings and queens became the muted-coloured dessert that began to be disliked for its stodgy texture and often bland flavour. In the 1950s it was served at the conclusion of the school dinner and it is engraved on many people's memories with such horror that most of them banished it from their lives forever. Little did these children know that this hated dish used to be something quite dainty and luxurious and the privilege of kings and queens.

Blancmange made with meat or fish is no longer eaten in Europe; however, a sweet blancmange made from chicken breast is very popular in Turkey. They call it 'tavuk göğsü'; the name literally means 'chicken breast' and some claims are made that it used to be served to the sultans of the Ottoman Empire in the Topkapi Palace.

What makes blancmange a dish worth recreating for the table today is that it is one of the few medieval dishes that have survived through the ages.

Blancmange

The original recipe reproduced below is the earliest in the English language. It uses capon meat, almonds, rice, sugar and salt. The blancmange was then decorated with red comfits: probably candied or dried fruits, such as dried pomegranate seeds, and roasted almonds.

Blank maunger. Tak capouns and seeth hem thenne tak hem up, take almaundes blaunched, grynde hem & alye hem up with the same broth, cast the mylke in a pot, waysche rys & do therto & lat is seeth, thanne tak brawne of capouns, tere it smal and do therto, take white grece, suger & salt & cast therinne, lat hit seeth, thanne messe hit forth and florysche it with anyes in confyt rede other whyte & with almaundes y fryed in oyle.
The Forme of Cury, c. 1390

Lenten versions using fish were given in most early books alongside the white meat blancmange as well. The fish used were pike, tench, lamprey and even lobster. If you'd like to make a fish version, just replace the chicken with an equal amount of poached fish fillet or lobster meat.

Serves 6–8

2 chicken breast fillets, about 300 g (10½ oz) in total

750 ml (26 fl oz/3 cups) chicken stock

30 g (1 oz) blanched almonds

1 teaspoon rosewater

150 g (5½ oz) arborio rice

400 ml (14 fl oz) milk

1 teaspoon butter

a pinch of sugar

a pinch of salt

Decoration

1 tablespoon vegetable oil

1 handful of blanched almonds

In a large saucepan, poach the chicken in the stock until cooked through. Remove the chicken from the stock and set it aside to cool.

Grind the almonds with the rosewater using a mortar and pestle and add to the stock, bringing it to the boil again. Rinse the rice under running water, and let it drain. Now add the rice to the stock, pour in the milk and boil until the rice is soft. Keep an eye on it so it doesn't burn and stick to the bottom of the pan.

Meanwhile, purée the poached chicken in a food processor and add it to the rice, then purée the rice and chicken together. Stir in the butter and add sugar and salt to taste.

Heat the vegetable oil in a frying pan and toss in the blanched almonds. Fry until brown on both sides. Scoop the blancmange into a shallow dish and decorate with the fried almonds.

This dish works well as a kind of dip like hummus, to eat with flatbread or crackers.

Strawberry Blancmange

This dish was simply referred to as 'Strawberry' in the fifteenth century cookery manuscript where I found it. It was listed along with the same dishes all using different flavourings, such as violets, primroses and red roses. However, when making this pudding it becomes clear that this is the ancestor of the modern blancmange, made without meat and using cornflour (cornstarch) as a thickener along with all kinds of flavourings.

Strawberye
Take Strawberys & waysshe hem in tyme of yere in gode red wyne; than strayne thorwe a clothe, & do hem in a potte with gode Almaunde mylke, a-lay it with Amyndoun other with the flowre of Rys, & make it chargeaunt, and lat it boyle, and do ther in Roysonys of coraunce, Safroun, Pepir, Sugre grete plente, pouder Gyngere, Canel, Galyngale; poynte it with Vynegre, & a lytil whyte grece put therto; coloure it with Alkenade, & droppe it a-bowte, plante it with the graynes of Pome-garnad, & than serve it forth
Thomas Austin ed., *Two Fifteenth-century Cookery-books*, 1888

This delicate pudding is one that I enjoy making the most of all the later medieval puddings. It has the power to intrigue people with its look and flavour. In the fifteenth century and earlier, the strawberries were of a different variety which can mostly be compared to European native wild strawberries. If you have a large quantity of these delightful little berries in your garden, you can re-create this dish with them. Otherwise, I suggest you use the smallest strawberries you can find.

The spices used in this recipe are typically those of medieval times. These days, some – such as galingale – might be difficult to find, but you can easily leave it out. By stewing this pudding, the colour gets quite bland; so, as the original recipe also suggests, you can colour it more brightly. I use beetroot powder, which is completely natural.

jellies, milk puddings & ices

6 small individual basins,
teacups or fancy moulds. Not
suitable for a large mould.

250 g (9 oz) strawberries,
hulled

100 ml (3½ fl oz) full-bodied
red wine, such as a merlot
(enough to cover the berries)

¼ teaspoon ground ginger

¼ teaspoon ground cinnamon

¼ teaspoon saffron threads

a pinch of pepper

40 g (1½ oz) raw sugar

40 g (1½ oz) rice flour

1 tablespoon unsalted butter

1 teaspoon red wine vinegar

2 tablespoons currants

1 tablespoon dried
pomegranate seeds

Almond milk

20 g (¾ oz) blanched almonds

½ teaspoon rosewater

250 ml (9 fl oz/1 cup) boiling
water

Strawberry blancmange

The day before, make the almond milk by grinding the
almonds with the rosewater using a mortar and pestle then
adding boiling water. Set aside to steep overnight for the
flavours to develop.

Immerse the strawberries in the red wine and soak them for
a minimum of 30 minutes, preferably overnight.

On the day of making, discard the wine (or drink it, or use
it for jelly-making, as it has a nice flavour). Purée the soaked
strawberries. Strain and pour the almond milk into a medium
saucepan. Bring to the boil and add the strawberry purée, all
the spices, the sugar and the rice flour.

When it starts to thicken, remove from the heat and add the
butter and vinegar followed by the currants. Combine well. If
the pudding seems too runny, you may add another teaspoon
of rice flour, dissolved in a little water.

Allow the mixture to cool slightly, then pour it into the moulds
or cups and put them in the fridge. Before serving, decorate
with dried pomegranate seeds if you can find them; otherwise
use fresh, or leave them out.

*If you want to turn the pudding out of the moulds, you need to
add an extra tablespoon of rice flour so it will thicken enough
to keep its shape. The original recipe doesn't use a mould, so you
can just as easily serve it in a dish as was intended by the author
in the fifteenth century.*

Jaune Mange

This recipe uses seville orange juice, while others recommend lemon and lemon peel. Later recipes by J.H. Walsh in *The British Cookery Book* (1864) instruct the cook to use sherry or 'raisin-wine'. Because the eggs give this jaune mange a set already, you don't need to use as much gelatine as you would for a blancmange.

Jaune Mange

Boil one ounce of isinglass three quarters of a pint of water, till melted, strain it; add the juice of two Seville oranges, a quarter of a pint of white wine, the yolks of four eggs, beaten and strained, sugar to the taste; stir it over a gentle fire till it just boils up; when cold put it into a mould or moulds; if there should be any sediment, take care not to pour it in.

Charlotte Mason, *The Lady's Assistant*, 1773

Makes enough for a fancy 400 ml (14 fl oz) mould

220 ml (7½ fl oz) white wine

1 teaspoon sugar

3 egg yolks

4 gelatine leaves

juice of 2 seville oranges

In a small saucepan, bring the wine and sugar to a simmer. In a separate bowl, whisk the egg yolks. Soak the gelatine leaves in the orange juice until soft.

Begin whisking the warm wine mixture into the egg yolks, followed by the soaked gelatine and juice. Allow to cool but not set, then pour into the mould and allow to set for 6 hours or overnight. The smaller the mould, the shorter the setting time.

To unmould, wet one of your hands and use it to loosen the jelly. Allow the jelly to slide out onto a wet plate (if the plate is wet, you can easily move the jelly around if necessary).

Almond Flummery

The original flummery was made by steeping oats or bran in water overnight and then straining the liquid to use. In the eighteenth century blancmange became known as flummery and it became more common to make it using a combination of sweet almonds – which are regular almonds – and bitter almonds, which come from a different type of almond tree and contain the poisonous substance cyanide. To prevent poisoning, the skins of the bitter almonds had to be completely removed. Because bitter almonds can be dangerous, apricot kernels are usually used to re-create these dishes today. They have a nearly identical flavour and you won't accidentally make yourself ill.

The almonds are blanched and have their skins removed, then they are crushed with rosewater using a mortar and pestle to keep the nuts from going rancid. When you crush bitter almonds or apricot kernels with rosewater you will immediately notice the marzipan scent. This is a chemical reaction and the substance you can smell is called benzaldehyde. You can also find it in the Italian liqueur amaretto and in amaretti biscuits; however, almond extract is usually used these days to work around using bitter almonds or apricot kernels, but unless you find an all-natural version, you are dealing with a chemical flavouring. Buy apricot kernels at a health food store, because those kernels have been checked for levels of harmful substances.

Mrs Raffald really loved her flummery: she was responsible for giving us the recipe for fancy flummeries such as the Hen's Nest on page 269, but also a flummery fish pond, flummery playing cards, eggs and bacon in flummery and much more of this extravagance. I've seen her flummery Solomon's Temple made by food historian Ivan Day, and it looked quite splendid.

To make Flummery
Put one ounce of bitter and one of sweet almonds into a bason, pour over them some boiling water to make the skins come off, which is called blanching, strip off the skins and throw the kernels into cold water, then take them out, and beat them in a marble mortar, with a little rosewater to keep them from oiling. When they are beat, put them into a pint of calf's foot stock, set it over the fire and sweeten it to your taste with loaf sugar, as soon as it boils strain it through a piece of muslin or gauze, when a little cold put it into a pint of thick cream, and keep stirring it often till it grows thick and cold, wet your moulds in cold water, and pour in the flummery, let it stand five or six hours at least before you turn them out; if you make the flummery stiff and wet the moulds, it will turn out without putting it into warm water, for water takes off the figures of the mould and makes the flummery look dull.
Elizabeth Raffald, *The Experienced English Housekeeper*, 1782

Mrs Raffald gives a recipe for almond flummery, which is used for all the elaborate creations, using a pint of calves foot jelly to a pint of cream. But she also gives a recipe for oatmeal flummery which is more an oatmeal porridge than it is a jelly.

30 g (1 oz) almonds

30 g (1 oz) apricot kernels

1 teaspoon rosewater

400 ml (14 fl oz) milk

400 ml (14 fl oz) thick
(double) cream

2 tablespoons white sugar

9 gelatine leaves

Almond flummery

Blanch and skin the almonds and apricot kernels by pouring boiling water over them to make the skins come off. Rinse under cold water and dry them in a clean tea towel (dish towel) to rub off the last of the skins.

Grind the apricot kernels and almonds with the rosewater using a mortar and pestle, until you get a purée. In a medium saucepan, add the almond purée to the milk and cream, add the sugar and bring it to the boil, then remove from the heat and allow to cool slightly in the pan to soak up all the flavours of the almonds.

Strain the cream mixture and discard the almond pulp. Soak the gelatine briefly in enough water to cover the leaves, until softened. Then gently squeeze the gelatine to remove the water and stir it into the warm almond cream mixture until fully dissolved. Allow it to cool, but don't leave it long enough to set. Pour it into a wet mould and put it in the fridge for a minimum of 6 hours, preferably overnight.

The larger the mould, the more gelatine you will require for it to stand up. You may have to experiment with your chosen mould. For flummeries in glasses you may use 1 leaf of gelatine to 100 ml (3½ fl oz) of liquid.

To unmould, wet one of your hands and use it to loosen the jelly. Allow the jelly to slide out onto a wet plate (if the plate is wet, you can easily move the jelly around if necessary).

An alternative way to make almond milk is to use 700 ml (24 fl oz) water and 40 g (1½ oz) each of almonds and apricot kernels. Put the mixture in the fridge overnight, then add 100 ml (3½ fl oz) thick (double) cream and warm the mixture in a saucepan over low heat.

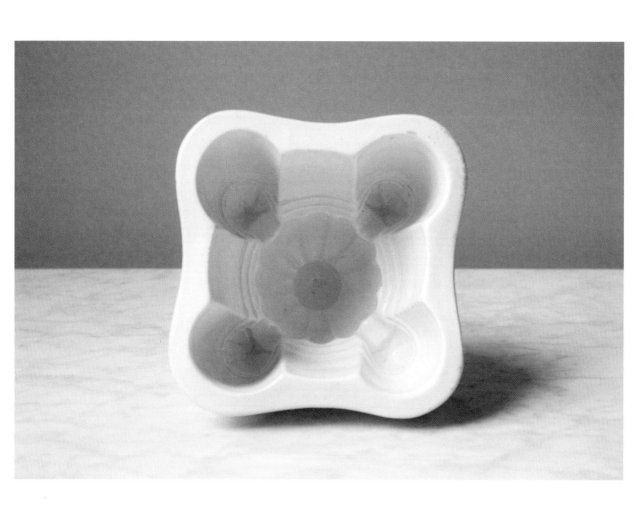

Piramidis Creams

Steeple creams, Spanish paps and piramidis creams were all seventeenth century leach-type opaque white jellies made with various gelling agents such as hartshorn, isinglass, calves foot jelly, ivory, gum arabic, etcetera. They were moulded in old-fashioned drinking glasses that were slightly fluted. Recipes would often mention that the jelly should look like a sugar loaf.

Moulds were produced for this kind of jelly too. They were conical and provided great amusement for dinner guests when the unmoulded jelly was brought to the table. They have a tendency to wobble in the most hilarious fashion. The Solomon's Temple moulds would also have a wobble but nothing surpassed the wobble of this one.

The recipes for these jellies are too long to include here, as the preparation of this jelly was no walk in the park. Luckily we have modern gelatine and don't need to create all kinds of concoctions to make this jelly stiff enough to stand up. The jelly was flavoured with almond and rosewater but also with musk and ambergris. These flavourings – also used in perfumes – were derived from animals, so they are no longer readily available today.

If you are using fluted glasses, these puddings can be really fun to make for a party. The original piramidis cream would have been decorated with pine nuts stuck into it. Although this might have looked the part in the olden days, I find a clean white conical jelly far more appealing. You can, of course, colour it as well.

For a recipe we are using the almond flummery from page 263 but doubling the gelatine so you get a good wobble and have a good laugh. I must admit this pudding is more for fun than it is for eating, as the large amount of gelatine might not be everyone's idea of a delicious pudding!

A Hen's Nest

Creating counterfeit meat or egg dishes out of something made to look like the real thing was a common practice in the Middle Ages; however, during the eighteenth century Elizabeth Raffald took inspiration from these medieval recipes for 'eggs for Lent' to create her Hen's Nest with flummery eggs. Her recipe calls for filling real eggshells with flummery and then peeling them as you would a real egg. The nest was made of a clear jelly in which thin threads of lemon peel were placed to look like straw.

Flummery 'eggs and bacon' was also a favourite of the Georgians. Chopped up green jelly would represent chopped spinach, and on top of it a flummery fried egg and bacon was placed. By the nineteenth century, special nest and egg moulds were manufactured from copper, so this dish must have been popular.

To make a Hen's Nest
Take three or five of the smallest pullet eggs you can get, fill them with flummery, and when they are stiff and cold, peel off the shells, pare off the rinds of two lemons very thin, and boil them in sugar and water, to take off the bitterness, when they are cold, cut them in long threds to imitate straws ...
Elizabeth Raffald, *The Experienced English Housekeeper*, 1782

Makes 4 eggs and the nest: one 17 cm (6½ inch/No. 30) basin (mould), filled half full with jelly.

½ quantity Almond
   Flummery (see page 263)

Nest

thinly sliced zest and juice
   of 2 small lemons

1 tablespoon sugar

6 gelatine leaves

40 g (1½ oz) raw sugar, extra

A hen's nest

To make the flummery eggs, pour the flummery mixture into egg-shaped moulds or, as Mrs Raffald suggests, real eggshells emptied out and rinsed. Allow to set.

Meanwhile, cut the lemon zest into fine strips to look like straw. Put the strips in a small saucepan with water to cover and 1 tablespoon of sugar. Bring to the boil then strain and allow to cool.

When the flummery eggs are set, peel the shell off or unmould them and set aside while you make the clear jelly. Soak the gelatine leaves in water until softened and then squeeze out the water when needed. In a medium saucepan, put 600 ml (21 fl oz) water and add the lemon juice and extra sugar, then bring to a simmer. Add the gelatine and stir well to dissolve. Remove from the heat and allow to cool.

Place the flummery eggs in a bowl or mould and arrange the lemon peel to look like a straw nest. Pour the clear jelly over them until they are nearly covered and allow it to set slightly.

Add the remaining jelly and allow it to set for a minimum of 5 hours or overnight.

Unmould very carefully onto a slightly wet plate.

If you have leftover flummery eggs, it's really fun to make a fake boiled egg! Cut the egg in half using a wet knife, then place a disc cut from apricot flesh where the yolk should be. It's super pretty.

jellies, milk puddings & ices |

Bacon & Eggs

Just like the hen's nest on page 270, I have taken my inspiration from Elizabeth Raffald's eighteenth century book, *The Experienced English Housekeeper*. This flummery dish is just too much fun not to include. It is a gimmick, but it sure makes your dinner guests laugh. It is also a dish that celebrity chef Heston Blumenthal has embraced and made his own.

Raffald instructs the cook to make part of the white flummery into a pretty pink colour; however, I have chosen to use a raspberry jelly instead. You can instead add raspberry sauce or natural beetroot colouring powder to flummery if you have some.

Serves 2

50 g (1¾ oz) raspberries

50 g (1¾ oz) raw sugar

5 gelatine leaves

½ quantity almond flummery (see page 263)

butter, for greasing

2 apricot halves, from a tin

Make raspberry jelly by putting 400 ml (14 fl oz) water with the raspberries and sugar in a medium saucepan over medium heat and bring to a simmer. Taste; if you find it too tart, add more sugar, one teaspoon at a time. Strain the liquid so you have no raspberry seeds and the juice is clear. Soak the gelatine in water until softened, gently squeeze out the water and add the gelatine to the warm raspberry juice, stirring until dissolved. Allow to cool slightly but not set.

Make the flummery according to the instructions on page 263 and allow to cool slightly but not set.

Lightly grease an 8.5 x 18.5 cm (3⅜ x 7¼ inch) cake tin with butter and line it with plastic wrap. The butter is there to keep the plastic from sticking to the tin. When the jelly and flummery are cooled, start layering. Pour in the jelly for the first layer to a depth of about 1 cm (⅜ inch). Transfer to the fridge and allow to set.

Meanwhile, wet a piece of baking paper, lay it on a tray or plate and spread a blob of flummery onto the paper. Flatten out with a spoon so it looks like an egg white and put it in the fridge to set. Make two of these.

When the first layer of jelly for the bacon is set, add a layer of flummery of about the same thickness as the first layer and put it in the fridge to set. Proceed in the same manner with more layers until you think you have a nice realistic bacon piece.

To assemble the dish, wet your serving plate or plates. Remove the 'bacon' from the cake tin and have a sharp knife ready and a bowl of water. Cut slices of bacon with a wet knife blade, and place on serving plates.

Carefully lift the 'egg white' off the baking paper and transfer it to the plate, using a wet knife or spatula. Cut the round cheek from an apricot half and place it on the egg white to make the yolk.

jellies, milk puddings & ices |

Ypocras Jellies

Mulled wine – called 'ypocras' in past centuries – has been around since the Middle Ages but mulled spirits predate even medieval times. There is a recipe for a fine spiced wine in a Roman cookery book (Apicius: *De Re Coquinaria*) that looks a lot like the recipe for ypocras. Ypocras was common enough in the fourteenth century to be mentioned by Chaucer and the first English recipe for it dates from that same period. The spice mixture for ypocras was known as 'ypocras Gyle' and usually contained cinnamon, cardamom pods and old varieties of pepper such as grains of paradise and long pepper. These spices were bruised using a mortar and pestle and left to steep in the red or white wine overnight, or possibly even longer, to soak up all the flavours.

Only the most noble and regal were able to afford ypocras, because in medieval times most spices were very expensive. The drink was usually taken at the end of a lavish meal as a digestive; later, the drink was turned into a jelly, which was eaten between courses. Unlike our mulled spirits today, it was enjoyed cold.

After the sixteenth century recipes for ypocras become richer, including more sugar, oranges, lemons, almonds and apples. Also ypocras jellies appear, with the earliest mention to be found in a book called *A Collection of Ordinances and Regulations for the Government of the Royal Household*, published in 1790. This book contains a menu with dietary prescriptions 'to be served to the King's Highnesse' dating back to a 1526 manuscript. Here the jelly is served as the first dish in the second course. In a later work written by Elias Ashmole (*Institution, Laws, and Ceremonies of the Order of the Garter*, 1672) we read that ypocras jelly was served to Henry VIII and Catherine of Aragon in Windsor Castle on Sunday, 29 May 1520, again in the second course of the dinner.

What we don't know is how the jelly was served in this period: was it in dainty glasses, moulds or cups? We know too little of the period's serving manners to be sure. For a specific recipe for ypocras jelly we have to wait until the Elizabethan period, although it is plainly called 'jelly'.

To make Ielly.
Take Calves feete and fley them, and faire washe them, and set them on to seethe in faire licour, and faire scum them, and when they be tender sod, faire straine out the licour, and see your licour be verye cleere, and put your licour into a pot, if there be a pottle of it, put a pottle of claret wine unto it, and two pound Sugar, a quartern of sinamon, half a quartern of ginger, an ounce of Nutmegs, an ounce of grains, some long Pepper, a fewe Cloves whole, a few Coliander sads, a little salt, Isonglasse being faire washed and laid in water a day before, Turnsole being aired be the fier and dusted, and when they be wel sod, let it run through a bag, and put two whites of Egs in the bag.
A.W., *A Book of Cookrye*, 1584

Clockwise from top left: antique pharmacy mortar and pestle; carafe of red wine; Georgian jelly glasses (see also following page); a Georgian 'toleware' spice dungeon; a nutmeg grater on a plate with nutmeg, long pepper, cloves, bay leaves and cinnamon; vintage salt spoon; muslin (cheesecloth) spice bag.

Makes enough for an 800 ml (28 fl oz) jelly mould or 8 small jellies

750 ml bottle red wine (not the cheapest nor the most expensive)

60 g (2¼ oz) raw sugar

2 long pepper buds, crushed

2 cloves

1 fresh bay leaf

1 teaspoon grated nutmeg

1 cinnamon stick

½ teaspoon ground ginger

1 marjoram sprig (optional)

1 cardamom pod, bruised (optional)

peel and juice of 1 clementine

60 ml (2 fl oz/¼ cup) sloe gin, or cherry brandy (optional)

1 gelatine leaf for each 100 ml (3½ fl oz) ypocras

Ypocras jelly

To make the ypocras, heat 200 ml (7 fl oz) of the red wine in a saucepan with the sugar, all of the spices (including the marjoram and cardamom, if using) and the clementine juice and peel until the sugar has dissolved. Bring to the boil and boil vigorously for 10 minutes, then reduce the heat and simmer for 5 minutes more. Allow to cool; when nearly cold or cold, add the remaining wine and the sloe gin, if using. Set aside to take up those lovely flavours overnight.

To make the jelly, strain the wine and measure the liquid. Soak the required number of gelatine leaves in water until soft. (If you are making one large jelly in a mould, add two extra leaves of gelatine to ensure that the jelly stays upright.)

Warm the ypocras in a saucepan but do not let it boil. Remove from the heat. Gently squeeze out the excess water from the gelatine, add it to the wine and stir until it has completely dissolved. Pour the mixture into dainty glasses or small moulds and allow to set for 3–4 hours, or 8–12 hours when using a large mould.

This makes a nice digestive.

You can freeze the boiled wine and spice mixture before adding the rest of the wine. The remainder of the wine will keep for a week in the fridge.

Ribbon Jelly

Although you might think this jelly looks quite modern with its colourful layers, it has been around for centuries. Today these jellies are called 'rainbow jellies', whereas in the past they were known as 'ribbon jellies'. Their ancestors are the medieval checkered leach jelly designs. In Georgian times, these ribbon jellies were made in the dainty jelly glasses of the period. They were served on glass comports especially made for this purpose.

To assemble this jelly, prepare one quantity of almond flummery (see page 263) and one of raspberry jelly (see page 272), or ypocras (see page 276) for a more spiced flavour; or use fruit juice of your choice set with gelatine according to the manufacturer's instructions.

Make the layers by pouring in a layer of flummery or jelly. Allow it to set in the fridge for about 20 minutes while you prepare the next layer. Proceed with the other layers, then return the jelly to the fridge for 1 hour.

If the jelly has set while you're waiting to use it for another layer, simply warm it over a hot-water bath and proceed.

I think the best effect is achieved in dainty glasses.

Only fools & trifles

When researching the dish with the peculiar name of 'fool' you soon find out that it can't be separated from another equally peculiar-sounding dish called a 'trifle'. These words mean something of little importance, but the puddings are quite the opposite. They usually grace the table at every special occasion and sons always prefer their mother's version to their wife's. It is a dish that boasts nostalgia, and made well, it is truly a feast for the eye as well as the palate.

A fool is a dessert made by blending puréed fruits – most commonly gooseberries or other tart fruit – with sweetened cream. It seems the exact origin of the name of this dish is lost in time. Some claim it's derived from the French verb 'fouler', which is used in the context of crushing grapes for wine; however, this doesn't make sense as, in the sixteenth century when the dish is first mentioned, the usage of the verb fouler didn't mean to crush or squeeze juice from fruit.

A trifle is a dish composed of layers of sponge cake soaked in sherry or other booze, jam or fresh fruit and syllabub, custard or whipped cream in a bowl. Sometimes a layer of jelly is added, and often the bowl is made of glass to show off the pretty layers of sweet pudding. The top of the trifle is often decorated with ratafia biscuits (see page 346), delicate almond flakes, glacé cherries or other candied fruit. A popular decoration of the Georgian period when confectionery was a highly regarded part of cookery are 'nonpareils', or what we know today as hundreds and thousands. Who would have thought these little things had such a history? Fresh and candied flowers and petals were also used to decorate a showstopper trifle. The key really is to use a decoration that is light and that will not sink into the cream.

Layered history

I'm afraid it is too easy to give these two explanations of each dish. The history of these dishes is as layered as a modern trifle and calls for some notes on their long history. Let's go back to the Tudor period, when *The Good Huswifes Jewell* by Thomas Dawson, written in 1596, gives us the very first recipe for a trifle:

> To make a Trifle.
> Take a pinte of thicke Creame, and season it with Suger and Ginger, and Rosewater, so stirre it as you would then haue it, and make it luke warme in a dish on a Chafingdishe and coales, and after put it into a siluer peece or a bowle, and so serue it to the boorde.
> Thomas Dawson, *The Good Huswifes Jewell*, 1596

Could this recipe have been the birth of the fool? It certainly doesn't look like the trifle we know today. Through history the names of these dishes were often used interchangeably. In 1598, Oxford-educated translator John Florio noted in his Italian/English dictionary, *A Worlde of Wordes*, 'a kind of clouted cream called a foole or a trifle'.

Gervase Markham's recipe for a Norfolk fool in his 1615 book, *The English Huswife*, is nearly the same as Dawson's trifle, only he adds thinly sliced 'manchet bread' which he places in the dish before pouring over the cream and egg mixture. A manchet is the word for a flat type of bread that was popular in that period and throughout the Middle Ages. In this recipe the bread was soaked with the fortified wine sack – like a sherry – just as in a modern trifle stale sponge cakes are soaked in booze. Markham then suggests to decorate the dish with caraway comfits, a custom that would also be favoured in Georgian times, when nonpareils would be strewn over the cream.

Markham's trifle, on the same page in his book, is again much like the first given here by Thomas Dawson. Only Markham says at the end of his recipe to use 'a spoonful of the best earning' – a spoonful of rennet – which means that this was a set cream like a junket.

At this point in history a trifle looks more like a fool, apart from setting it with rennet as Markham does, and a fool is starting to get layers with bread and custard, which looks like a modern trifle …

It begins to appear that a 'Norfolk fool' would later be known as a trifle, while a 'fool' would become a fruit-flavoured cream and nothing more. In fact Robert May (*The Accomplisht Cook*, 1660) even instructs the cook to create two or three layers of bread and custard in his Norfolk fool. He then finishes off the dish with dates, red and white biscuits and 'sippets', which were small pieces of thin toasted bread, to put around the edge of the dish on the cream. Again very much like the ratafias and macaroons which are used as a decoration on the trifles from the eighteenth century. May's trifle recipe is nearly the same as Markham's, also using rennet to set the cream.

I have found the first recipe for a fool containing fruit in *The Compleat Cook* by W.M., from 1658. Stewed gooseberries are used in an egg mixture. In this fool recipe there is no mention of cream, in fact many early fool recipes continue to use an egg mixture rather than just cream, as we know it today.

Hannah Wolley, in *The Queen-like Closet* of 1672, also sets her trifle with rennet and adds French comfits. It looks like she was taking the comfits used to decorate the fool and put them on her trifle. Mary Eales, in *Mrs Mary Eales's Receipts* in 1718, has a trifle recipe in her book which is similar to Robert May's, although she uses orange flower water instead of cinnamon and mace; she also says specifically that after the rennet has been put in, 'let it stand 'till it comes like Cheese'. A junket would very much look the same as this trifle.

The first fool

The first recipe for a fool as we know it today is Eliza Smith's Strawberry or Raspberry Fool in her delightful book *The Compleat Housewife*, first published in 1727 (see the notes about the recipe on page 296). The fruit is squeezed and orange flower water is added, then cream. The recipe is simple and straightforward and could be made by any cook today. Eliza Smith does not give a recipe for a trifle.

The first trifle

In the fourth edition of *The Art of Cookery, Made Plain and Easy*, published in 1751, Hannah Glasse published a recipe for a trifle (see page 290) that would change the nature of trifles forever. Hannah Glasse is famous for having copied most of the recipes in her books from other cooks and authors without disclosing it, so it is likely that in those 30 years after Mary Eales published her trifle recipe, someone created what we know as a trifle today; and that someone gave it the name 'trifle' when a dish like that would previously have been known as a 'Norfolk fool'. Glasse must have picked up the recipe somewhere and decided to add it to the fourth edition of her book, as it doesn't appear in her first editions.

Hannah Glasse's trifle story doesn't end here: she also published a lesser known book called *The Compleat Confectioner* in 1760, in which she gives a recipe for 'A grand trifle'.

> Take a very large china dish or glass; that is deep, first make some very fine rich calves-foot jelly, with which to fill the dish about half the depth; when it begins to jelly, have ready some Naples biscuits, macaroons, and the little cakes called matrimony; take an equal quantity of these cakes, break them in pieces, and stick them in the jelly before it be stiff, all over very thick; pour over that a quart of very thick sweet cream, then lay all round, currant jelly, raspberry jam, and some calves-foot jelly, all cut in little pieces, with which garnish your dish thick all round, intermixing them and on them lay macaroons, and the little cakes, being first dipped in sack. Then take two quarts of the thickest cream you can get, sweeten it with double-refined sugar, grate into it the rind of three fine large lemons, and whisk it up with a whisk; take off the froth as it rises, and lay it in your dish as high as you can possibly raise it; this is fit to go on the King's table, if well made, and very excellent when it becomes to be all mixed together.

Again it is not certain that Hannah Glasse invented this dish, but it appears to be the earliest in print to this day and also the first to include a layer of jelly as a base.

In a sweet little book named *Trifle*, written by Helen Saberi and the author of the *Oxford Companion to Food*, Alan Davidson, I found a recipe that is dated a year earlier than Hannah Glasse's. It is a recipe from a manuscript recipe book owned by the owner of Prospect Books, Tom Jaine, and the recipe is as good as identical to Glasse's, though not in wording.

To Scotland with the trifle

In 1755 the first trifle recipe was published in Scotland by Elizabeth Cleland in her book *A New and Easy Method of Cookery*. She includes an apple purée made by first roasting the apples, then mixing the soft flesh with sugar and egg white as the final layer of her trifle. She is the first to publish a trifle recipe using stewed fruit. Another recipe from across the Scottish borders came from Susanna MacIver's *Cookery & Pastry* in 1786 and also suggests using apples. Mrs MacIver ran a cookery school in Edinburgh with Mrs Frazer who also gives us a trifle recipe in her book, *The Practice of Cookery, Pastry & Confectionery*, in 1795. Her recipe is like no other trifle of that period. She instructs to make a sponge cake first, in a separate recipe that contains 12 eggs, 450 g (1 lb) of sugar and 225 g (8 oz) of flour, seasoned with the grated rind of 3 or 4 lemons.

Mrs Frazer instructs to create layers of sponge cake with preserves, either raspberry, strawberry, or sliced apples. The layers should look like a 'small sugar loaf' she says, which means it should be pyramid shaped. Then she instructs to stick a sprig of myrtle in the top and then fill the dish with cream all the way round the pyramid of soaked cake and fruit preserve. Finally she says to garnish the trifle with currant cream, angelica and whole redcurrants. She also mentions that you can use some preserved gooseberries around the border of the plate.

Victorian trifles

Eliza Acton presents us with several different trifles and trifle-like recipes – such as a 'Tipsy cake' and 'Swiss Cream' – in her 1845 book, *Modern Cookery for Private Families*. Often described as 'the real Mrs Beeton', along with Agnes B. Marshall, she was one of the finest cookery writers of her time and beyond. Acton writes with convincing determination in her voice and gives clear instructions. She also tells us to use an extraordinarily large quantity of alcohol in this trifle!

Mrs Beeton's trifle in *The Book of Household Management* (1861) has sponge cake, macaroons and ratafias soaked in wine and brandy, a layer of grated lemon zest with sweet almonds, a raspberry or strawberry jam layer, a custard layer and a whipped cream topping – made of cream with egg white, sugar and sherry – that she calls 'whip'; it resembles a syllabub (see page 302) but with added egg white.

She also has recipes for trifles using stewed apple purée or gooseberry purée and there is an Indian trifle recipe. In her regular trifle recipe she states to garnish the top with strips of bright currant jelly, crystallised sweetmeats or flowers, and notes that the small coloured comfits that are sometimes used for the purpose of garnishing a trifle are now considered rather old-fashioned.

Queen of trifles and zuppa Inglese

In 1895 Theodore Francis Garrett gives a recipe for a 'Queen of Trifles' in his book *The Encyclopaedia of Practical Cookery*. He goes about his recipe in the same way as other authors before him, but gives the option to use lady fingers or savoiardi (see page 350) and a layer of fruit jelly instead of jam. At the end he instructs to decorate the trifle not with a syllabub but with regular whipped cream as we know it today.

Garett also wrote a note about trifle in his book: 'Trifles: These are exceptionally English dishes, and are held in very poor esteem by the foreign pastry-cook …'

Contradicting his note, trifle appears to be well enough esteemed by foreigners for an Italian to mention it in his book: Pellegrino Artusi gives a recipe for a 'Zuppa Inglese' (English soup) in his *La Scienza in Cucina e l'Arte di Mangiare Bene* in 1891. He instructs to place a layer of apricot, pear or quince preserves in a greased bowl first – in fact he instructs to use a mould, which is a first for this dish – then instructs to place lady fingers on top soaked in either a white rosolio, a light-coloured rose petal liqueur, or a mix of soaking the biscuits in the rosolio and a red alchermes, which is a traditional deep scarlet-coloured liqueur in Italy.

The biscuits are followed by a layer of custard thickened with cornflour (cornstarch), then more biscuits and so on until the bowl or mould is full. Then the zuppa Inglese is turned out of the mould.

I think Artusi just liked certain English recipes, as on the page before the zuppa Inglese he gives a recipe for a plum pudding and then a plum cake, explaining that despite the English calling it a plum pudding, it is not made with plums. Artusi even uses the English names for these two dishes. The reason he translated the trifle to zuppa Inglese is, I think, because trifle would have been harder to explain, or maybe he couldn't explain the etymology of the word himself. Or perhaps it is another one of his jokes, as he is quite funny at times in his book.

Some claim, that the English trifle is inspired by the zuppa Inglese but, as we have seen so far, the trifle goes centuries further back in history than Artusi's recipe, which is the first to appear with that name. Another similar dish called a 'zuppa del Duca' (Duke's soup), is also attributed to be the inspiration for the trifle; however, no early recipes survive of this pudding to my knowledge and the only thing we have to go by is a legend.

The story goes that chefs created the pudding in honour of Cosimo III de' Medici in the seventeenth or early eighteenth century to celebrate his visit to Sienna. The dish created was named zuppa del Duca and the duke took the pudding back with him to Florence.

In the nineteenth century, zuppa del Duca became popular among the English who lived in Florence which would be the reason the dish was renamed to zuppa Inglese. It is claimed that the zuppa Inglese was then brought to England where it was renamed a trifle … only, the trifle was then already going strong in several cookery books of the century and for two centuries before that!

Tiramisu

Tiramisu, although very similar to the trifle, is said to be the dish that evolved out of the zuppa del Duca or the zuppa Inglese; it is the youngest recipe of the bunch as it was invented in the 1960s in Treviso. The creator of the tiramisu, Carminantonio Iannaccone, claimed in a *Washington Post* interview (with Jane Black, 11 July 2007) that it took him two years to perfect the recipe in the kitchen of his restaurant, Piedigrotta in Treviso. His story is believed to be true, as no mention is made of a tiramisu in major works on Italian food prior to the 1960s. Elizabeth David for example, doesn't mention it in her *Italian Food* in the 1950s.

Stories claiming that the tiramisu was created centuries ago as a 'pick me up' – as this is the translation of the word – for Venetian ladies of pleasure to help them through the nights, are intriguing but completely untrue.

Retro

Back to our English trifle, now arriving in the twentieth century. In 1902 a recipe for a 'Trifle à la Old Century' was published by Mrs Salis in *A La Mode Cookery*. It shows that by then the trifle was already considered a 'retro' dessert rooted into English culture. May Byron, author of what must be the thickest pudding book in history (*May Byron's Pudding Book*, 1917), gives 18 trifle recipes! In her book she explains that a trifle might be difficult to define, but not to devour. She also notes that the trifle requires elaboration, imagination and ingenuity to be a success, and also some recklessness with regards to economy; meaning that it wasn't a cheap dish to prepare, if you used decent ingredients anyway.

jellies, milk puddings & ices |

May Byron was the first to publish a recipe for a baked trifle. It looks more like the Queen of Puddings (see page 181) we know today. Stewed pears are placed in the bottom of a pudding basin on top of slices of sponge cake sprinkled with coconut. The dish is then baked before a layer of meringue is added and returned to the oven to colour.

Wartime trifle

Then the wartime years came and shortages meant that milk and eggs, the key ingredients for trifle, weren't available. Dried eggs, custard powder and grated potato or potato flour were used instead. You couldn't bake cakes so a tea bun soaked in fruit juice was often suggested.

After the Second World War, it seems like the trifle was largely considered an unfashionable dessert. This was mostly to do with the fact that during the years of food rationing the glorious boozy trifle went to a stale bun soaked in juice with fake custard. Nothing of the previously celebrated tipsy trifle pudding remained. Tinned fruit became fashionable in the postwar years with Marguerite Patten, one of the earliest TV celebrity chefs, as a major influence. Patten shared many trifle recipes over the several decades that she wrote books, articles and did TV shows. She uses a set jelly and custard powder in her trifles and also advises typically retro-looking decorations such as glacé cherries and nuts to go on top. I do like a retro trifle from time to time.

Layers, booze and cream

The trifle now lives on in many different styles but they are all defined by layers made of soaked sponge fingers, a fruit of some sort and a cream topping. Some swear by using tinned fruit, some only use fresh, while others use jam. Some are particular about a layer of jelly while others dream of a smooth boozy syllabub. Chocolate, of course, is never far away, and works well with soaked boozy sponge and cream.

Presentations vary in retro-ness. Some idolise their mother's trifle with glacé cherries, angelica or perhaps some pineapple, a recipe she probably inherited from her mother in turn. Others want a more dainty look with candied flower petals or plain cream piping. Small amaretti biscuits from a pack are also popular, as are colourful macaroons.

To serve the mighty trifle some people swear by their large crystal punch bowl as a vessel while others prefer a more elegant bowl with a stem. As the formidable food writer M.F.K. Fisher noted in *With Bold Knife and Fork* (1968): 'A trifle can be a pretty thing, and it needs a pretty dish.'

The dish that started its early life as a Norfolk fool is now a British favourite and an integral part of every festive occasion. Who doesn't instantly want to dip their spoon into an untouched trifle, all the way down to that bottom layer, to slowly scoop out a velvet-soft, fruity alcohol-soaked mouthful, just for yourself alone?

Devonshire Junket

Junkets are made by setting milk with rennet. They appear first in the fifteenth century, when they were called 'Iouncat', 'Ioncate' or 'Iunket' in Middle English. The earliest mention of this dish can be found in John Russell's *Boke of Nurture* of about 1460: 'Milke, crayme, and cruddes, and eke the Ioncate.' From the sixteenth century, recipes for trifle look a lot like junket. The early seventeenth century writer Gervase Markham explains in his recipe for trifle to use 'a spoonful of the best earning [rennet]' to set the cream. Later junkets appear more often in books and by the early 1800s it had become a popular dish in Devon. It was traditionally eaten topped with cream, which was a Devon speciality.

I have discovered a late nineteenth century postcard depicting a junket in its traditional junket bowl, and clotted cream in a Torquay Pottery bowl. Both these vessels have become extremely rare but after months of searching I managed to reproduce the old postcard with the original pottery as the image that accompanies this recipe.

The dish disappeared when junket tablets, along with ready-made jellies, gave it a bad name in the postwar years. This is a great shame as junket is a most delicate pudding, simply made of set milk and whey, flavoured with spices and sometimes some alcohol. The vintage recipe reproduced below uses cinnamon, but I suggest you try nutmeg or mace too.

To make an excellent Junket
Take new Milk warm; then add Runnet, and let it cool; then ftrow on it Cinnamon and Sugar, over that caft Cream, and ftrow sugar upon the cream with Rose-water.
Henry Howard, *England's Newest Way in Cookery*, 1703

Serves 8–10, using a 1 litre (35 fl oz/4 cup) bowl or teacup-size individual moulds

1 litre (35 fl oz/4 cups) milk

flavouring, such as
  1 tablespoon brandy,
  or 1 teaspoon rosewater
  or orange flower water
  (optional)

2 teaspoons vegetable rennet

ground nutmeg, mace or
  cinnamon, to dust

Clotted cream (see page 336),
  to serve

Have a serving bowl or individual glasses ready.

Pour the milk and flavouring, if using, into a clean saucepan and heat to 37°C (98°F), otherwise known as body temperature or blood heat. Stir in the rennet in one large movement to spread it through the mixture and swiftly transfer the combined liquid into the bowl or glasses. Allow it to set for 15 minutes and then serve it dusted with nutmeg, mace or cinnamon and a bowl of clotted cream on the side.

Some fresh fruit, such as strawberries or raspberries, is a lovely addition to this delicate pudding. Blueberries are also suggested in some old texts.

Junket bowl: S Fielding & Co, The Devon Pottery, Stoke-on-Trent, c. 1879; cream bowl: Longpark Torquay Pottery motto ware, c. 1860

jellies, milk puddings & ices |

The First Trifle

As you have read in the previous pages, this is most probably the first recipe for a trifle as we know it today. Hannah Glasse was also the first to add a layer of syllabub. The trifle is much simpler than those that appear in the later cookbooks, but I enjoy its simplicity.

To make a Trifle
Cover the bottom of your dish or bowl with Naples biscuits broke in pieces, mackeroons broke in halves, and ratafia cakes. Just wet them all through with sack, then make a good boiled custard not too thick, and when cold pour it over it, then put a syllabub over that. You may garnish it with ratafia cakes, currant jelly, and flowers.
Hannah Glasse, *The Art of Cookery, Made Plain and Easy*, 1751

A trifle can truly be grand when made with good cream and eggs and, if you can spare the time, homemade biscuits and sponge cakes. As with so many other puddings in this book, the quality of the products used elevates the dish to a whole other level.

Serves 6 people, made in a 30 cm (12 inch) bowl

1 quantity lady fingers (savoiardi) (see page 350)

1 quantity ratafia biscuits (see page 346)

sherry or Madeira, to taste

½ quantity custard sauce (see page 338)

½ quantity everlasting syllabub (see page 304)

Make a nice layer of lady fingers and ratafia biscuits in the bottom of the bowl. Sprinkle a generous amount of sherry on the biscuits.

Gently pour a layer of custard over the soaked biscuits, followed by a layer of everlasting syllabub.

Store in a cool place or in the fridge until ready to serve, then decorate with fresh flowers, ratafia biscuits and, if you like, some hundreds and thousands (nonpareils); which, weirdly enough, are my favourite since I am always amazed that they were also used centuries ago.

Retro Trifle

As far as retro trifles go, you can come across constructions made with layers of custard, cream, jelly, fruit encased in jelly, tinned fruit, fresh fruit, Swiss roll cake, stale cake, lady fingers; just about anything you can soak in booze and layer in a bowl.

Compared to some of the fantastic trifles of which I wish I had fond childhood memories, my retro trifle is very simple. My favourite trifle is still the first trifle on page 290, so this one isn't very far removed from it. This trifle is just as 'soupy' as the first trifle, but if you prefer a more solid consistency, add a tablespoon of cornflour (cornstarch) to your custard when putting it back on the stove for thickening.

Serves 8–10 people, made in a 30 cm (12 inch) bowl

1 quantity lady fingers (savoiardi), (see page 350)

1 quantity ratafia biscuits (see page 346)

brandy, to taste

½ quantity custard sauce (see page 338)

500 g (1 lb 2 oz) strawberries, hulled and halved

1 quantity everlasting syllabub (see page 304)

500 ml (17 fl oz/2 cups) thick (double) cream, whipped

Make a layer of lady fingers followed by a few ratafia biscuits, just enough so that every serving will have one. Drizzle the biscuits with enough brandy to cover them generously. Pour the cold custard over the biscuits and put it in the fridge to rest for about 15 minutes. Make a crown of strawberry halves all around the outer edge of the custard layer and fill the centre with more strawberry halves.

If you are a jelly lover, you could add a jelly layer at this point. Simply pour in cooled but not set jelly over the berries and refrigerate until set.

Scoop the syllabub on top of the strawberries. Add another layer of boozy lady fingers and a couple of broken up ratafias, if you still have some left, followed by a layer of whipped cream. Decorate the top with sliced or halved strawberries.

Stand in the fridge for an hour, or until you need it, so the flavours can develop and mature. This trifle can easily be made in the morning for an evening dinner.

For a variation use peaches or nectarines stewed with cinnamon and sugar; allow the fruit to cool before assembling the trifle. You can also omit the whipped cream and use more syllabub instead.

Fruit Fools

Both strawberry or raspberry fool and gooseberry fool can be made in the same way. Another nice fool is one with rhubarb. For a gooseberry or rhubarb fool, stew the fruit with some honey or sugar. For a raspberry or strawberry fool, I prefer not to stew the fruit, as it is so good as it is.

To make Strawberry or Raspberry Fool
Take a pint of raspberries, squeeze and drain the juice with orange flower water; put to the juice five ounces of fine sugar; then set a pint of cream over the fire, and let it boil up; then put in the juice; give it one stir round, and then put it into your basin, stir a little in the basin, and when it is cold use it.
Eliza Smith, *The Compleat Housewife*, 1727

Makes enough for 6 glasses or jam jars

150 g (5½ oz/1 punnet) raspberries

½ teaspoon orange flower water

½ teaspoon sugar, or to taste

500 ml (17 fl oz/2 cups) thick (double) cream

Crush two-thirds of the raspberries with a fork, leaving some large chunks for texture. Mix with the orange flower water. Add the sugar to the cream, taste and add more if you have a sweet tooth.

Stir half of the cream into the crushed fruit so you get a nice pink colour.

Now layer the remaining cream with the pink fruit cream into the jars or glasses.

Decorate with the remaining fruit.

jellies, milk puddings & ices

Syllabubs & possets

Syllabubs and the closely related 'possets' are dairy dishes for which we find the first recipes in the sixteenth century. They were initially a kind of frothy drink but over time evolved to become a pudding.

Possets were made by pouring hot spiced cream from a height into eggs beaten with wine, such as sack. They were usually served hot in the spouted ceramic posset pots in which they were made. Syllabubs were cold and served in dainty spouted glasses that were nearly identical in shape to posset pots. In the eighteenth century, special bell-top glasses were produced which were a little less fragile than the spouted syllabub glasses. In both cases the liquid part would separate from the cream and was sucked through the spout while the creamy froth was eaten with a spoon.

Syllabub under the cow

In the seventeenth and eighteenth centuries there were three different, yet similar, kinds of syllabubs. In one of them, the milk was sweetened, spiced and mixed with cider or ale. It was treated as a drink, often reputedly made by milking a cow straight into a bowl with the alcohol, sugar and spices. The whole thing was then left to curdle so a froth would form on top and a boozy whey would be left underneath. This was probably the syllabub enjoyed by people in the countryside, and poems from the period confirm this.

However, it is not entirely certain that one can create a syllabub by milking a cow directly into ale or cider. Several food historians have tried it without obtaining the desired effect, including Ivan Day, who attempted the method for the first time when he was just a 14-year-old schoolboy. Maybe the whole 'real cow' thing was a misunderstanding? There were recipes which mentioned a 'wooden cow' or a 'dry cow', which was an instrument made to push out milk.

One of the first printed recipes for syllabub comes from a book called *The Compleat Cook*, published in 1658.

> An excellent Sillabub.
> Fill your Sillabub-pot with Syder (for that is the best for a Sillabub) and good store of Sugar and a little Nutmeg; stir it well together, put in as much thick Cream by two or three spoonfuls at a time, as hard as you can, as though you milke it in, then stir it together exceeding softly once about, and let it stand two hours at least ere it is eaten, for the standing makes the Curd.
> W.M., *The Compleat Cook*, 1658

Robert May copied this recipe nearly completely in his book *The Accomplisht Cook* (1660) which was published a few years later. And then in 1723, John Nott copied May's recipe in his *Cooks and Confectioners Dictionary* as a recipe for 'A Worchester Syllabub'. But it is what he adds to it, which is of significance: 'If it be in the field, only milk the cow into the cider, and so drink it.'

Top: eighteenth century syllabub glasses on a glass stand; eighteenth century syllabub glass with a spout, from the private collection of food historian Ivan Day. Below: reproduction of a seventeenth century posset pot from Ivan Day.

A whipped syllabub

A more solid version of the syllabub was made by the well-to-do using cream instead of fresh milk and adding more expensive alcohol such as sack. The cream was whipped into froth and this froth was continuously removed and set on a fine sieve to drain. The next day the syllabub glasses were filled with sweetened wine or sack, and the froth was laid on top, supported by the bell-shaped glass.

An everlasting syllabub

Then the everlasting syllabub became popular: by adding less alcohol to the cream it made a more solid version that would not separate and could be made in advance. It would become the topping of a trifle after Hannah Glasse published her recipe (in *The Art of Cookery, Made Plain and Easy*, 1747); and Eliza Smith claimed in her book of the same period (*The Compleat Housewife*, 1727) that her syllabub would 'keep good for nine or ten days'. I wouldn't recommend you try this at home.

In the early nineteenth century possets and syllabubs start to disappear from recipe books. It would not be until the 1970s that these dishes would get attention again, when Elizabeth David and Jane Grigson wrote about them. Even then it would take a while before the general public was aware of them again. Elizabeth David wrote a booklet devoted to syllabubs and fruit fools: in it she goes into great detail about the history of these puddings, shares several historical recipes and also one of her own. She sold it in her cookery shop in London.

Now, the internet has recipes for possets and syllabubs aplenty, and they also feature in the most creative combinations in modern cookery books. But few know the provenance of these ancient dishes, and the modern versions are quite different from the originals.

Syllabub

This is a recipe for a separating syllabub. In the seventeenth century these were served in the most delicate, spouted, glass syllabub pots and in the eighteenth century they were served in dainty bell-top glasses to support the froth. A spoon was provided, so guests could scoop out the froth.

A Syllabub

My Lady Middlesex makes Syllabubs for little Glasses with spouts, thus. Take 3 pints of sweet Cream, one of quick white wine (or Rhenish), and a good wine glassful (better the ¼ of a pint) of Sack: mingle with them about three quarters of a pound of fine Sugar in Powder. Beat all these together with a whisk, till all appeareth converted into froth. Then pour it into your little Syllabub-glasses, and let them stand all night. The next day the Curd will be thick and firm above, and the drink clear under it. I conceive it may do well, to put into each glass (when you pour the liquor into it) a sprig of Rosemary a little bruised, or a little Limon-peel, or some such thing to quicken the taste; or use Amber-sugar, or spirit of Cinnamon, or of Lignum-Cassiae; or Nutmegs, or Mace, or Cloves, a very little.

Sir Kenelm Digby, *The Closet of the Eminently Learned Sir Kenelme Digbie Knight Opened*, 1669

I find syllabubs quite fitting for a stylish occasion. Place them all together on glass compotes as they would have done in the eighteenth century; your guests will be impressed.

The recipe for this syllabub is, in essence, the same as the everlasting syllabub (see page 304), only omitting the lemon juice.

Serves 6, made in fluted
100 ml (3½ fl oz) glasses

425 ml (15 fl oz) thick (double) cream

50 g (1¾ oz) raw sugar, processed to a fine powder

125 ml (4 fl oz/½ cup) white wine, such as riesling

60 ml (2 fl oz/¼ cup) sherry or Madeira

6 rosemary sprigs, to garnish

In an electric mixer fitted with the whisk attachment, whisk together the cream and the sugar on low speed. Combine the lemon juice with the alcohol and add that to the cream, whisking constantly until it becomes thick. You may whisk this by hand, but it needs at least 10–15 minutes of whisking. Fill the syllabub glasses or use for a trifle.

Add a sprig of rosemary to each syllabub glass.

Allow to rest in the fridge until the mixture separates, then serve with a straw and a little spoon so people can suck out the liquid part and scoop off the froth.

Whipped syllabub

Take off the froth after it has separated from the liquid and fill the glasses with more white wine, add a sprig of rosemary and then return the froth to the top.

For extra decoration, you can use either fresh zest of a lemon cut into thin strips as for cocktails, or thin slices of candied peel.

Everlasting Syllabub

This syllabub can be served in pretty little glasses or in pots. Since the mid-eighteenth century, it has also been used as one of the layers of a trifle (see page 290).

To make Everlasting Syllabubs
Take three pints of the thickest and sweetest cream you can get, a pint of rhenish, half a pint of sack, three lemons, near a pound of double refined sugar, beat and sift your sugar, and put it to the cream; grate off the yellow rind of three lemons, put that in and squeeze the juice of three lemons into your wine; put that to the cream, beat all together with a whisk just half an hour, then take it up all together with a spoon, and fill your glasses.

Hannah Glasse, *The Compleat Confectioner*, 1760

Serves 6, made in fluted
100 ml (3½ fl oz) glasses

425 ml (15 fl oz) thick (double) cream

50 g (1¾ oz) raw sugar, processed to a fine powder

80 ml (2½ fl oz/⅓ cup) lemon juice

125 ml (4 fl oz/½ cup) white wine, such as riesling

60 ml (2 fl oz/¼ cup) sherry or Madeira

rosemary sprigs

Using an electric mixer fitted with the whisk attachment, whisk together the cream and the sugar on low speed. Combine the lemon juice with the alcohol and add that to the cream, whisking constantly until it becomes thick. You may whisk this by hand, but it needs at least 10–15 minutes of whisking. Fill the syllabub glasses, add a sprig of rosemary or use for a trifle.

It was traditional to put a sprig of rosemary in the glass. The original recipe states to add lemon zest, too; however, I found it too aggressive and left it out.

jellies, milk puddings & ices

Nineteenth century syllabub glass

Sack Posset

Although similar to a syllabub, the posset is much richer because it is more like a custard than a cream. Possets were served in a ceramic posset pot, which looked a little like a teapot with two handles. They were usually very decorative and were extremely expensive to buy. This dish is therefore, again, one of high standard.

Possets were originally more drinks than they were puddings and were often given to people in rich households when they were feeling unwell.

My Lord of Carlisle's Sack-Posset
Take a pottle of Cream, and boil in it a little whole Cinnamon, and three or four flakes of Mace. To this proportion of Cream put in eighteen yolks of eggs, and eight of the whites; a pint of Sack; beat your eggs very well, and then mingle them with your Sack. Put in three quarters of a pound of Sugar into the Wine and Eggs, with a Nutmeg grated, and a little beaten Cinnamon; set the Bason on the fire with the Wine and Eggs, and let it be hot. Then put in the Cream boiling from the fire, pour it on high, but stir it not; cover it with a dish, and when it is settlede, strew on the top a little fine Sugar mingled with three grains of Ambergreece, and one grain of Musk, and serve it up.
Sir Kenelm Digby, *The Closet of the Eminently Learned Sir Kenelme Digbie Knight Opened*, 1669

*Makes 8–10 posset pots
or teacups*

850 ml (29 fl oz) thin (pouring) cream

1 cinnamon stick

1 mace blade

6 egg yolks

3 egg whites

230 ml (7¾ fl oz) sherry or Madeira (for an alcohol-free posset, use orange or lemon juice)

100 g (3½ oz) raw sugar

In a medium saucepan, bring the cream to a simmer with the spices, then remove from the heat.

Whisk the egg yolks and whites in a clean saucepan, then pour in the sherry (or juice, if preferred) and sugar. Put the saucepan over medium–high heat and bring to a simmer, stirring constantly; do not let it boil. Turn down the heat and pour the cream into the egg mixture, whisking constantly. Remove from the heat.

Pour the mixture into pots or teacups and rest for a couple of minutes. Serve with a spoon while still warm or chill in the fridge if you prefer.

Custard Creams

I n the eighteenth century, plain custards were served in delicate little custard glasses. They would be served with jellies, syllabubs and other creamy puddings.

To make a common Custard
Take a quart of good cream, set it over a slow fire, with a little cinnamon, and four ounces of sugar; when it has boiled take it off the fire; beat the yolks of eight eggs, put to them a spoonful of orange flower water, to prevent the cream from cracking, stir them in by degrees as your cream cools, put the pan over a very slow fire, stir them carefully one way till it is almost boiling then put into cups and serve them up.
Elizabeth Raffald, *The Experienced English Housekeeper*, 1782

Makes 6 small cups or glasses

4 egg yolks

1 teaspoon orange flower water

425 ml (15 fl oz) thick (double) cream

20 g (¾ oz) raw sugar

1 cinnamon stick

Whisk the egg yolks with the orange flower water in a large bowl. In a medium saucepan, bring the cream, sugar and cinnamon to a simmer. Remove the cinnamon stick. Pour a little of the hot cream mixture into the egg yolk mixture and whisk thoroughly. Now continue to add the hot cream mixture in batches, whisking constantly, until it is fully incorporated and you get a smooth custard.

Pour the mixture back into the saucepan, put it over low heat and stir with a spatula until just thickened, making sure the eggs don't scramble. Remove from the heat and allow to cool a little in the saucepan until the custard is cold enough to scoop into glasses or small teacups.

Dust some mace or nutmeg on the custards before serving.

Almond custard

To make this into an almond custard, omit the orange flower water and whisk the egg yolks. Crush 50 g (1¾ oz) blanched almonds with 1 teaspoon of rosewater using a mortar and pestle and mix this with the cream before bringing it to a simmer with the sugar and cinnamon. Remove from the heat, strain and proceed to mix the hot cream mixture with the eggs as above. For a more marzipan flavour, add a few blanched apricot kernels to the mix.

jellies, milk puddings & ices |

Eighteenth century glass custard cup

Rice Pudding

Cookery writer Dorothy Hartley wrote in *Food in England* (1954) that 'East End women make a rice pudding using broth ... when cooked it is finished under the joint of Mutton.' This is very similar to the 'Ryse of Flesh' recipe found in *The Forme of Cury* (ed. Samuel Pegge, c. 1390). Rice was an expensive import and therefore rice dishes would only appear on the tables of kings.

> Ryse Of Flesh. IX. Take Ryse and waishe hem clene. and do hem in erthen pot with gode broth and lat hem seeþ wel. afterward take Almaund mylke and do þer to. and colour it wiþ safroun an salt, an messe forth.
> *The Forme of Cury*, ed. Samual Pegge, c.1390

The Forme of Cury also gives a recipe for a rice pottage, virtually identical to 'Ryse of Flesh'. The rice pottage is what would become the modern day rice pudding and the recipe just omits the salt and broth, using water instead of broth to cook the rice the first time.

Sugar isn't added in *The Forme of Cury*; for a sweetened rice pudding we have to wait until the fifteenth century Austin manuscripts, which include a pudding sweetened with honey and sugar. In 1660, Robert May (*The Accomplisht Cook*) adds eggs, beef suet, salt, nutmeg, cloves, mace, currants, dates and powdered coriander seeds.

A recipe for rice plainly cooked as a side dish only appears in 1669, but even then it is still served as a sweet dish spiced with cinnamon. This rice pudding is very savoury and might not be suited to modern tastes.

Serves 4

120 g (4½ oz) short-grain rice, such as arborio rice

500 ml (17 fl oz/2 cups) beef broth

500 ml (17 fl oz/2 cups) almond milk

a few saffron threads

Put the rice and broth in a deep saucepan and heat gently. Stir well and bring gently to the boil. Simmer and stir often so the rice doesn't stick to the bottom of the pan.

When the liquid is almost completely absorbed, after about 15 minutes, add the almond milk and saffron. Stir well, then simmer gently for 20–30 minutes, stirring every now and then until all the liquid is absorbed and the rice is cooked and thick. Spoon the cooked rice pudding into a serving dish.

Not up to using the broth? You can use 1 litre (35 fl oz/4 cups) almond milk, or regular milk instead, for a plain and simple rice pudding. If you have a sweet tooth, add vanilla and sugar to taste.

A pewter porringer dish, a design that stayed the same for centuries

Icy creams & princess bombs

I ces have been adored for centuries, either by kings on their feasting tables, or by working class folk from a 'penny lick' glass. They were moulded into various shapes; encased cake or fruit; were topped with chocolate, fancy sugar treats and meringue. Some prefer three different-flavoured scoops on their cone, some want plain vanilla and nothing else, nearly melted in a bowl.

The bill of fare for Charles II's banquet course at the 1671 Garter feast, according to Elias Ashmole in *The Institution, Laws, and Ceremonies of the Most Noble Order of the Garter* (1672), mentions 'One plate of Ice Cream' as one of the dishes for the sovereign's evening table. This is the first record of the term 'ice cream' in England. However, the earliest English ice-cream recipe dates from about 10 years earlier and is by the hand of Lady Ann Fanshawe (who called it 'Icy Cream' rather than ice cream) in her manuscript recipe book of 1625–1680. This recipe predates the first recipe to appear in print in *Mrs. Mary Eales's Receipts* from 1718 and is the earliest in the whole of Europe. Mary Eales's recipe 'To Ice cream' had long been assumed the first English recipe before Lady Ann's recipe for an 'Icy Cream' was discovered.

I can't claim that the ice-cream freezing technique was invented in England: it was most probably invented in Italy where it was described by an Italian scholar in his *Problemata Aristoteles* in 1530. A popular myth – which has been disputed by the formidable Elizabeth David – is that the Florentine Catherine de Medici and her confectioners brought the art of making ices to the French capital in the sixteenth century.

Georgian ices

French and Italian confectioners came to England and set up shops in London in the 1760s. In these first ice-cream parlours you could enjoy an ice cream or take a larger quantity home for a special occasion. One vendor, the Italian Domenico Negri, had a shop called 'The Pot and Pineapple' in Berkeley Square where he sold 'all sorts of English, French, and Italian wet and dry sweetmeats', according to his trade card. One of his apprentices was Frederick Nutt, who published his fabulous book *The Complete Confectioner* in 1789. Nutt gives 32 recipes for ice cream and 24 for water ices.

Negri's shop eventually came into the ownership of one of his apprentices, James Gunter of the Gunter family, who continued the trade into the twentieth century. In the early nineteenth century Gunter employed the Italian confectioner William A. Jarrin as an ornament maker. Jarrin's book, *The Italian Confectioner* (1820) has an impressive chapter on ices. He also gave us the very first recipe for an ice-cream bombe, which became very popular at that time. Copper bombe moulds – plain, melon-shaped or in the form of beehives – were manufactured to create these ice-cream puddings. They each had a screw to dispel the vacuum inside the mould so the ice would be easier to unmould.

jellies, milk puddings & ices

Pewter ice-cream moulds, part of the collection of food historian Ivan Day

Victorian ices

Ice puddings and ice cream were very popular in the eighteenth century, but saw their heyday in Victorian times. The moulded ice puddings were one of the most technically challenging dishes for a cook to make. Variously shaped copper and pewter ice-cream moulds were produced to look like domes, beehives, flowers, fruit, vegetables, swans, peacocks and other animals.

Other elaborately shaped and presented iced puddings were made, too. The cover design of the book *The Royal Confectioner* (1891) by Queen Victoria's chef de cuisine, Charles Elmé Francatelli, showed a spectacular iced pudding named after the queen. The pudding sat on a comport moulded out of ice in the form of two entwined dolphins, a mould of which he also had in an advertisement in the back of his book. The ice itself was made in a melon mould with 'Plombières ice cream' to which 'diavolini' – ginger comfits, dried apricots and dried cherries – were added. The 'Plombières ice cream' was made with bitter and sweet almonds; orange flower water and apricot jam. Then the finished puddings were sprinkled with shaved almonds and chopped pistachios to look like a real melon. The top and base of the pudding was garnished with 'small fancy fruit-shaped water ices', which were also a popular treat.

Ice-cream flavours were versatile: there are recipes for bergamot water ice, diverse fruit and cordial sorbets, chocolate ice cream, burnt filbert ice cream, brown bread ice cream and various fruit ice creams. A peculiar one is a recipe for a parmesan ice cream by Frederick Nutt.

The challenge wasn't only in creating the most sensational of puddings, it had to be frozen at a time when freezers weren't yet invented. Today we have all kinds of fancy freezing equipment, but in the eighteenth and nineteenth centuries the techniques were a little more primitive, although at the same time quite inventive.

jellies, milk puddings & ices

Pewter and copper ice-cream moulds, part of the collection of Ivan Day

Georgian ice-cream makers

In the seventeenth century ice cream was made in a closed tin box that was left to freeze, producing a solid ice cream. By the mid-eighteenth century the ice-cream mixture was frozen by pouring it into a pewter canister with a handled lid called a sorbetière. The sorbetière was placed in a wooden bucket containing a mixture of ice and salt, or saltpetre. The right ratio of salt to ice would prevent the ice from melting. The ice-cream mixture was then turned by the handle of the sorbetière to mix and an ice spaddle or houlette was used to scrape down the frozen mixture from the sides and into the rest of the soon-to-be ice cream.

When the ice cream was thoroughly frozen, it was removed from the sorbetière and either transferred to a pewter ice-cream mould, or to an ice-cream pail. These pails were incredibly inventive things and benefited from a double bottom on which the ice was placed; the pail that held the ice cream was placed on top; and then finally the lid was placed on top of the pail and also filled with ice. This was created to have a fashionable item to bring to the table and keep the ice cream cold. They were made in France, but also by the English potteries. As they were an item only for the highest of the elite, they were rare, and are even more rare to find today.

jellies, milk puddings & ices |

Icehouses

Ice cream wasn't a privilege only for city dwellers. Ice creams were also made in the large country houses, which had icehouses built in the gardens of their estate as early as the seventeenth century. James I is attributed with ordering the building of the first icehouse in Britain in Greenwich Park. Icehouses have been known from the Romans, the ancient Greeks and even as far back as Mesopotamian civilisation. A clay tablet from around 1780 BCE records the foundation of an icehouse in Terqa, a city on the banks of the middle Euphrates.

These early examples of icehouses looked a little like brick-built igloos and were often located in a sheltered area close to freshwater lakes or ponds. This is because the location would be coolest, but also to be able to easily transport ice from the frozen lake into the icehouse when it happened to freeze solid. Ponds, such as the one at old Eglinton Castle estate in North Ayrshire, were sometimes created especially to supply ice for the icehouse.

The icehouse would often have more than one door, acting as an airlock to keep the warmth outside. The inside of the building was often further insulated with straw, an insulation Mary Eales also mentions in her 1718 recipe.

After being a privilege to the upper class for centuries, by the middle of the nineteenth century, ices had become available to ordinary people. Henry Mayhew (in *London Labour and the London Poor*, 1851) mentioned that ices were being sold on the streets of London in 1850, and that it appeared the working-class folk didn't enjoy these ice-cold treats at first. The two first street sellers of 'penny lick' ices went out of business; however, trade did pick up, despite having one of the smallest numbers of traders on the streets.

Bringing natural ice to London

Change came when immigrants from Italy and Italian-speaking Switzerland came to London; by 1860, Italian ice cream became a familiar sight in the streets. One of these early entrepreneurs, Carlo Gatti, founded his first ice-cream shops in London in 1851. He became possibly one of the first wholesale ice-cream makers in England. Gatti also transported large blocks of natural Norwegian ice by boat to London. The building now occupied by the Canal Museum just off Regent's Canal is a former ice warehouse of his, originally constructed around 1863 to store the imported ice.

In 1899 the 'penny lick' was banned due to fear of the spread of diseases such as tuberculosis. 'Penny licks' were glasses made of thick pressed glass and were sold as a half penny, penny or twopence lick. After the customer had licked the small glass clean, it would be washed in a basin of dirty, greasy dishwater. Luckily the ice-cream vendors could still sell their cheap blocks of ice called 'Hokey Pokey' which was a slang term for ice cream in general and often resembled a Neapolitan layered ice. But sales did drop until the ice-cream cone was introduced.

The Queen of Ices

Agnes Bertha Marshall, crowned with the title 'Queen of Ices' by ice-cream afficionados today, was an English culinary entrepreneur. She published two books entirely devoted to ices: a thin blue volume named *The Book of Ices* (1888) and her later book *Fancy Ices* (1894). They remain much sought after books to this day.

She also invented an 'ice cave' to keep ices cold and an ice-cream machine capable of freezing a pint of ice-cream mixture in five minutes, for which she was granted a patent. Her inventions would further develop ice-cream making in England. She quite remarkably suggests using liquid oxygen to freeze ice cream, which was quite modern for the day.

In addition to publishing her books she had a weekly magazine called *The Table* and ran her own cookery school as well as an agency for domestic staff. She had her own shop selling her ice-cream maker, ice caves, cabinet freezers and other kitchen utensils and supplies. Marshall's pewter ice-cream moulds in all imaginable sizes and shapes, and fancy entrée moulds in tin and copper, were all compiled in *The Catalogue of Moulds* (c. 1880) which contained more than 400 engravings of the moulds available in her shop. This really shows the scale of her business, which must have been unique for its day, particularly having a woman at its head.

Ice-cream cones

It is assumed that Italo Marchiony invented the waffle ice-cream cone in New York in 1896. He received a patent for 'a molding apparatus for forming ice cream cups' in 1903. However, in 1902 Antonio Valvona, an ice-cream manufacturer of Manchester, received a patent for his 'Apparatus for baking biscuit-cups for ice-cream'. These two men, however, are not the inventors of an ice-cream cone, although they created devices to mould wafer cups.

Food historian Ivan Day notes, in *Ice Cream: A History* (2011) that wafer cones are first mentioned in Bernard Claremont's *The Professed Cook* in 1769. They were initially not used for ice cream but to serve with other sweetmeats during the dessert course. The first record of someone actually filling one of these wafer cones or cornets with ice cream is Charles Elmé Francatelli, who mentioned them in *The Modern Cook* in 1846 as a garnish in a recipe for his 'Chesterfield Cream Ice'. The illustration in his book shows the tall ice-cream pudding decorated with a crown of ice-cream cones at the base. He instructs to fill the cones with ice cream.

Ice cream for everyone

In the early twentieth century, ice-cream making experienced a decline because of wartime shortages of milk and sugar. The production and selling of ice cream was banned by the Ministry of Food in 1917 but, as soon as the war was over, the ice-cream trade came back as strong as it was before. In 1922, T. Walls and Sons Ltd became the first nationwide ice-cream wholesaler. They had tricycle ice-cream carts driving around London with the words 'Stop me and buy one' painted onto the front; by 1939 their numbers would be 8500 nationwide. Lyons Ices followed with their ice-cream parlours and others followed suit. After the Second World War and into the 1960s ices and ice lollies (iceblocks/popsicles) were factory-made on a large scale and had become an important part of a good night out at the cinema. Soon the American-style soft ices such as the still-popular 'Mr Whippy' followed. The contrast with the artisanal ice cream of the Italian and French ice-cream sellers and confectioners of Victorian England was immense.

Flavours went from natural to artificial: the quality of the milk, eggs and cream were questionable and so ice cream became another mass-produced food worldwide. Luckily, in the last 20 years it has become fashionable again to make homemade ices and restaurants are experimenting with new and exciting flavours. The quality of the ingredients plays an important role, and dairy farms market their ice creams made with milk and cream from their own herd. The future of ices is bright: maybe they will never look as dazzling and dramatic again as they did in the eighteenth and nineteenth centuries, but they will taste fantastic. Because when the best ingredients are used, you will get the best result.

jellies, milk puddings & ices

Pewter sorbetière, spaddle and bucket
from the collection of Ivan Day

Ice cream without an ice-cream machine

Homemade ice cream is exceptionally nice, but personally, I don't want to buy an ice-cream machine: they are big and ugly and will gather dust and take up space. I do have an ice-cream maker, but it's made of pewter, small, quaint and dates from the early 1800s: it's called a 'sorbetière'. Because not everyone is lucky enough to have a traditional sorbetière, the following method will do the trick just fine.

Early ice-cream recipes do not use egg yolks, but do feel free to use this technique for making ices with eggs as well. Eggs will keep the ice cream frozen for longer, and will also make it creamier. I find ice cream with egg yolks a little too heavy, while eggless ice cream feels nice and thin on the tongue. If you find the ice creams here too delicate for your liking, you may add up to 5 egg yolks per 500 ml (17 fl oz/2 cups) of cream; however, keep in mind that with 5 egg yolks, you essentially have frozen custard.

I find that with delicately flavoured ice creams, you need to use the minimum amount of egg yolks to keep the flavour nice and fresh. So give the eggless version a try, and if you don't find it creamy enough, add a yolk, and then another.

An important thing to note is that you cannot reduce the sugar content of the recipes, as the sugar is of importance to prevent the ice cream freezing into a solid brick. As much as I like to reduce sugar content in most recipes, you just can't do it with ice cream.

What you need

A plastic or pewter vessel, or an aluminium cake tin (make sure you can fit the vessel into your freezer); a wooden spatula; a whisk, or handmixer; a towel; an ice-cream mould, chilled (optional).

Method

Put the vessel in the freezer to get cold.

Using the recipe of your choice, bring the cream to a simmer with the flavourings and the sugar, then remove it from the heat and leave to infuse for at least 1 hour, after which you may remove any flavouring items, if necessary. Allow the mixture to cool completely.

Pour the cooled mixture into the ice-cold vessel and return it to the freezer for 45 minutes. After 45 minutes, whisk the mixture with a whisk, mixer or spatula. Return it to the freezer for 30 minutes. After 30 minutes repeat the whisking and return it to the freezer for a further 30 minutes. After 30 more minutes repeat the whisking and return it to the freezer for a further 30 minutes.

The mixture should be getting thicker and thicker at the edges of the vessel. Make sure you scrape the frozen mixture back into the centre and whisk well each time. Return it to the freezer for 30 minutes between whisking and repeat until you get ice cream.

It will take 2–3 hours, but it's totally worth the time you'll spend.

When the ice cream is ready, you can scoop it out and into an ice-cream mould, or you can transfer it to a freezer-safe airtight container. It will keep for a week, after which the texture will begin to be less pleasant.

Keep in mind that if you are not using egg yolks, the ice cream will melt more quickly.

Icy Cream

This is the first English ice-cream recipe, written down by Lady Ann Fanshawe's clerk in her manuscript recipe book around the mid 1660s. Luckily Lady Ann's contemporary and friend Grace Carteret, Countess Granville, gives more detailed instructions in her near-identical recipe in her manuscript recipe book of 1654–1744. Both ladies instruct to use a lidded silver or tin box, which will make the ice cream into a brick that would be easily portioned. It is very possible that this ice cream could have been the kind served to Charles II, as reported by Elias Ashmole, in the *Insititution, Laws and Ceremonies of the Order of the Garter*, 1672.

To make Icy Cream;
Take three pints of the best cream, boyle it with a blade of mace, or else perfume it with orange flower water or Amber-Greece sweeten the Cream, with sugar let it stand till it is quite cold, then put into Boxes, either of silver or tin then take, Ice chopped into small peeces and putt it into a tub and set the Boxes in the Ice covering them all over, and let them stand in the Ice two hours, and the Cream Will come to be Ice in the Boxes, then turne them out into a server with some of the same seasoned cream, so serve it up to the table.
Lady Ann Fanshawe, MS.7113 at the Wellcome Trust Library, London

Following these instructions would make the ice cream rather hard, as it wasn't churned as would be done later using sorbetière ice makers.

Serves 4–6

600 ml (21 fl oz) thick (double) cream

50 g (1¾ oz) raw sugar

1 mace blade

In a medium saucepan over low heat, bring the cream, sugar and mace to a simmer. Remove from the heat and allow it to cool in the saucepan, then freeze according to the instructions on page 319.

For an original feel, use a brick mould or loaf (bar) tin.

As a variation, use 1 tablespoon of orange flower water instead of the mace.

jellies, milk puddings & ices

Brown Bread Ice Cream

T he first time I heard about brown bread ice cream was when I read Jane Grigson's *English Food* (1974) years ago. In the introduction to her recipe she tells the story of a conversation she had with a hotelkeeper in a small village in France who was telling her: 'your ices are so wonderful. We have nothing like them here. I remember at Gunter's …' Sadly the quote in her book ends there, but we know of which Gunter she speaks: James Gunter of the Gunter family took over the famous Domenico Negri's confectioner's shop in London.

The recipe for Brown Bread Ice in *Gunter's Modern Confectioner* (by his apprentice William Jeanes, 1861) is very different to an earlier recipe by Frederick Nutt in *The Complete Confectioner* (1789). Nutt, like Gunter, had been an apprentice of Negri.

> Brown Bread Ice Cream.
> Do the same with a pint of cream as in the plain ice cream, only when you have frozen it, rasp two handfuls of brown bread and put it in before you put it into your moulds.
> Frederick Nutt, *The Complete Confectioner*, 1789

Agnes Marshall in *The Book of Ices* (1888) instructs to soak the breadcrumbs, while Nutt adds them without soaking. You get two different ice creams when you follow these recipes, although I must say I prefer the version when the bread hasn't been soaked; that way you have little bits of crunch in your ice cream, which is very nice to eat.

I prefer larger and more rustic breadcrumbs than those Nutt would have used in his ice cream. To get the effect of his ice cream, just use a finer breadcrumb. I also like to use brown sugar in this ice cream.

Serves 4–6

600 ml (21 fl oz) thick (double) cream

1 cinnamon stick

50 g (1¾ oz) brown sugar

butter, to fry the bread chunks

80 g (2¾ oz) wholemeal, rye or spelt bread, torn into chunks no larger than a pea

40 g (1½ oz) raw sugar

In a medium saucepan over low heat, bring the cream, cinnamon and brown sugar to a simmer. Remove from the heat and allow it to cool in the saucepan, then remove the cinnamon and freeze according to the instructions on page 319.

Meanwhile, melt the butter in a frying pan, toss in the bread and sugar, then fry until the bread chunks are crisp.

When the ice cream is ready for the final freezing, fold in the fried bread chunks just before putting it into the mould. You could also fold them through just before serving. If you wish, keep some of the fried breadcrumbs aside to use as decoration.

323

Tamarind Ice Cream

T amarinds are curious fruits that grow in pods and have tough strings. The flavour is very tart and tamarinds are one of the prime ingredients of Worcestershire sauce. In the eighteenth century, little balls of tamarind were placed in custard tarts, but they were also turned into a beautiful ice cream.

786. Tamarind Cream Ice
Take half a pound of tamarinds, three spoonfuls of syrup (No. 675); warm it together, and add one pint and a half of cream; rub it through a sieve; and freeze, as No 759.
John Conrade Cooke, *Cookery and Confectionery*, 1824

I learned to make this ice cream using the Georgian method at the home of food historian Ivan Day, using a pewter sorbetière to freeze the ice cream. It is truly refreshing on a hot summer's day, or after a festively rich meal, as the tartness of the tamarind cuts right through the richness of the ice cream. The unusual flavour of the tamarind will ensure your dinner guests will be curious and wanting seconds.

Serves 4–6

600 ml (21 fl oz) thick (double) cream

80 g (2¾ oz) raw sugar

50 g (1¾ oz) unsweetened tamarind purée

In a medium saucepan, bring the cream to a simmer with the sugar and tamarind purée. Simmer over low heat for 7–10 minutes, constantly poking the tamarind purée with a fork until it comes away from the threads it still has and starts to dissolve. The tamarind will colour the cream a pale chocolate milk colour.

Strain out the tamarind threads by pushing the cream through a sieve. Allow to cool completely. Now freeze the mixture according to the instructions on page 319.

Make sure you use tamarind purée that contains 100 per cent tamarind pulp and no other additives or sugar. You can find tamarind purée in shops specialising in Indian groceries.

jellies, milk puddings & ices |

A one-quart pewter sorbetière, left, and a nineteenth century pressed glass 'Penny Lick' ice-cream glass

Princess Surprise Bombe

The original recipe for this impressive Victorian ice pudding comes from Mrs Marshall's book *Fancy Ices* (1894). This pudding is similar to the baked Alaska, an ice pudding that was said to have been invented in New York in 1867 by Charles Ranhofer. A popular claim is that it was created to celebrate the United States' purchase of Alaska from the Russians. The recipe for baked Alaska is, however, not based on this one by Mrs Marshall, so we may assume that it represents a variety of ice pudding that was popular throughout the Victorian period.

Princess Marie d'Orléans Surprise Bomb
Prepare and freeze a white coffee ice (*Book of Ices*, page 13), and when frozen put it into a plain bomb mould with a pipe, and place the shape into the cave to freeze for two and a half hours; remove the lid and pipe, and fill the hollow space with pieces of fresh sponge cake steeped in Marshall's Maraschino Syrup; then turn out the ice on to a layer of sponge cake that is placed on the centre of the dish, and by means of a forcing bag with a large rose pipe cover it well in an ornamental style with a stiff meringue mixture prepared as below, and sprinkle it with Marshall's Icing Sugar. Stand the dish containing the bomb in a tin with water, and place it in a quick hot oven to brown the outside of the meringue, or glaze it with a salamander, and serve it immediately with a purée of peaches (prepared as below) round the base.
Agnes B. Marshall, *Fancy Ices*, 1894

This particular ice-cream pudding was often made in a copper bombe mould with a pipe in the middle that would leave a cavity to fill with other ice cream, or in this case, maraschino-soaked sponge cake. The ice cream surrounding the soaked cake is white coffee ice, made by infusing coffee beans in simmering cream. To serve, the pudding is placed on a disc of sponge cake – not soaked – of the same size and a meringue topping is added, which is then burnt using a blowtorch, originally a salamander.

327

jellies, milk puddings & ices |

19th century copper ice-cream bombe mould

White coffee ice cream

50 g (1¾ oz) roasted coffee beans

600 ml (21 fl oz) thick (double) cream

50 g (1¾ oz) raw sugar

Filling & base

sponge cake (see page 349)

maraschino liqueur

Sauce (optional)

410 g (14½ oz) tin peaches, or fresh boiled peaches

1 teaspoon rosewater

1 tablespoon rum

1 teaspoon sugar

Meringue

4 egg whites, at room temperature

225 g (8 oz) raw sugar

If you do not fancy maraschino liqueur, you can use amaretto or hazelnut liqueur instead. If you don't like to use the coffee beans, 5 crushed amaretti biscuits used instead also makes a lovely ice cream. The coffee ice cream is very nice on its own without making it into this elaborate ice pudding.

Princess surprise bombe

Make the ice cream a minimum of 2 hours in advance. In a medium saucepan, bring the cream to a simmer with the coffee beans and the sugar, then remove from the heat and leave to infuse for at least 1 hour. Allow to cool completely, then strain out the coffee beans. Proceed to make ice cream as instructed on page 319.

Meanwhile, place the mould you are going to use for the final freeze on the sponge cake and cut around it so you have a disc of cake the same size as the mould. Cut the remaining cake into chunks and soak them lightly in maraschino.

Transfer the ice cream to the mould, and set a small bowl into the ice cream so you will have a cavity in which to stuff the soaked cake.

Make the sauce, if using, by puréeing the peaches and adding the rosewater, rum and sugar. Keep cool until needed.

Remove the ice-cream mould from the freezer, take out the small bowl – this might stick – and stuff the cavity with the soaked pieces of cake, making sure it is filled up to the brim. Return to the freezer while you whisk up the meringue.

Put the egg whites into a large, ultraclean mixing bowl: it helps to clean it with some lemon juice, as any greasiness will ruin the meringue.

Beat the egg whites using an electric mixer fitted with the whisk attachment, until the mixture stands up in stiff peaks, then continue whisking while you add the sugar, 1 teaspoon at a time. Set aside while you unmould the ice-cream pudding.

Dip the mould into warm water to make it easier to unmould, then place the disc of sponge cake on top of the mould followed by a plate. Turn over carefully to unmould. Take it easy: it might pop out at once, or it might take a little while.

When unmoulded, use a palette knife or piping (icing) bag to spread or pipe the meringue over the pudding as neatly as you can manage. Toast the outside of the meringue using a kitchen blowtorch, or if you have a salamander you can use that instead. Be quick, as the pudding will melt very quickly as you brown the meringue.

Serve at once, with the peach sauce, if using.

Mock Plum Pudding Ice

We know by now that the English have always loved to serve one dish under the guise of another. This imitation plum pudding is no different. It also resembles the Nesselrode pudding, an ice-cream pudding that was very popular in Victorian England but designed in France for Count Nesselrode. Food historian Ivan Day reckons the count's chef, Monie, probably designed his Nesselrode pudding as a joke to poke fun at the English plum pudding.

There are Nesselrode pudding recipes aplenty in the nineteenth century books, but I was only able to find one version described as an 'imitation plum cake'.

> Imitation plum cake ice
> Prepare a custard cream ice with six ounces of chestnut farina added to the other ingredients composing the custard, and mix therewith stoned raisins, currants, candied peels, shred pistachios, and a wine-glassful of curacoa; mould the ice in a Charlotte mould, and when dished up pour a vanilla cream ice half frozen over it.
> Charles Elmé Francatelli, *The Royal Confectioner*, 1891

This pudding requires chestnut flour, where Nesselrode pudding often uses chestnuts that are boiled then puréed. I find the second version has a much nicer flavour than using chestnut flour, which is only really good if you can get it fresh. You can easily use the chestnuts bought ready peeled in a jar or vacuum pack; I use a small brand from the Ardennes. Boiling and then peeling the chestnuts is a tedious task you don't want to get into.

Makes enough for a 600 ml (21 fl oz) basin (mould); serves 4–6

20 g (¾ oz) raisins

20 g (¾ oz) currants

10 g (⅜ oz) candied peel

a shot of Cuarenta Y Tres or any other citrus liqueur, or dark rum

600 ml (21 fl oz) thick (double) cream

50 g (1¾ oz) brown sugar

4 egg yolks

5 chestnuts, boiled or roasted and peeled

20 g (¾ oz) peeled unsalted pistachios, halved

Soak the dried fruits, including the candied peel, in the liqueur overnight: this will prevent them from freezing dry.

In a medium saucepan, bring the cream to a simmer with the sugar, then remove it from the heat. Whisk the egg yolks in a bowl then start adding the warm cream gradually, as for a custard. Allow to cool.

Proceed to make ice cream as instructed on page 319.

Meanwhile, grind the chestnuts using a mortar and pestle.

When you are ready to transfer the ice cream to the mould for the final freezing, mix the ground chestnut into the ice cream, along with the soaked fruits and soaking liquid and pistachios.

Serve, as suggested by Francatelli, with melting ice cream so it looks like a plum pudding with cream poured over, or just as it is.

jellies, milk puddings & ices

CHAPTER 6

MASTER RECIPES

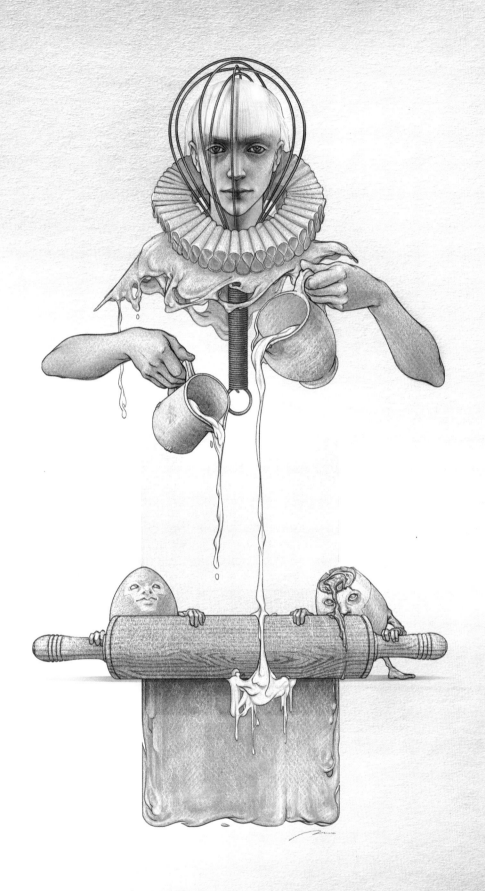

Master recipes

The following recipes for traditional sauces, pastries, cakes and biscuits are used in many recipes throughout this book. To get the most satisfying result from these recipes it is important to use the best possible quality ingredients. Good fresh butter and cream, free-range eggs and the best bread you can afford or make yourself.

For those of you living outside of Britain, or even far removed from the West Country – also known as 'Clotted Cream Central' – you will be happy to know that I have included a recipe to make this most divine buttery cream yourself. You don't need a cow, you don't need special bacteria or an open fire, just good thick cream, a tray, time and the recipe on these pages.

I won't be disappointed in you if you do buy ratafia biscuits or lady fingers (savoiardi); we don't always have the time to make these biscuits ourselves. You can save your efforts for special occasions, for those guests who will appreciate the trouble. There are a couple of good Italian biscuit brands out there, so look out for those.

Sponge cake, however, is best made to the recipe in these pages, because store-bought sponge cake can often be too sweet and too dense. (I'm not even considering that mass-produced sponge cake often contains more artificial ingredients than you might imagine.)

A pudding is a proud thing, and deserves to be made from the best possible components, so see what is possible for you.

Clotted Cream

Clotted cream is one of the most wonderful things that milk can produce. I remember vividly the first time I tasted this delightful mix between butter and sweet thick cream.

The earliest recipe I could find came from Thomas Dawson's *The Good Huswifes Handmaide for the Kitchin*, written in 1594. In the olden days it was called Clouted Cream, referring to the clouted top. The clouted top develops when warming fresh milk for hours: recipes usually state to use the cow's morning milk and warm it till the evening when a crust develops on the top. It is that crust that is so distinctive to this cream.

> When you have taken the milke from the Kine, straight set it on the fire, but see that your fyre be without smoake, and soft fire, and so keepe it on from morning till it be night, or nigh thereabout, and ye muste be sure that it doeth not seeth all that while, and ye muste let your milke be set on the fyre, in as broad a vessell as you can. Then take it from the fire, and set it vpon a board, and let it stande al night: then in the morning take off the cream, and put it in a dish or where ye wil.
>
> Thomas Dawson, *The Good Huswifes Handmaide for the Kitchin*, 1594

Recipes through the ages vary little: the pot of milk is placed on the embers or a small fire and the milk is either left alone until a crust develops, or a hole is made in the skin and cream is poured in and then the mixture is left to develop a crust. It is quite simple to make clotted cream with modern methods, we just have to keep the cream warm for a very long time and, luckily, we have safe ovens for that.

Not only is clotted cream an essential part of the English afternoon tea, it is also used in baking and in ice cream. Imagine that: buttery clotted cream ice cream, it should be illegal! In fact, in many places, it is. I prefer to use unpasteurised cream that I get from a local farm, but I strongly advise that you do not use raw cream or milk if you cannot be certain of the source or if you are unwell. It is illegal to sell or give unpasteurised products for consumption by humans in many places. Pasteurised cream will work but produces less clotted cream.

To be successful you need to know your oven. It really needs to be precisely 80°C (175°F) to work, as a higher temperature will colour the clouted top too much and will not leave you with clotted cream. A lower temperature will not work either. To prevent disappointment, you can measure the temperature in your oven with an oven thermometer if you have one.

1 litre (35 fl oz/4 cups) thick (double) cream

Preheat the oven to 80°C (175°F).

Pour the cream into a shallow roasting tin or tins to a depth of about 2 cm (¾ inch). Set the tins in the middle of the oven for 9–10 hours. Remove the cream from the oven and stand in a cool place for another 10–12 hours. The fridge is allowed if you have the space.

Don't be alarmed if the cream is very runny underneath; this is normal. Think of it as being similar to butter, which is also runny when warm. Just put in a cold place or the fridge and forget about it for the time being.

After 10–12 hours, scoop off the yellow crust or 'clouted cream' with a spoon, put it into a clean airtight container and refrigerate before use.

Any leftover runny cream can be used for other cooking.

18th century

Custard Sauce

Gloriously flavoursome full-fat milk and cream and deep orange coloured egg yolks will give the flavour you need to make this a truly enjoyable sauce. Mace is excellent as a flavouring, a bay leaf added to it gives a more spiced flavour. When using cinnamon, the flavour is quite similar to using vanilla, I find, but vanilla – now commonly used – was never traditional.

Makes about 2 litres
(70 fl oz/8 cups)

10 egg yolks

500 ml (17 fl oz/2 cups) milk

500 ml (17 fl oz/2 cups) thick (double) cream

50 g (1¾ oz) raw sugar

1 mace blade or cinnamon stick

1 bay leaf (optional)

Whisk the egg yolks in a large bowl. Bring the milk, cream, sugar, spice and bay leaf, if using, to a simmer in a saucepan. Strain the hot milk mixture and discard the flavourings. Pour a little of the hot mixture into the egg yolks and whisk thoroughly. Now continue to add the hot milk mixture in batches until fully incorporated and you get a smooth sauce.

Pour the mixture back into the saucepan and cook over low heat, stirring constantly with a spatula until just thickened, making sure the eggs don't scramble.

When just thickened, remove from the heat and pour into a cold sauceboat for serving. If you don't want the custard to develop a skin, cover the sauceboat with plastic wrap.

Vanilla custard

Adding vanilla isn't traditional to Britain but is delicious and often done today. Please use a real vanilla bean and not the essence, which has often not a seed of vanilla in it. Split a vanilla bean lengthways and simmer with the milk and cream. Take the bean out of the liquid when you are adding it to the egg yolks. Keep the vanilla bean, rinse it gently and dry it. It will still give off enough flavour to make your own vanilla sugar when placed in a jar with sugar.

master recipes

Sack Sauce

This is a very traditional sauce for pudding. It has been forgotten during the past hundred years, but because the flavour is so good, and everyone I serve it to enjoys it; it really ought to be revived.

Sack was a fortified wine; the flavour can be compared to sherry today. It was used a lot in cooking and also in puddings. You may also use Madeira or another sweet wine if you have that in your larder.

Take equal quantities of butter, sherry and sugar. Melt the butter until it starts to brown, then add the sugar and sherry and stir until the sugar has dissolved and the sauce is creamy. Serve hot.

Raspberry Vinegar

Raspberry vinegar can be served with very heavy puddings, or as a little sour lift in very sweet ones. Vinegars were an important part of the medieval and renaissance cuisine.

Makes 500 ml (17 fl oz/2 cups)

100 g (3½ oz) raspberries or leftover raspberry pulp

250 ml (9 fl oz/1 cup) good-quality cider vinegar

Rinse the raspberries and put them in a ceramic bowl. Crush the fruit with a fork and add the cider vinegar. Cover the bowl with plastic wrap and store in a cool, dark place for 3 days. After 3 days strain the vinegar and discard the pulp.

Transfer the vinegar to a clean bottle(s) using a funnel. Leave the bottle(s) for a month in a cool, dark place – it will be autumn by then. The vinegar will keep for at least 6 months, but I have used it for far longer. The taste doesn't really change much as it ages, it just gets a little more pungent.

Candied Citrus Peel

In the Tudor period these candied fruits or sweetmeats were known as 'wet suckets' because they were kept in syrup. They were an important addition to the banqueting courses and displayed to show off their beautiful colours.

Before these sweetmeats were made in England, they were imported from the Mediterranean; however, by the Tudor period they were made in England with imported fruits. By the eighteenth century candied fruits were available to buy from professional confectioners.

The method for making candied fruit hardly changed over the centuries. In fact the method I use is inspired by Eliza Smith's 1727 book, *The Compleat Housewife*.

whole oranges, citrons or lemons

an equal weight of sugar to the fruit

100 ml (3½ fl oz) water to each 100 g (3½ oz) of sugar

Day 1. Wash and peel the citrus fruit, discarding the flesh. Cut the peel of each piece of fruit into six equal pieces.

Poach the peel in fresh water until tender, making sure the fruit is kept underwater at all times. This takes 30–40 minutes.

Put the peel in a clean saucepan and cover with the sugar and water. Bring to a boil, stirring to dissolve the sugar and continue to cook for 30 minutes. Leave to steep overnight.

Day 2. Bring the syrup and peel back to the boil, then immediately remove from the heat and use tongs to transfer the peel to a clean, warmed glass jar. Pour the syrup over the peel and allow to cool. When cool, put on the lid and store in the fridge.

Day 3. Strain the syrup into a pan and return the peel to a warmed glass jar. Bring the syrup to the boil, then pour it back over the peel and return to the fridge when cool. Repeat this step daily for 10 days.

After 10 days the peel looks translucent and soft. Keeping them in syrup keeps them moist. If you like the peels dry, drain the syrup and dust some caster (superfine) sugar over them while leaving them to dry to a consistency that you prefer.

Keep the peel in the fridge at all times, when it looks like it is starting to ferment, simply boil the syrup again and pour it back over the peel.

master recipes

Shortcrust Pastry

Most medieval recipes for tarts and pies do not tell you anything about the kind of pastry that should be used for the crust. Recipes usually only describe how to make the filling. Contrary to what has been assumed, most pie and tart pastry was eaten and edible. Sometimes just the sides and top were removed.

This sixteenth century recipe is one of the earliest for making shortcrust pastry. The addition of eggs and saffron give it a wonderful flavour.

> To make short paest for tarte. Take fyne floure and a cursey of fayre water and a dysche of swete butter and a lyttel saffron, and the yolckes of two egges and make it thynne and as tender as ye maye.
> *A Proper New Booke of Cookery*, 1575, edited by Catherine Frances Frere, 1913

The recipe below is for a basic shortcrust pastry.

Makes enough for one 20–22 cm (8–8¾ inch) tart with a little left over

a pinch of saffron threads

1 tablespoon cold water

100 g (3½ oz) cold butter

180 g (6¼ oz) plain (all-purpose) flour

20 g (¾ oz) icing (confectioners') raw sugar

tiny pinch of salt

1 egg yolk

Soak the saffron in the water so it can give off its colour. Cut the butter into small pieces.

Put the flour into a food processor and add the butter, sugar and salt. Pulse for 8 seconds until the mixture looks like breadcrumbs. To mix by hand, simply use a blunt knife, cutting the knife through the butter and flour to work them together.

Add the saffron water and egg yolk and pulse until you get big lumps, then turn the pastry onto a lightly floured work surface and knead briefly until smooth.

Wrap the pastry in plastic wrap and refrigerate for at least 30 minutes or until you are ready to use it.

Turn the dough out onto a lightly floured work surface and knead and press the dough into a flat disc, then roll it out to a circle larger than the base of the tart tin.

Place the pastry over the tart tin and let it sink in, pushing it nicely into the corners, then cut off the excess pastry and prick the pastry with a fork, making sure you don't pierce through it.

To blind bake, preheat the oven to 180°C (350°F). Line the pastry with baking paper and weigh it down with baking beads, rice or dried beans. Bake for 25 minutes, remove the weights, then fill and bake at the required temperature.

Hot-water Pastry

T his pastry was used in the Middle Ages for custard or cheese tarts. The pastry was hand raised and hot water is used because it softens the gluten and makes the pastry easier to handle and less prone to break. It also holds its shape nicely for baking. Later lard and butter were added to the recipe and it evolved to the hot-water pastry we know today.

The pastry is incredibly fun to handle; when baked it will appear tough but this is the traditional pastry for these tarts and pies. This pastry was also used to make castles, which often had fillings of custard or meat; these were called 'subtleties' and were placed on the tables for theatrical effect. Dinner was theatre, remember!

Makes enough for a 20 cm (8 inch) tart tin

225 g (8 oz/1½ cups) plain (all-purpose) flour

150 ml (5 fl oz) boiling water

Preheat the oven to 200°C (400°F). Lightly grease and line the tart tin with baking paper.

Put the flour into a heatproof bowl and make a well in the centre into which you will pour the boiling water.

Use a blunt knife to form a stiff dough by making circular movements combining the water and flour. If the dough is too dry, you may add more water, 1 teaspoon at a time, but not after you knead it for a few minutes. The dough should come together nicely without adding extra water, but some flours can take up more moisture than others.

Turn the dough out onto a lightly floured work surface and knead and press the dough into a flat disc, then roll it out to a circle larger than the base of the tart tin.

Place the pastry over the tart casing and let it sink in, pushing it nicely into the corners, then cut off the excess pastry and prick the pastry with a fork, making sure you don't pierce through it.

Line the pastry with baking paper and weigh it down with baking beads, rice or dried beans. Blind bake for 25 minutes, remove the weights, then fill and bake at the required temperature for the recipe.

Puff Pastry

It is remarkable to see how little puff pastry recipes have changed over the centuries. The recipe I give here is a standard rough puff pastry recipe that is really easy and will convince you to make your own instead of using ready-made puff pastry. The difference is that this is done and dusted in 10 minutes and the butter goes in all at once, while with standard puff pastry you need to fold the butter into the pastry, roll and fold and repeat a few times with resting in the fridge in between rolls. For the recipes in this book you don't really need to make the more time-consuming standard puff pastry, as rough puff pastry works perfectly.

Makes enough for two 20 cm (8 inch) pies. It works better to make the whole recipe and freeze the remainder if you only need half the pastry.

225 g (8 oz/1½ cups) plain (all-purpose) flour

½ teaspoon fine salt

240 g (8¾ oz) cold butter

130 ml (4¼ fl oz) ice-cold water

The quickest way to make this is to use a food processor. I'd never really used a food processor for pastry until I was experimenting with this recipe and I must say I found it an absolute improvement.

Put the flour in a large bowl, or the bowl of a food processor, and put it in the fridge to get cold. Meanwhile, cut the butter into small cubes and put it into the freezer with the water for a few minutes.

Put the flour into the food processor and toss in the butter. Before you start the processor, use a knife to stir the mixture so every cube of butter is covered in flour.

Give two short pulses of about 1 second, then add half the water, pulse again for 3 short pulses, then add the rest of the water and pulse 6 times.

Turn out the dough onto a lightly floured work surface. Don't be alarmed if you think the dough is too crumbly; it's supposed to be that way.

Pat the dough into a sausage, then use a rolling pin to flatten it out to a rectangle. The dough should be quite rough and very marbled with butter. If it is barely holding together at the edges, this is normal.

Fold the right side of the rectangle to the middle and then do the same with the left side of the pastry. Flatten the dough slightly with the rolling pin, then fold up the bottom third of the dough, followed by the top third, to make a small square of dough.

Again, flatten the dough slightly, wrap in plastic wrap and put it in the fridge for at least 30 minutes.

Roll out when needed and proceed as instructed in the recipe.

Ratafia Biscuits

These biscuits are a type of macaroon that were made with sweet and bitter almonds, now apricot kernels. They have the marzipan flavour also found in Amaretto, which is a ratafia liquor, hence the name ratafia biscuits. They were used in trifles, but also served as sweets at dinner parties and as an accompaniment to a syllabub. In Italy these biscuits are known as amaretti, also like the drink Amaretto.

Ratafia Biscuits
Take a pound of sweet almonds, and half a pound of bitter almonds, and pound them in a mortar very fine, with the whites of eggs; put three pounds of powdered sugar, mix it well with the whites of eggs, to the proper thickness unto a bason; put two or three sheets of paper, on the plate you bake on; take your knife, and the spaddle made of wood, and drop them on the paper, let them be round, and about the size of a large nutmeg; put them in the oven, which must be quick, let them have a fine brown, and all a like, but be careful they are not burnt at bottom, else they will not come off the paper when baked: let them be cold before you take them off.
Frederick Nutt, *The Complete Confectioner*, 1789

Makes 60–65 small biscuits

55 g (2 oz) sweet almonds

30 g (1 oz) apricot kernels

½ teaspoon rosewater

4 egg whites

85 g (3 oz) raw sugar,
  processed to a powder

Preheat the oven to 180°C (350°F). Line a baking tray with baking paper.

Blanch and skin the almonds and apricot kernels and pound them with the rosewater, using a mortar and pestle. You may use a food processor if you have one, as you need quite a large mortar and strong arms to finish the job properly.

Whisk the egg whites to a froth, gradually adding the sugar. Now fold it into the almond and apricot kernels. Don't overwork it as the biscuits will become flat. (Don't worry if it does, it happens to me all the time.)

Transfer the mixture to a piping (icing) bag and pipe small drops evenly onto the baking tray: make them the size of a nutmeg, as Nutt instructs.

Put the tray in the middle of the oven and bake until golden brown, which will take about 15 minutes. Cool on the tray.

When fresh, the biscuits are quite chewy, but when stored for a couple of days in a paper bag (not an airtight container) they become crisp and just the right texture to be used in trifle, semolina or cabinet pudding, or just as a nibble.

After they have become crisp, you can store them in an airtight container for a couple of weeks.

Sponge Cakes

Sponge cakes, or 'Savoy biscuits' as they were also known, often feature in recipes as an ingredient, such as cake layers in a tort de moy, or general satisfaction, or soaked in booze in a cabinet pudding. Sometimes lady fingers (savoiardi) are used instead, as in a trifle, but for some dishes you really need sponge cakes.

Although one might think, by looking at old recipe books, that they were never eaten on their own, on rare occasions – as in *The Cookbook of Unknown Ladies* (c. 1690) – they are mentioned to be 'proper with tea in an afternoon'.

Basically they are no-butter sponge cakes, often with flavourings like orange flower water or rosewater. I find a little butter added improves them, as does the use of self-raising flour.

Makes enough for two 20 cm (8 inch) cakes, or you can use muffin tins to make about 24 individual cakes

butter, for greasing

50 g (1¾ oz) unsalted butter, softened

220 g (7¾ oz/1¼ cups) raw caster (superfine) sugar

4 eggs

½ teaspoon orange flower water, rosewater or lemon zest (optional)

225 g (8 oz/1½ cups) self-raising flour, plus extra for dusting

Preheat the oven to 180°C (350°F). Grease the cake tins lightly with butter and dust with flour.

In a bowl, combine the butter and sugar together, adding the eggs one at a time and whisking thoroughly until the mixture is creamy. Add the flavouring, if using. Sift in the flour and fold in well.

Pour the batter into the cake tins and bake in the middle of the oven for 30 minutes. Insert a toothpick: when it comes out clean, the cakes are done. Do not open the oven before 30 minutes have passed or your cakes will collapse.

They should not have a lot of colour on top.

Keep sponge cakes in an airtight container for up to 1 week.

19th century

Lady Fingers

Snappy lady fingers used to be called 'sponge fingers' and they evolved from the classic sponge cakes of the nineteenth century. They are the English version of an Italian savoiardi biscuit, which means 'from Savoy', explaining the link with the English sponge cakes which were also called Savoy biscuits. The Aosta Valley of Italy, in the Alps, was once known as the Duchy of Savoy, and the biscuits were said to have come from these parts.

It is hard to determine where the biscuit was first made; it seems to me it is a normal evolution of a biscuit that has been lovingly prepared in so many different ways for centuries. It appears the biscuit was popular and used all over Europe, as other countries have their own name for it.

master recipes

Frederick Vine gives a recipe in his book *Saleable Shop Goods* (1898) and also shares an engraving of what the sponge finger pan – or 'frame', as they called it – looked like. His recipe is very clear, though he doesn't mention an important step: to beat the egg whites to soft peaks, which is important to create that snappy biscuit. His recipe and instructions are too long to share here, but I leave you with William Kitchiner's version, which is very similar.

Sponge Biscuits.
Break into a round-bottomed preserving-pan nine good-sized eggs, with one pound of sifted loaf sugar, and some grated lemon-peel; set the pan over a very slow fire, and whisk it till quite warm (but not too hot to set the eggs); remove the pan from the fire, and whisk it till cold, which may be a quarter of an hour; then stir in the flour lightly with a spattle; previous to which, prepare the sponge frame as follows: – Wipe them well out with a clean cloth, rub the insides with a brush dipped in butter, which has been clarified, and sift loaf sugar over; fill the frames with the mixture; throw pounded sugar over; bake them five minutes in a brisk oven: when done, take them from the frames, and lay them on a sieve.
William Kitchiner, *The Cook's Oracle*, 1820

Makes enough for 2 lady finger trays

clarified butter, melted, for greasing

60 g (2¼ oz) plain (all-purpose) flour, plus extra for dusting

3 eggs, separated

90 g (3¼ oz) raw sugar

grated zest of ½ lemon

icing (confectioners') sugar, for dusting

Preheat the oven to 110°C (230°F).

Prepare the baking trays – preferably sponge finger trays, or plain trays will do – by greasing them with melted clarified butter and dusting with flour.

In a clean bowl, whisk the egg whites to soft peaks, then add half the sugar and continue to whisk until you get a glossy shine. This should take no longer than 1 minute.

Mix the egg yolks with the remaining sugar and the lemon zest and whisk until creamy. Sift the flour – yes, you really do need to sift it to get the best result here – over the yolk and sugar mixture and fold it in until combined.

Now fold in the egg whites, then scoop the batter immediately into a piping (icing) bag with a plain 1 cm (⅜ inch) nozzle and start piping 8 cm (3¼ inch) long fingers into the lady finger tray or onto the plain tray. Dust lightly with icing sugar.

Bake in the oven for 45 minutes.

Remove from the oven, allow the biscuits to cool in the tin for 5–10 minutes only, then remove them before they stick to the tin.

In an airtight container, they keep for weeks and are good to use in trifles and other puddings. If you want to eat them on their own, it's best to eat them as fresh as possible.

References

A., W., *A Book of Cookrye*, 1584

Acton, Eliza, *Modern Cookery for Private Families*, 1845, new edition with a foreword by Jill Norman, 2011; *The English Bread Book*, 1857

Adamson, Melitta Weiss: *Food in the Middle Ages: A Book of Essays*, 1995; *Food in Medieval Times*, 2004

Albus, Liber, *The White Book of the City of London, Introduction by H. T. Riley*, 1861

Alcock, J.P., *A Brief History of Roman Britain*, 2011

Allaire–Graham, Erin Sunshine, 'From Fast to Feast: Analyzing the Ubiquitous White Dish Called Blancmange', paper, 2012

The Anglo-Saxon Chronicle, Everyman Press, 1912

Apicius: *De Re Coquinaria, Project Gutenberg's Cooking and Dining in Imperial Rome*, Editor: Cesare Giarratano, Friedrich Vollmer

Apicius: *Cookery and Dining in Imperial Rome*, edited and translated by Joseph Sommers Vehling

Ashmole, Elias, *Institution, Laws, and Ceremonies of the Order of the Garter*, 1672

Artusi, Pelegrino, *La Scienza in Cucina e l'Arte di Mangiare Bene*, 1891; translated as *Science in the Kitchen and the Art of Eating Well*, University of Toronto Press, 2003

Austin, Thomas, ed., *Two Fifteenth-century Cookery-books*: Harleian MS. 279 (ab 1430), & Harl. MS. 4016 (ab. 1450), with extracts from Ashmole MS. 1439, Laud MS. 553, & Douce MS. 55, Oxford University Press, 1964

Awkbarow, Thomas, *Thomas Awkbarow's Recipes (MS Harley 5401)*, 15th century

Barham, Peter; Brears, Peter; Deith, John; and Weir, Robin, *Mrs Marshall, The greatest Victorian ice cream maker*, 1998

Bede, The Venerable, reported in Banham, Debby, *Food and Drink in Anglo–Saxon England*, 2004

Beeton, Isabella, *The Book of Household Management*, 1861

Bibbesworth, Walter of, see Walter of Bibbesworth

Black, Jane, 'The Trail of Tiramisu', *Washington Post*, 11 July 2007

Blankaart, Stephaan; Hoorn, Jan Claesz ten, *Nieuw Lichtende Praktyk der Medicynen*, 1678

Book of Common Prayer, 1549

Borella, *The Court and Country Confectioner*, 1770

Bradley, Richard, *The Country Housewife and Lady's Director*, 1732

Brears, Peter, *The English Kitchen: Jellies and Their Moulds*, 2010; *All the King's Cooks: The Tudor Kitchens of King Henry VIII at Hampton Court*, 2011, *Cooking and Dining in Medieval England*, 2012, see also Barham, Peter

Briggs, Richard, *The English Art of Cookery, According to the Present Practice*, 1788

Brookes, Stuart; Harrington, Sue; Reynolds, Andrew, *Early Anglo–Saxon Art and Archaeology: Papers in Honour of Martin G. Welch*, Archaeopress 2011

Buckner, Phillip Alfred; Francis, R. Douglas, *Rediscovering the British World*, 2005

Burney, Fanny, *Diary and Letters of Madame D'Arblay 1797–1840*, 1876

Burns, Robert, 'To a Haggis', *Burns Illustrated : The Poetical Works of Robert Burns*, c.1856

Byron, May, *May Byron's Pudding Book*, 1917; *Pot-luck*, 1932

Camden, William, *Remaines of a Greater Worke, Concerning Britaine*, 1605

Carême, Marie Antonin, *Le Patissier Royal Parisien*, 1815

Carey, Henry, *A Learned Dissertation on Dumpling; its Dignity, Antiquity and Excellence with a Word upon Pudding*, 1726

Carlin, Martha, *Food and Eating in Medieval Europe*, eds Martha Carlin and Joel T Rosenthal, London and Rio Grande, 1998

Carter, Charles, *The Complete Practical Cook*, 1730

Chambers, Robert, *The Book of Days*, 1862

Chaucer, Geoffrey, *The Canterbury Tales*, 1475

Chieregati, Francesco, *Calendar of State Papers and Manuscripts Relating to English Affairs Existing in the Archives and Collections of Venice and in Other Libraries of Northern Italy*, Vol. VII, 1558–1580, London, 1890; see also Parsons, Frank Alvah, *The Psychology of Dress*, 1920, 'Chieregati's letter to Isabella d'Este 1547'

Claremont, Bernard, *The Professed Cook*, 1769

Cleland, Elizabeth, *A New and Easy Method of Cookery*, 1755

A Collection of Ordinances and Regulations for the Government of the Royal Household, Society of Antiquaries of London, 1790

The Cookbook of Unknown Ladies, Westminster City Archives, c. 1690

Cooke, John Conrade, *Cookery and Confectionery*, 1824

Cooper, Artemis, 'David, Elizabeth (1913–1992)', Oxford Dictionary of National Biography, Oxford University Press, 2004; *Writing at the Kitchen Table: The Authorized Biography of Elizabeth David*, 2011

Cotton, Charles, *Wonders of the Peak*, 1681

Das Buch von guter Speise (The Book of Good Food), 1350

David, Elizabeth, *Mediterranean Food*, 1950; *French Country Cooking*, 1951; *Italian Food*, 1951; *Summer Cooking*, 1955; *Spices, Salt and Aromatics in the English Kitchen*, 1970; *English Bread and Yeast Cookery*, 1977; *An Omelette and a Glass of Wine*, essay 'Syllabubs and Fruit Fools', 2009

Davidson, Alan, *The Oxford Companion to Food*, 1999; 3rd edition, 2006

Davidson, Alan; Saberi, Helen, *Trifle*, 2009

Dawson, Thomas, *The Good Huswifes Handmaide for the Kitchin*, 1594; *The Good Huswifes Jewell*, 1596, transcribed by Daniel Myers, 2008

Day, Ivan, 'From Murrell to Jarrin: Illustrations in British Cookery Books, 1621–1820', *The English Cookery Book: Proceedings of the Twelfth Leeds Symposium on Food History*, 2004; 'Further musings on syllabub, or why not "jumble it a pritie while"?', 1996, accessible at www.historicfood.com/Syllabubs%20Essay.pdf; *Ice Cream: A History*, Shire Library, 2011; Day's website and blog at www.historicfood.com; www.foodhistorjottings.blogspot.be

Deith, John, see Barham, Peter

Digby, Sir Kenelm, *The Closet of the Eminently Learned Sir Kenelme Digbie Knight Opened*, 1910, originally published 1669

The Domesday Book, c. 1086

Eales, Mary, *Mrs. Mary Eales's Receipts*, 1718

Eaton, Mary, *The Cook and Housekeeper's Dictionary*, 1822

Ellis, William, *The Country Housewife's Family Companion*, 1750

Encyclopædia Britannica, 9th ed., Vol. XI, 1880

Fanshawe, Lady Ann, *Recipe Book of Lady Ann Fanshawe, 1625–1680, MS.7113* held at the Wellcome Trust Library

Farley, John, *The London Art of Cookery*, 1783

Fernie, William Thomas, *Herbal Simples Approved for Modern Uses of Cure*, 1897

Fettiplace, Elinor, *Elinor Fettiplace's Receipt Book* (17th century), 1987

Finberg, H.P.R.; Thirsk, Joan, *The Agrarian History of England and Wales*, Vol 2, Cambridge University, 1988

Fisher, M.F.K., *With Bold Knife and Fork*, 1968

Fitzstephen, William, *A Survey of London*, reprinted and translated by John Stow, 1598

Florio, John, *A Worlde of Wordes, Italian/English dictionary*, 1598

The Forme of Cury, Rylands MS7, c. 1390

Fowler, J.T., *Extracts from the account rolls of the Abbey of Durham, from the original MSS, Durham*, published for the Society for Andrews & Co, 1898, p 106

Francatelli, Charles Elmé, *The Modern Cook*, 1846; *A Plain Cookery Book for the Working Classes*, 1852; *The Royal English and Foreign Confectioner*, 1862; *The Cook's Guide*, 1867; *The Royal Confectioner*, 1891

Frazer, Susanna, *The Practice of Cookery, Pastry & Confectionery*, 1795

Frere, Catherine Frances, ed., *A Proper Newe Booke of Cokerye*, (1575) Cambridge: W. Heffer & Sons Ltd, 1913; electronic version: Thomas Gloning, VII/2001

Garrett, Theodore Francis, *The Encyclopaedia of Practical Cookery*, 1895

Gasteiz, Vitoria, 'El Cocinero de los Reyes y el Rey de los Cocineros', Spain, September 2000, in *Zapardiel: revista de cultura y gastronomía*, No 1

Getz, Faye M., *Healing and Society in Medieval England, A Middle English Translation of the Pharmaceutical Writings of Gilbertus Anglicus*, 1991 (original: 1250)

Gibson, Alex M., *Prehistoric Pottery for the Archaeologist*, 1997

Glasse, Hannah, *The Art of Cookery, Made Plain and Easy*, 1747; 4th edition, 1751; *The Compleat Confectioner*, 1760

Goodwin, Gillian, 'Blancmange', *History Today*, Vol 35, no. 7: 60, 1985

Granville, Countess, *manuscript recipe book of Grace Carteret, 1654–1744, MS.8903* held at the Wellcome Trust Library

Grieco, Allen J., 'From the Cookbook to the Table: A Florentine Table and Italian Recipes of the Fourteenth and Fifteenth Centuries,' in *Du Manuscrit a la Table*, Paris: Champion – Slatkine, 1992, ed. Carole Lambert

Grigson, Jane, *English Food*, 1974; *Charcuterie and French Pork Cookery*, Michael Joseph, 1967

Grimm, Jacob und Wilhelm, *Deutsches Wörterbuch*, 1854

Gwynarden, Baroness Faeris, trans., *A Treatise of Portuguese Cuisine from the 15th Century*, (Collection of recipes, some very original, for the preparation of most varied delicassies)

Hagger, Conrad, *Neues Saltzburgisches Kochbuch*, 1719

Halliwell-Phillipps, James Orchard, *The Nursery Rhymes of England*, 1842

Hardy, Thomas, *Tess of the d'Urbervilles*, 1892

Harper, Douglas, Modern Language Association (MLA): 'pudding', *Online Etymology Dictionary*, 27 February 2015

Harpestræng, Henrik, *Libellus De Arte Coquinaria*, c. 1240

Hartley, Dorothy, *Food in England*, 1954

Heath, Ambrose, *From Garden to Kitchen*, 1937; *Good Sweets*, 1937; *More Kitchen Front Recipes*, 1941

Hieatt, Constance B., 'Sorting Through the Titles of Medieval Dishes: What is, or Is Not, a "Blanc Manger",' in *Food in the Middles Ages: A Book of Essays*, New York: Garland, 1995, ed. Melitta Weiss Adamson; 'The Middle English Culinary Recipes in MS Harley 5401: An Edition and Commentary', *Medium Ævum* Vol 65 no 1 (1996): 54–71; *Cocatrice and Lamprey Hay, Corpus Christi College, Oxford MS F 291*, edited and translated by Constance B. Hieatt, 2012; 'A miscellany of household information', Cambridge University Library, MS Ll.1.18 in *The Culinary Recipes of Medieval England*, 2013

Hieatt, Constance B.; Butler, Sharon, 'Curye on Inglish: English Culinary Manuscripts of the Fourteenth Century (Including the Forme of Cury)', for The Early English Text Society by the Oxford University Press, 1985

Hill, Georgiana, *Everybody's Pudding Book, or puddings, tarts, etc., In their proper season, For all the year round*, 1862

Holmes, Urban Tigner, *Daily Living in the Twelfth Century: Based on the Observations of Alexander Neckham*, 1952

Homer, *The Odyssey*, c. 800 BCE, translated by Samuel Butler, 1999

Howard, Henry, *England's Newest Way in Cookery*, 1703

Hudson, William, ed., *Leet Jurisdiction in the city of Norwich during the XIIIth and XIVth centuries*, Selden Society, 1891

Hughes, Kathryn, *The Short Life and Long Times of Mrs Beeton*, 2006

Hunt, Tony, *Teaching and Learning Latin in Thirteenth-century England*, Texts By Tony Hunt, 1991

Jacob, Elizabeth (& others), *Physicall and Chyrurgicall Receipts. Cookery and preserves, 1654–c.1685*, MS.3009 held at the Wellcome Trust Library

Jarrin, William Alexis, *The Italian Confectioner*, 1820; 3rd edition 1827

Jeanes, William, *Gunter's Modern Confectioner*, 1861

Jewry, Mary, *Warne's Model Cookery and Housekeeping Book*, 1868; *Warne's Every Day Cookery*, 1887

Joyce, James, *A Portrait of the Artist as a Young Man*, 1922

Kalm, Pehr, 'Kalm's account of his visit to England on his way to America in 1748', translated by Joseph Lucas, 1892

Kelly, Ian, 'Crème du Carême, Manchester', *The Guardian*, 12 October 2003

Kettleby, Mary, *A Collection of Above Three Hundred Receipts in Cookery, Physick and Surgery*, 1714

Kidder, Edward, *Receipts in Pastry and Cookery*, 1720

Kitchiner, William, *The Cook's Oracle*, 1822

La Chapelle, Vincent, *The Modern Cook*, Vol 1–2–3, 1733

The Ladies Companion: or, An infallible guide to the fair sex, 4th edition, Vol I and II, 1743

Leamington Spa Courier, Saturday 15 August 1891, The British Newspaper Archive

Leyel, Mrs C.F. (Hilda), *The Gentle Art of Cookery, with 750 recipes*, with Hartley, Olga, Chatto & Windus, 1925; *Puddings: baked, boiled, fried, steamed, iced*, 1927

Liber Cure Cocorum, circa 1430, translated into modern English by Cindy Renfrow, 2002

The Liverpool Training School of Cookery, *Plain Cookery Recipes*, 1902

Lozinski, G, *Enseingnemenz qui enseingnent a apareillier toutes manieres de viandes*, c. 1300, *La bataille de caresme et de charnage: édition critique avec introduction et glossaire* (Lutetiae 1933) pp. 181–87

M., W., *The Compleat Cook*, 1658

McIntosh, Jane, *Ancient Mesopotamia: New Perspectives*, 2005

MacIver, Susanna, *Cookery & Pastry*, 1786; *Mrs. MacIver's Cookery*, 1773

McNeill, F. Marian, *The Scots Kitchen*, 1929

The Magazine of Domestic Economy, 1836

Markham, Gervase, *The English Huswife*, 1615

Marshall, Agnes B., Mrs. A.B. *Marshall's Book of Cookery*, 1888; *The Book of Ices*, 1888; *Mrs. A.B. Marshall's Larger Cookery Book of Extra Recipes*, 1891; *Fancy Ices*, 1894; *Catalogue of Moulds*, c. 1880

Mason, Charlotte, *The Lady's Assistant*, 1773

Massey and Son's Comprehensive Pudding Book, 1865

Massialot, Françoise, *Nouveau Cuisinier Royal et Bourgeois*, 1691

May, Robert, *The Accomplisht Cook*, 1660

Mayhew, Henry, *London Labour and the London Poor*, 1851 or 1864

Miller, G., 'Classification and economic scaling of nineteenth century ceramics', in *Documentary Archaeology in the New World*, ed. M. Beaudry, Cambridge University Press, 1988, pp. 172–83

Ministry of Food, war cookery leaflet no. 4 – *Carrots*, WWII

Misson, Francois Maximilian, *Mémoires et observations faites par un voyageur en Angleterre*, 1698, published in English as *M. Misson's Memoirs and observations in his travels over England*, 1719

Mollard, John, *The Art of Cookery Made Easy and Refined*, 1802

Monasteriales Indicia: the Anglo–Saxon Monastic Sign Language, edited by Debby Banham, British Library – Anglo–Saxon Books, 1991

Montiño, Francisco Martinez, *Arte de Cocina*, 1763 edition, first published in 1611 by Francisco Martinez Montiño, head chef to King Felipe IV of Spain

Mooers, Colin, *The Making of Bourgeois Europe*, 1991

Muir, Bernard J., *Exeter Book of Old English Poetry*, 2000

Murrell, John, *A Newe Booke of Cookerie*, 1615

Napier, Mrs A., ed., *A Noble Boke Off Cookry, MS c. 1480*; published 1882

Neckham, Alexander, *Nominibus Utensilium*, c. 1190

A Noble Book of Festes Royalle and Cokery, 1500

Norwood, Colonel, 'A Voyage to Virginia', *A Collection of Voyages and Travels by Awnsham Churchill and John Churchill*, 1745, Vol 6 p.153

Nott, John, *The Cooks and Confectioners Dictionary: Or, the Accomplish'd Housewifes Companion*, 1723

Nutt, Frederick, *The Complete Confectioner*, 1789

The Original Mother Goose's Melody as First Issued by John Newbery of London About A.D. 1760, 1889

Partridge, John, *The Treasurie of Commodious Conceits*, 1573, transcription by Johanna Holloway, 2010

Pegge, Samuel, ed, *The Forme of Cury*, c.1390

Pepys, Samuel, *Diary of Samuel Pepys*, 1660–1669

Percy, T., ed., *The Northumberland Household Book: The Regulations and Establishment of the Household of Henry Algernon Percy*, new ed., 1905

Phillips, Sarah, *The Ladies Handmaid*, 1758

Pigot's Directory, Derbyshire, 1835

Platina, Bartolomeo, *De Honesta Voluptate*, 1475

Potter, Beatrix, *The Tale of Samuel Whiskers or The Roly-poly Pudding*, first published 1908

Price, Rebecca, *The Compleat Cook*, 1681

Problemata Aristoteles, 1530

Rabisha, William, *The Whole Body of Cookery Dissected*, 1661

Raffald, Elizabeth, *The Experienced English Housekeeper*, 1769 and 1782, facsimile edition

Renfrow, Cindy, *Take a Thousand Eggs or More: A Translation of Medieval Recipes from Harleian MS. 279, Harleian MS. 4016, and Extracts of Ashmole MS. 1439, Laud MS. 553, and Douce MS. 55, with More than 100 Recipes Adapted for Modern Cookery*, Unionville, Royal Fireworks, 1997; and *Liber Cure Cocorum*, from the Sloane MS. 1986 by Richard Morris, 2002

Riley, Mr., '*Introduction to the Liber Custumarum*' included in Thomas Becket's biography as a preface, *Descriptio Nobilissimi Civitatis Londoniae*, Henry Thomas Riley ed. *Liber Custumarum. Rolls Series no.12*, 1860

Rodrigues, Domingos, *Arte de Cozinha*, 1758 edition

Rogers, B., *Beef and Liberty: Roast Beef, John Bull and the English Nation*, 2003

de Rossi, Martino, *Libro de Arte Coquinaria*, c. 1450/1465

Rothwell, William, ed., *Walter de Bibbesworth Le Tretiz*, Anglo–Norman Text Society, 1990

Rundell, Maria Eliza Ketelby, *A New System of Domestic Cookery*, 1806/1807

Russell, John, *Boke of Nurture*, c. 1460

Saberi, Helen, see Davidson, Alan

Salis, Mrs., *A la Mode Cookery*, 1902

Sandford, Francis, *History of the Coronation*, 1687

Sayer, William, 'The Genealogy of Haggis', *Miscelénea 39*, 2009: p. 103–110. http://www.miscelaneajournal.net/images/stories/articulos/vol39/103_misc39_.pdf

Science magazine, 'DNA recovered from underwater British site may rewrite history of farming in Europe', http://news.sciencemag.org/archaeology/2015/02/dna-recovered-underwater-british-site-may-rewrite-history-farming-europe

Scully, Terrence, *The Art of Cookery in the Middle Ages*, 1995

Sharpe, *Calendar of Letter-Books of the city of London: 1400–1422*, 1909

Smith, Eliza, *The Compleat Housewife*, first edition 1727, later editions 1737, 1758

Society of Antiquaries of London, 'A collection of ordinances and regulations for the government of the royal household, made in divers reigns: from King Edward III to King William and Queen Mary, also receipts in ancient cookery', 1790

Soyer, Alexis, *The Modern Housewife or, Ménagère*, 1849; *A Shilling Cookery for the People*, 1854; *Soyer's Charitable Cookery*, 1884

Spencer, Colin, *British Food: An Extraordinary Thousand Years of History*, 2011

Spry, Constance; Hume, Rosemary, *The Constance Spry Cookery Book*, 1956

Stow, John, *A Survey of London*, 1598, ed William J. Thoms, Esq, F.S.A, 1842

Swallow, Henry J., 'The Installation Feast of George Neville, Archbishop of York, 1465' in *De Nova Villa or The House of Nevill in Sunshine and Shade*, 1885

Taillevent, *Le Viandier de Taillevent, c. 1315–1395*, translated by James Prescott, 1989

Teonge, Henry, *The Diary of Henry Teonge*, 1825

Thacker, John, *The Art of Cookery*, 1758

Thackeray, William Makepeace, *Notes on a Journey from Cornhill to Grand Cairo*, 1846

Thirsk, J., *Food in Early Modern England: Phases, Fads, Fashions, 1500–1760,* Hambledon Continuum, 2007

Traditional Fare of England and Wales, The National Federation of Women's Institutes, 1948

Turner, Thomas, *The Diary of Thomas Turner 1754–1765*, ed. David Valsey, 1985

la Varenne, Francois, *Le Cuisinier François*, 1653

Vine, Frederick, *Saleable Shop Goods*, 1898

W., A., *A Book of Cookrye*, 1584

Walsh, J.H., *The English Cookery Book*, 1858, second edition published as *The British Cookery Book*, 1864

Walter of Bibbesworth, *The Treatise of Walter of Bibbesworth*, c. 1234, translated by Andrew Dalby, 2012

Watkins, Ann E., *Aelfric's Colloquy, translated from the Latin*, www.kentarchaeology.ac/authors/016.pdf

Weber, Henry, 'Kyng Alisaunder', in *Metrical Romances of the Thirteenth, Fourteenth, and Fifteenth Centuries*, 1810

Weir, Robin; Weir, Caroline, *Ice creams, sorbets & gelati, the definitive guide*, 2010, see also Barham, Peter

White, Florence, *Good Things in England*, 1932; *Good English Food*, 1952

The Whole Duty of a Woman, 1737

Willan, Anne; Friedma, Amy, *One Soufflé at a Time: A Memoir of Food and France*, 2013

Wilson, Anne C., *Food and Drink in Britain: From the Stone Age to the 19th Century*, 2003

Wolley, Hannah, *The Queen-Like Closet*, 1672

Woodforde, James, *The Diary of a Country Parson 1758–1802*, The Canterbury Press, 1999

Wright, Thomas, *A Dictionary of Obsolete and Provincial English*, 1857

'A Y Chromosome Census of the British Isles', *Current Biology*, Elsevier Science Ltd., Vol. 13, pp. 979–84, 27 May, 2003

Index

Thank You

First of all I would like to thank those of you who have been supporting me from the very beginning: the readers of my blog, my instagram followers and you, for buying this book. My friends: I'm thinking of two very special ladies, Vanessa and Giulia. Also Sarka, Pavel, Emiko and so many others. Ex-boss and top friend Miguel for believing I should make my own way in this world and become freelance before I even dared thinking of it. Thank you my English friends for indulging me when I was quizzing you about your pudding habits and other English traditions. (There will be more of that, I must warn you.) To Loes and Krikke for making me a care pack with bread and beef when I was in the final stages of writing this book and racing against time. A special thanks to Stef, my mate from culinary school, who insisted on helping me cook one day a week while I was doing the photography and recipe testing of this book. Those were the best workdays, even if we had to make that pastry over and over again to get it right. Thank you Charlie McSherry from Cherry Pie Lane. Thank you Solomia Zoumaras. Thank you Christine McClellan, my trusty proofreader, the first to read this book while still in its rough state. Thank you to my family, for understanding my absence and silence the past two years, with the knowledge I was just trying to create this book and make it beautiful and perfect.

Thank you David Loftus for your support when I started out as a photographer, something you said has really made a difference. Thank you Jamie Oliver for being so very kind to me, for giving your opinion on the design and concept of this book even when you were so busy. I'm beyond proud to have your quote on the cover. Oh, and thanks for the *Naked Chef* because without that cheeky guy I would probably never have started cooking when I was a teen! Thank you Trevor and Sally Oliver: I had my first ever steamed sponge pudding in your lovely Clavering pub, and shortly after I decided to write this book.

Thank you Dr Annie Gray, for your support and excitement for this project, for giving your seal of approval by writing the foreword to this book. Thank you Ivan Day, for letting me photograph your beautiful collection, for sharing your knowledge and for one of the most magical weekends, and meals, in my life by the fire in your Cumbrian kitchen.

Thank you Adam Balic, for sharing your knowledge, and Dave Rayner, for your help with translating medieval Latin. Thank you to Burleigh, Denby and to Barrington pottery. Long live English pottery. Thank you to P&O North Sea Ferries for making my trip from Belgium to Bakewell happen.

Thank you to the lovely and patient people who tested recipes: Matt Cook, Paula Bacchia, Inge-Marie Drachter, Joanne Sayce, Eloïse Pontbriand, Inês Mendes, Hanna Kukkonen, Naomi Kooijmans, Catarina Herculano, Salima Tiamani, Elinor Hill, Joanna Straburzyńska, Adelina Marghidan, Mandy Ng, Lia Teixeira, Kaitlin Flannery and Lauren Petri.

A massive thanks goes to my English-language publisher Murdoch Books. Thank you Corinne Roberts and Sue Hines for being captivated by my book and wanting to publish it. Thank you Melody Lord for sublime and thoughtful editing and for understanding my voice. Thank you Katie Bosher and Megan Pigott for making this book as beautiful as it could be.